> Mike —
> Our word is our best hope for the future. With kind regards.
> [signature]

Journeys of Conscience

CURTIS L. IVERY

Acknowledgements

This book is fervently dedicated to my beloved father and mother. I warmly acknowledge the nurturing experiences I received from both of them, which molded and shaped me. There were many lessons I took to heart from each of them.

My wife Ola has been a constant source of encouragement and strength in all my endeavors. Without her words of guidance, support and comfort, I would not have been able to achieve appointment to so many leadership roles.

Moreover, she was a critical reviewer of my columns. Her intense scrutiny of my words and opinions aided me tremendously. I thank you, Ola, for being a loving wife and supporter.

My many references to my son and daughter in my columns reflects my intense desire to be a good husband and father. Our loving interactions during their formative and early adult years opened my eyes to the challenges young people face today. I am deeply indebted to my son, Marcus and daughter, Angela for their insight and comments all along the way.

While I have led them, they also have led me toward a greater level of conscience and dedication and a higher level of achievement.

Finally, it is important for me to acknowledge the major impact, influence and guidance of my longtime colleague, friend, and mentor, Wright L. Lassiter, Jr. in my professional and intellectual development. It was he who insisted that I stop delaying the production of this work and "do it now." I am deeply indebted to him in many ways.

Curtis L. Ivery

A Mentor's Perspective: A Man Of Passion And Purpose

Upon meeting Curtis L. Ivery nearly 20 years ago, I quickly realized that he was a man of honesty, integrity and passion, whose sole goal was to uplift those who had been forgotten on the sometimes turbulent adventure called life. Shortly after forming our professional relationship, I further discovered his talents as a communicator and writer, and I urged him to build on his journalism background and share his views with a much larger audience, free of the confines of "local" conversation.

True to his personality as a rather dogged individual, Curtis saw this as an opportunity to serve others in a capacity where he could mesh his writing capability with his strong commitment to justice, fairness and hope.

As soon as his first columns appeared in several newspapers, people took notice of his views and whether they agreed with him or not, came to the conclusion that his was a unique voice unfettered by the opinions of others. His refreshing honesty in bringing details about his professional and personal life to print not only served to illuminate what makes him tick, but served as an indicator to others that they were not alone in their triumphs and tragedies.

Journeys of Conscience is a smart collection of commentaries that defines the world in which we live. This collection puts on display not only the immense range of his interests, but also the full panoply of gifts for physical description and imagery, for the satirical moment and the transformative detail and dazzling prose that is at once mathematically precise and lyrical.

Journeys of Conscience represents the body of a passionate man who demonstrates a talent for penetrating the heart of the matter, for advancing far beyond events to find their true meaning.

I am extremely proud of my friend. Those who choose to read *Journeys of Conscience* will be impressed, informed and inspired.

Dr. Wright L. Lassiter Jr.
President
El Centro College

Copyright © 2005 by Curtis L. Ivery

All rights reserved. No part of this book may be used or reproduced in any manner whatsoever without written permission of the publisher.

Printed in the United States of America

ISBN:
Library of Congress Catalog Control Number:

Word Association Publishers
205 Fifth Avenue
Tarentum, Pennsylvania 15084
800-827-7903
www.wordassociation.com

Book Design by Larry Zelensky

"While the tale of how we suffer, and how we are delighted, and how we may triumph is never new, it always must be heard…in every country and…in every generation"

James Baldwin

Table Of Contents

Introduction – Manning Marable — xvii
Advance Reviews — xix
Preface – Clarence Page — xxii
Essay by Marcus Brandon Ivery — xxiv
The Inspiration: Author's Introduction — xxvi
Author's Note to the Reader — xxx

PART I — LESSONS FROM THE SANDBOX — 3
   In The Midst of Life — 5
   Superstitions Linger Well Into The 20th Century — 8
   Investing In A Child's Future Makes A Difference — 11
   Miles of Understanding — 14
   Peas, Punishment, But No Penance — 17
   It's Only Words — 21
   Strength For The Journey — 24
   Kindergarten's Life Long Advantage — 26
   Everyone Loves The Fight — 28
   Lunch Room Choices Mean Lifelong Returns — 30
   Cultural Awareness Opens Minds To Many Possibilities — 32
   New Skills, New Life — 35
   Excellence Is Ripe For The Picking — 39
   The Lessons Of Life And Time — 42
   Handicaps Are What You Allow Them To Be — 45
   There Is Nothing To Fear But Fear Itself — 48
   Time To Live Our Dreams — 51

Instant Karma 53
Lessons About Learning 56
Love On A One-Way Street 59
Have Hot Dogs For Breakfast 62
Winning Truly Takes A Team 64
The Young & The Restless 66

PART II— COMMUNICATION: THE KEY TO LIFE AND LOVE 71
Communication Is An Art Form 73
Written Communication Skills Cut By Television Time 76
What I Learned About Writing 78
Communication – The Real Answer To Trusting 82
Misunderstandings Can Begin With Simple Words, End With Dire Results 85
The Most Important Pronoun 88
Don't Fear, Change Is Inevitable 91
Computer Age Brings Changes 95
Deciphering Meaning From Language Can Be Subjective 98
The Other Digital Divide 101
Put People First – No Matter The Cost 103
Speech Difficulty Shapes Outlook On Life And Others 106
Ageless Mind, Ageless Spirit 109
Circumstances Yield Our Best 112
Needless Risk As Dangerous As No Risk 114
Making Excuses Won't Bring About Success 117
Country, Friends Suffer From Illiteracy 120
Revenge: Fight With Fist Or Brain Power? 123
Written To Distraction 126
Building A Good Vocabulary Versus Becoming Child Couch Potatoes 129

PART III — ETHICS AND MORALITY 135
Ethics And Attitudes 137
Actions Reflect Ethics 139
The Dichotomy Of Defining Morality 141
Role Models Are Chosen, Not Necessarily By The Role Models Themselves 144
Negative Ads Come From Negative People 147

Living By Golden Rule Lifts Society With Value System	*150*
Are Churchgoers More Moral?	*153*
Can't They Stop Killing for Christmas?	*156*
Violent Criminals Must Pay For Their Crimes	*160*
Guns Can't Protect Us From Fear	*164*
Ending Crime Starts At Home	*167*
Study of Human Sexuality Shows Need For Change	*170*
Law Can't Deal With Euthanasia	*172*
Political Correctness Shouldn't Become Stumbling Block	*175*
Families Without Fathers	*178*
Without Honesty, Social Interaction Becomes Impossible	*181*
Trust: The Center Of It All	*184*
Second Chances	*187*
Don't Be So Quick To Judge	*190*
Ethics And Morals	*192*
Ministers Miss Chance To Promote Electoral System	*194*
Was Stevie Ever Really "Cute?"	*196*
The Prospect-Killing Aspects of Rudeness	*199*
PART IV — THE FAMILY AND CHILDREN	*205*
The Heart And Soul Of Family Values	*207*
Father Doesn't Always Know Best	*210*
Strict Discipline Policy May Not Be Bad Idea	*212*
Role Models And Their Responsibility To Children	*215*
Cuban Boy And All Youth Need Our Help	*218*
Children Should Remain Top Factor In Welfare Equation	*221*
Teenage Pregnancy: Once A Disgrace, Now The Norm	*223*
Children Suffer From Inadequate Parenting	*226*
Reforming Families Only Way To Improve Welfare	*228*
It Truly Takes A Village To Raise A Child	*230*
Love Lets Kids Be Kids and Grow Safely Into Adults	*235*
Responsibility For Teenage Pregnancy Must Be Shared	*238*
To Stop Violence, Focus On Children, Not Guns	*241*
Children Need To Know About Death	*244*
What Do The Opinions Of Others Matter?	*246*

Gun Law Creates Environment of Fear	248
Children And Violence	251
Key To Healthy Living Is Taking Time For Healthy Activities	254
Domestic Terrorism: Family Violence	257
Why Babies Are Dying	260
Communication Breakdown	263
Flipping Channels	265
Protecting Our Children	268
Rethink And Restructure	271
Returning America To Prominence	274
Welfare System Needs To Find Reform, Lose Misconceptions	276
Giving Is The Greatest Gift Of All	280
Don't Blame The Children	283
America Was Built On Immigration	286
Mandatory School Attendance Not Always Beneficial	289
Parental Involvement Is Mandatory	291
The Curse of The Elderly	294
PART V — WIT, WORDS AND WISDOM	299
Keeping The Brass Polished	300
Changes In Health Care Must Be Carefully Charted	302
Why Me?	305
One Step At A Time	307
College Leader Finds Brave, Old World	310
Please Hold For Further Assistance	315
Detroit's Future: It's Up To Us	318
PART VI — CULTURAL COMPETENCE AND UNDERSTANDING	323
Despite Tragedy, Americans Remain Resolute, United	325
Diversity: The Key To Understanding	328
At What Point Are We Grown Up?	331
What Is Our Most Defining Characteristic	334
Take Time To Reflect On Triumphs, Struggles Of Black Americans	337
Loyalty Is A Motivating Force	340
Workplace Equality Will Only Come With Change Of Attitude	343

Vignettes On Racial Awareness	*347*
The Scourge Of Hip-Hop	*351*
Visit To Cape Town	*354*
Smiles Are Universal When Bridging Differences Between Cultures	*357*
Slowly, The Times Are Changing	*360*
The Fog Of War	*362*
Vote, Or Else!	*365*
Beggars And Vagrants Pose Threat To Civic Security	*367*
Midnight Basketball No Panacea	*369*
Banish The Language Of Our Culture?	*372*
The Case Against Reparations	*375*
Guns Are Merely Weapons Of Choice For The Violent	*378*
Hope For A Color Blind Society May Be Dwindling	*381*
Saving The Jewel	*384*
A Final Word	*389*
APPENDIX:	
Bibliography	*395*

Introduction

Curtis L. Ivery is one of America's most gifted and remarkable educators and communicators. Throughout his long and distinguished public career as a scholar, educational administrator, columnist and community leader, he has earned numerous awards and honors, along with setting a high standard for both academic excellence and compassionate civic engagement that few have equaled.

Yet this is only a small portion of Curtis Ivery's story. More attractive by far are the richly human dimensions of his life experiences – how the stories and episodes from his own life helped to produce the man he has become. *Journeys of Conscience* is an eloquent, moving and intimate collection of essays that reveals the fabric and texture of his character. The writing here is direct and clear, accessible to all readers, yet at the same time holding powerful, timeless lessons drawing upon wellsprings of knowledge and critical reflection.

Journeys of Conscience provides practical lessons for a life of excellence and service, and illustrates the necessity for educators to ground themselves within a passionate commitment to justice and fairness for all members of society.

Rarely have I learned more from any person than Curtis L. Ivery. *Journeys of Conscience* is an extraordinary testament to a remarkable man.

Manning Marable
Professor of Public Affairs, History and African-American Studies
Director, Center for Contemporary Black History
Columbia University
January 11, 2005

Advance Reviews

It is always a pleasure to write something on the behalf of someone doing positive things.

I have been involved all my life to make our society fairer, more just and more progressive, and have been privileged to speak to national and world leaders about these issues. Dr. Ivery readily brings these issues to the forefront in this book.

Dr. Ivery's collection of newspaper columns paints a vibrant picture of someone who has been involved with the efforts of social change and the reality of segregation and polarization. Dr. Ivery's efforts in world politics and education are greatly noted and reflect a lifetime commitment to the betterment of others.

Journeys of Conscience is a testament to one man's commitment to improving society in every way he can.

Judge Greg Mathis

Curtis Ivery is a man of many firsts. But first and foremost in his mind is the generational responsibility we must all share to make things better, to always reach higher and to constantly demand more of ourselves. Those ideas radiate throughout his latest work, *Journeys of Conscience*.

The ideas in the book transcend generational gaps, ideological boundaries and socioeconomic differences. He expresses ideas and sentiments that apply to humanity as a whole, not to specific types or classes of men and women. The thoughts and words are laid out in a logical manner that everyone can easily understand. The book expresses in clear terms what it means to be human. It illustrates how to most effectively relate the concepts to your own experiences, apply them to your interaction with others, and communicate the ideas so they can be passed on to future generations.

Dick Gregory
Author, Humorist, and Civil Rights Activist

Journeys of Conscience carries for all of us simple lessons and profound wisdoms. It reflects Dr. Ivery's high level of critical thinking and his perseverance to do more for the betterment of generations to come. His work speaks volumes of this powerful personality, who continues to make long-lasting impressions on a multitude of people. This collection of essays is a must read for the reassuring effect in its message of hope and a reminder of the strength that all of us have to make our lives more meaningful.

Les Brown
Speaker, Entrepreneur

A steady force of constructive change, Dr. Curtis L. Ivery has observed first-hand the challenges facing urban America, and has come up with practical solutions. His work has touched the lives of a broad spectrum of people – from the wealthiest communities to the poorest, and every demographic in between.

In *Journeys of Conscience*, Dr. Ivery presents topics that we can all relate to as his insights and ideas are easily adaptable to each reader's circumstances. It is part self-help, part philosophical; and entirely focused on fulfilling more of our human potential.

David Dinkins
Former Mayor, New York City

Preface

The most important thing that we columnists do is explain things. News reporters bring you the news. Some of it offers hope. Most of it too often sounds pretty depressing.

We columnists and commentators try to make some sense out of the news. The best of us, in my view, offer you some hope, not just gripes. That's what makes Dr. Curtis Ivery's writings so welcome. In a time of great change, anxiety and polarization, his essays offer a rare and welcome voice of reflection and reason.

He brings wit, wisdom, experience and encyclopedic knowledge to the page with an elegant candor and simplicity to which everyone can relate.

His years of experience in education, civil rights and other public service make him a valuable voice in the cause of closing economic and cultural gaps, opening doors of opportunity and helping all of us to take full advantage of opportunity once it has been opened up to us. Dr. Ivery helps the reader to understand that each of us has the power to do great things and that the world is still a manageable place, if we work at it.

He understands how far America has come in dealing with the complexities of its own racial, ethnic and religious diversity and how far we still have to go.

He also understands that the battle for true equality involves a lot more than civil rights. It also requires education, the most important force for liberation on this planet.

In a world where plenty of writers and commentators are raising a lot of heat, *Journeys of Conscience* brings a welcome light.

Clarence Page *Syndicated columnist*

Essay *by* Marcus Brandon Ivery

My name is Marcus Brandon Ivery and was born in Fort Smith Arkansas on August 30, 1980. I don't remember much about my life before age three. I remember spending time with my grandfather while my mother and father went off to work. I was the second child born in my family. I have one sister who was born four years earlier. My father was born and raised in Texas. My mother was born and raised in Arkansas. My father met my mom on Valentines day after he had moved to Arkansas to work at a college in Fort Smith.

The thing I remember most when I was just a little boy was that my father traveled a lot. Sometimes I would only see him on weekends. My father worked for the Governor, Bill Clinton of Arkansas which kept him very busy. He was always on television and in the newspapers. I remember always looking forward to Friday evenings, because thats when my father would come home. He would always pick me up and hold me in his big arms. That was very special to me.

My very first dog was a german shepard named bullet. We did not keep him very long because my mother did not like pets. We gave him to my uncle. My first big trip was on an airplane from Arkansas to Texas. I was four years old when the family went with my dad because he had to make a

AUTHOR'S NOTE: *My son, Marcus, wrote this at age 10. Today, I am very proud to say that Marcus is a successful professional, devoted son and a kind and generous person.*

To me, this essay from a young mind truly reflects the importance of life's lessons learned during the early childhood development stages...as early as the sandbox.

speech in Amarillo.

The first grade was my best grade ever. I guess because I was so excited about finally being in school. My favorite subject was math and my favorite teacher was Mrs. Boswell. I liked her because she was always really nice. The special event in my life was moving from Arkansas to Desoto. When I left Arkansas I left many good friends and relatives. But when I got to Desoto, I made many new good friends. I really like going to school. I have a chance to be with my friends. I don't like being by myself or being bored. I like having lots of fun things to do.

My parents believe going to college is really important and so do I. I will go to college and eventually become a Doctor. I plan to marry when I finish college and have and bigger.

The Most special person in my life is my mother. She has taught me many thing about being a good person. Also, she is smart and know how to fix almost anything. I have a great ten years thanks to mom.

The Inspiration: Author's Introduction

My long-time friend, colleague and mentor, Dr. Wright L. Lassiter, Jr., has often urged me to share with a larger audience in the form of a book a series of columns I have written through the years for newspapers and magazines.

He was a loyal reader of my columns and has heard many of my speeches, and sensed that I was writing and speaking from the heart about my own unusual odyssey from a poor childhood in a large African-American family to a position of leadership in the worlds of education and politics.

God blesses some of us by helping us travel a life journey that is meaningful – and He so blessed me. It seems that at every turn of the road, there was a person to inspire me or an incident containing a lesson to be learned.

This book is really a collection of those people and incidents.

I believed I could best express my feelings by giving the reader the opportunity to examine some of my favorite editorial and opinion pieces I have written over the last 15 years.

In the sections that follow, I share my feelings, emotions, dreams and aspirations on a variety of subjects in six areas:

- Lessons From The Sandbox
- Communication: The Key to Life and Love
- Ethics and Morality
- The Family and Children
- Wit, Words and Wisdom
- Cultural Competence and Understanding

The driving objective in my writing has been to express my deepest feelings of conscience. The tales of how we suffer, how we are delighted and how we may triumph are never new, but always they must be heard anew in every country and in every generation.

Because each of these experiences takes the writer – and the reader – from a beginning point to a new perspective, I have called these essays "Journeys of Conscience."

A column that I wrote for the *Michigan Chronicle* titled "The Pain and Power of Words," does a very effective job of capturing that which has inspired me to write and speak, and I present it here as an essential segment of my "author's inspiration."

The Pain and Power of Words

No doubt everyone has heard the cliché "Sticks and stones may break my bones, but words will never hurt me."

As children, this was some comfort against the harassing words and slurs from fellow playmates. As adults we reach back for it sometimes in an attempt to move beyond the abrasive comments of insensitive adults. We are supposed to take comfort in the message and help maintain a "stiff upper lip" when we are victims of verbal curves or abuse.

It is embedded in our minds: we now repeat it to our children even though we realize that it's a lie. We know better, and we knew better as children. It only took one "fatty" or "four-eyes" or any other popular facial or ethnic or sexist slur to destroy the myth that words don't hurt, that certain words don't send chills of horror or fear or anger down our spines. We learned early on the power of words to make us feel isolated, embarrassed and inferior.

It's easy to overlook the power of words as it becomes easier and more convenient to trivialize their significance and impact. In a world ruled by swiftness, words can cut to the quick. They are a perfect fit into today's world where verbal brashness is accepted as the norm. Insensitive remarks – the slurs, put-downs, ethnic or sexist remarks can only be meant to hurt those who are different.

Words that not many years ago would not have been printed in the general press or spoken on television or radio barely make us blush. We have become desensitized.

The biggest source of destructive and insulting language is the entertainment industry, where abusive and abrasive remarks and insensitive jokes abound. In most TV shows or movies – even those classified as family oriented – you'll hear a barrage of foul language. Innuendoes are made about other cultures, and people with physical or mental challenges are imitated and ridiculed. Comedians often joke about certain cultures and lifestyles to get a laugh. The laugh, of course, is always at the expense of others.

Recently, I was appalled at what I saw and heard on a well-known talk show where people were arguing profusely about an issue that should never have been aired on national television. The one-hour segment consisted of the panel members shouting obscenities at one another and, at times, even making physical advances toward each other. Had there not been intervention, they surely would have physically attacked each other.

The danger in such behavior is that children are the sponge-like observers of these behaviors, absorbing all of this verbal venom. What do they learn about human beings, human relationships and human communications from such trash?

In some cases, words are used to gain power and control over a situation or another person. This verbal abuse is a very real form of personal destruction. According to Patricia Evans, author of *Verbal Abuse Survivors Speak Out*, abusive people stop at nothing to squelch, put down, correct, criticize, belittle, trivialize, ignore, snub, sneer and, when all else fails, put on displays of rage for the sole purpose of dominating and controlling their mates. This form of oppression unfortunately permeates our society.

Verbal abuse falls quietly under the umbrella of violence, and demeans and handicaps people from all socio-economic levels. This behavior and pattern of verbal abuse is passed from generation to generation, either actively or passively, and rips at the core of our human fabric. The victims of such abuse suffer from low self-esteem and lack of self-confidence.

Given the damaging effects of our disparaging verbal expressions, it is imperative that we become more attuned to what we say and how we say it and change our passive attitudes toward verbal insensitivity and abuse. We need to stop ridiculing others who are different – in culture, lifestyle, or socio-economic status – stop making people into cheap jokes for television comics. Stop speaking as if words don't matter.

They do.

Curtis L. Ivery

Author's Note To The Reader

This book is a collection of newspaper columns written over the course of many years. Many of the columns have references to current events at the time they were written.

Some of these references have been made more universal. However, in order to retain the flavor of some of the columns, references to contemporaneous events have usually been retained.

I have clarified such references as much as possible, but I ask the reader to understand when references to events or related matters are not totally clear to today's readers.

I also realize that from year to year the way one should refer to various ethnic and social groups changes. I kept my references to racial, religious and social groups as more true to the original writing.

CLI

Part I
Lessons From
The Sandbox

*"Is nothing in life
ever straight and clear,
the way children see it?"*

Rosie Thomas

Storytelling has been used for centuries to pass the wisdom of one generation to the next, carry forward family and community traditions, transmit the culture and engage the listeners in the experiences of an earlier time. No chronology or historical record can convey what a heartfelt story can.

When a storyteller shares the story of his or her personal life's journey, he or she imparts the knowledge and wisdom gained from that journey. Listeners learn about what lies under the surface of the historical record and see revealed the values, emotions, feelings and yearnings of the storyteller. Listeners identify with the triumphs, sufferings, failures, joys, and delights of the storyteller and gain from the lessons learned from these experiences.

These lessons become a part of the experience of the listeners, and may serve as a guide as their own life story unfolds. It is my objective in these passages to share the knowledge and wisdom gained from my life's experiences with the hope of encouraging others, particularly young adults who are making key choices that will shape their search for meaning and significance and their lifelong journey of self-discovery.

The first set of stories, or passages, is entitled "Lessons From The Sandbox." I am very aware of the importance of education, starting at the earliest age, in shaping the course of one's life. I mean education in all its forms, from positive learning experiences in the home and school, to negative learning experiences that may result from watching *inappropriate television programs, or life on the "mean streets." I do not limit my definition of education to the development of the intellect or "brain work" –learning the methods, structures, and rules of math, writing, reading, science and the like. I also include the nurturing of the inner self – the heart and soul – through experiences with art, poetry, literature, drama, ethics, and philosophy.*

Education is the key to the enlightenment of all. However, for children, education – the right kind, steeped in common sense, in addition to traditional subject matter – is also crucial for developing a sense of strength and purpose, along with critical thinking skills.

We are all on a personal journey of self-discovery from the earliest age. We discover who we are through all life experiences, especially from our interactions with others. I recall as a child my deeply felt reaction when a family member, neighbor, teacher or coach would give me a word of praise and encouragement. This simple gesture made me feel more like the real me. In spite of my awkward immaturity and self-doubts, someone thought that I was OK. I was valued and loved. Of course, I also recall being criticized in ways that I took as an attack on my fragile sense of self. As I grew to adulthood, I began to sense from these experiences that being an encouragement to others could define my life's work, and that my vocation could center on shining the light of hope, love and encouragement onto and into the lives of others. That is the path my life has taken. I trust that these stories, or passages, will illuminate in some way the lives of those who read them. The passages in this section deal with the realm of education that encompasses our brains, our hearts and our souls. No matter what stage of life we are in, learning should be an ongoing, and never-ending, process.

In The Midst Of Life

Across one of the streets from our school was a funeral home, which we could see from our sixth grade classroom. Since it had always been there, we thought nothing much about it in the early years of school. But by the time sixth grade came around, we had begun to discover other things to interest us than just reading and writing.

Whenever a group of cars appeared in the small parking lot next to the funeral home, we knew that someone had died. None of us had ever been inside this place that was already inherently spooky, and that was fine. But one day when there were cars parked across the street, Charles said we should go around back and sneak inside to look around.

It was a dare – he said he was going and asked who was not too chicken to go with him. Fear suddenly overcame my curiosity about the back of a funeral home, and I no longer really wanted to go there. But it was too late now. In the sixth grade you can't run out on a dare, not even involving dead bodies. The best I could hope for was to go last.

After school we met as planned and, with Charles leading the way, walked down the street and came back up the alley behind the funeral home. At any moment from then on I would have been really happy if someone had come out and seen us, or if Charles had second thoughts, but no, there was no one in the back. The door was partially open and after Charles peeked in and around, he motioned us to follow him in. My heart pounded now, and I jockeyed for last position with the other two guys, but eventually we all wound up inside.

We saw several caskets, boxes, buckets, a big sink, shelves – it looked like a messy workroom of some kind. Except for the caskets. There was one in the middle of the room and Charles walked over and lifted up the lid. Inside I could see the head and neck of an old, ugly, shriveled up dead lady. Gasping, I stared almost trance-like, and the spell was only broken when I thought her eyes turned and looked over at me. That was enough, I was out of there, dare or no dare. I don't know how long the others stayed, but I took off running out the door and into the alley, and down to the street and was halfway home before I could even stop and look back to make sure the old dead lady wasn't chasing me down the sidewalk.

It was a few weeks before I stopped seeing those eyes and finally could sleep easily again. I was afraid of going into dark rooms and always looked behind doors when I went into a dark room, not really expecting to find anyone, yet unsure enough to need to look.

It was also around that period in my life that several older family members began to die and so I became reacquainted with the funeral home, this time through the front door and viewing open caskets. Each time I had to walk past the open casket of another dead uncle or aunt, I would glance quickly inside and then look away before the eyes could find mine. Sometimes going through the line I noticed some people reaching over and touching the person lying in the casket. I don't remember the source of my fear anymore, but touching a dead body was about as scary as anything I could think of.

One day I remember walking home from school and as I got near the house I saw my uncle's truck parked in the driveway. Perhaps it was quick logic – the uncle was always at work during the day, his truck was never at our house, something serious must be wrong. It must be my grandmother, she must have died. All that in a split second or so, but I felt scared. I slowed my pace, delaying the bad news I was anticipating, but eventually I made it home.

Sure enough, I was right. My grandmother had died that day, following an extended illness. It was not a surprise that she was going to die, only a matter of when.

I can't remember much about the day other than going to the funeral home that evening to view the body and greet visitors. I was careful to avoid making contact with her even as she lay quietly in her casket. Whenever I was alone, both then and long after, thoughts of her came up and I would quickly focus on something else.

There were more funerals of aunts and uncles from time to time, and each time I avoided letting myself think about it. Death was just too big and too final and too scary.

Superstitions Linger Well Into The 20th Century

I was probably about 10 years old when I was introduced to the world of superstitions. One morning while hurrying through one of a few household chores, which on this particular occasion was sweeping the kitchen floor, I ignored the fact that my father was standing over the sink fetching something from the cabinet.

It never occurred to me that it would matter if his feet became a part of what was being swept. After all, those ugly and dirt-stained boots he was wearing had seen their best days.

Well, after I got up from the kitchen floor, I knew sweeping his feet, no matter how well intentioned, was not the thing to do. Enter my introduction to the meaning of superstition. My father explained to me that my sweeping his feet would surely mean that some unfortunate set of circumstances would lead him to jail.

Since my early encounter with superstitions, I have kept a count of the ones I take seriously. My magic number is three. Many of you have them but are probably unwilling to admit it. The essence of superstition is that it is a bad omen and it is irrational. And who wants to be irrational? But people do have superstitions.

It does not matter who we are and how we might feel about superstitions. We still have to deal with them in some form or fashion. For example, my administrative assistant and dear friend has some. Let me tell you about a couple of them.

If she is driving and a black cat crosses the street in front of her, she will not cross its path. She will stop, turn around and go around the block.

The next one says never step on a crack. If you do, surely you will break your back or some other unforeseen accident will befall you.

Superstition, supernatural, custom, manners, rituals, folklore – call them what you wish but all have a common origin in the occult. Even those of us who are skeptical of the supernatural will be shocked to discover its enormous effect on our everyday lives. Although superstitions originated in less enlightened times than our own, they still maintain a powerful hold on the imagination of our technological society.

When I decided to explore the subject of superstitions, I had no clue as to the extent our society is influenced by the implicit acceptance of magic as a rule of life. Deep down, I have always felt that superstitions were to be taken lightly, something to be made fun of, something to be dismissed as illogical fantasies.

Only recently, I became aware of the fact that in many large high-rise buildings the labeling of a 13th floor is avoided, especially in hotels and hospitals. In the American culture, many consider the number unlucky. R. Broach, the author of *Strange Customs: How Did They Begin*, explains it this way:

"The ability of primitive man to count was limited. He could do so up to 12 but no further. That is why no numbers beyond…12 have an individual and independent name, but are merely composed of a combination of the description of the previous numbers. This might also explain why for no apparent reason the traditional multiplication table stops at 12 times 12."

If 12 were the end of the line, 13, which followed it, had no exact value and definite meaning at first. Hence, it was an uncertain number, fraught with mystery. This enigmatic quality of the number 13 made man fear the numeral and render it fateful and foreboding.

In this moment of reflection, I also wonder why many of us also avoid doing anything of particular significance on Friday the 13th. The notion that Friday the 13th is unlucky is indelibly imprinted on my mind.

Fear of the number 13 can even be applied to space technology and decisions made at the Johnson Space Center in Houston. Do you remember the 13th Apollo mission? The mission was aborted on April 13, 1970.

Some say it was because it was launched at 1313 hours Central Time from Pad 39 (the third multiple of 13). The newspapers were especially enthusiastic in calling these wicked numbers to our attention. Today the real significance of many superstitions has been forgotten. However, the essence of most of them lives on to shape and influence our behavior.

Many of us cherish superstitions that have been handed down in our families. We remember things like our grandfather saying, "My joints are aching, so we are going to have cold weather." I have long been fascinated with my father's superstition about sweeping his feet with a broom. I also know several other black families who have spoken of the superstitions surrounding the mysticism of the broom.

During my research on this topic, I discovered that there is an interesting parallel between the lore of white and black in the old slave superstitions that held that to sweep dust from the doorstep at night meant that the sweeper would have the misfortune to be sold in the slave market, which is closely allied to the European belief that sweeping dust out of the house sweeps away the household luck. There is apparently more than coincidence in the fact that the witch is so closely associated with the magic broom.

Some superstitions are so popular that they have become part of our language. We find ourselves automatically saying, "Knock on wood," when something positive happens and we don't want to "jinx" it by mentioning it or appearing to brag about it.

What can we do about those who hold dear to their superstitions? Nothing, absolutely nothing. No matter at times how irrational they may be, superstitions will continue to color our judgment.

Oh yes, if it's raining today, be sure not to open the umbrella in the house!

Investing In A Child's Future Makes A Difference

I remember sitting in study hall in seventh grade when Rodney Caldwell rolled a *National Geographic* magazine tightly, bound it with several rubber bands and from the back of the long room, heaved it forward with all of the strength of his quarterback arm, over the head of its intended victim, Charlie Bray, and smack into the plaster wall.

For the more than two minutes it took Mr. Hishon to walk from his desk in the back of the room, all the way to the front and over to the corner where it stuck out, like a Bowie knife in a tree, the room howled until we hurt.

He yanked the magazine out of the wall, dusted it off, rolled off the rubber bands, and straightened it out as he huffed back to deal with David.

It took several months for the hole to be patched, and those of us who witnessed that day would point to the spot where it landed and retell the story.

It's funny what we remember about our school.

The time five of us got in trouble in the library for carving up a wooden newspaper holder to make toothpicks to eat the olives I had smuggled to school that day.

Lining up outside the old cafeteria for lunch, running across the grounds to be early in line so we could eat fast and go out to play.

Studying and then eating crawfish – for the first time – in biology lab, drawing angles and designs with a compass in geometry, our history teacher/coach drawing plays on the board every Friday, explaining to every history class our plan for that night's football game.

Writing a short essay on love for English. Giving a speech on sound, which terrified me beyond reason.

Typing on old manual typewriters, and having a turn once every week to use the only electric one in the room. Welding and cutting in the old, ill-equipped machine shop.

It all happened in the same school district for me. I started in one building, and I moved to another one when I got older.

It was a long time ago for me. But my memories of my school years, and my school building and facilities, meager as they were, are still vivid and important.

I didn't always appreciate school, but I did have enough sense to know that it was important, and I did like and respect my teachers – who cared and often went on fairly soon to better paying jobs.

But it was the place that I still visualize. I still drive by once in a while when I return to my home, just to look, and see how it's changed.

Despite the changes, it still represents my community's collective interest in its own future, its investment of time and energy and care and financial resources in its children's education.

Many years have passed since my own public school days. But I can still remember my teachers in elementary and high school: Mrs. Witaker and Miss Marshall in first and second grade; Mrs. Cameron and Mrs. Kelly in third/fourth; Mr. Dixon and Mr. Booker in fifth/sixth; and the legendary Miss Smith in seventh/eighth – whom everyone feared and few liked, but who in her dying days, years after I was in her classroom, presented me with a cross-stitched picture that had hung in her room for probably 40 years.

I could name most of my high school teachers, too, but I would be hard-pressed to name more than a few of my college professors from either undergraduate or graduate school.

Our school and our teachers do have an impact on us, they do make a difference, often in ways that we are not always aware of at the time.

My high school principal made a complimentary remark to me one time, almost in passing; yet that small courtesy made a tremendous impact for it made me study hard and strive to make something of myself.

I didn't want to disappoint him because of the confidence he'd shown in me, and I owe him more than I can ever repay.

Just as our school days are a vital part of our personal growing and learning experience, so schools are a vital part of a community.

Almost three decades later, after my high school days when we made our decision to move to the Dallas area, I was lured to DeSoto in large part because of what I had read and heard about its schools.

Quality education is very important to me for my children. I want to provide them with the best opportunity they can get in order to meet the challenges they will face in life and work.

I recently asked my son's friend Robert about his experience so far in ninth grade. "It's OK, but it's too crowded," he said. "Too crowded" summarizes our present school situation simply and clearly.

What is essential? What is non-essential? Every community should address the issue honestly and openly.

For when a community reaches consensus, when its educational expectations are reasonable, and when it will commit adequate resources for the realization of those objectives, it will not be disappointed in the performance of its schools or the achievement of its youth.

Putting our children's educational needs first by building to meet their future, showing our belief and value in quality education, we show this as our priority by supporting school bond proposals. When our school boards ask the question, let's say, "Yes" to our children.

Miles Of Understanding

In fourth grade we picked up Billy Martin, who had the distinction of flunking each of the first three grades once. Of course, by then he was three years taller and bigger and meaner than any of us, and I guess he had decided some time the preceding summer that he was tired of having to take every grade twice. He made it known to us before the first test that he wasn't going to fail it, and we were going to make sure that didn't happen, or else he'd meet us after school.

We assumed an after-school meeting with Billy Martin who had flunked a test would not be a tutoring session. We might learn something, but it would be lying flat on the ground looking up at this giant boy who had just knocked you down. Nobody wanted an afternoon school encounter with Billy.

For the first few weeks of school, Billy mostly ignored us except during tests, going off somewhere else during recesses and lunch. After a while we settled into a routine and sometimes on the playground he would decide to play baseball, and of course, both sides wanted him since he could knock balls over the back fence. In football whenever he had the ball, we just stood back out of the way or else he'd knock us all down and step on us as he bullied his way to the goal.

Billy came around to at least tolerating us and we became friendly, if not friends. That is, as long as we made sure he was to pass his classes. He arranged for that by selecting strategic seats in different classes, behind and to the left of the person likely to make the best grade who would let him copy. I was never very happy about sharing my spelling words with him, and while I never said he could copy (giving me a moral leg up, my reasoning went), I also didn't try to cover my answers when I knew he was looking. Since I was a pretty good speller, Billy amazed the teacher that year with his spelling ability. My less-than-legible handwriting no doubt made it hard for Billy to copy everything correctly, but he got by.

He was a little less lucky in English class. One day he was copying a test from Henry sitting up one row and to the right, while Miss Stern was busy grading papers. Henry was not my choice to copy from if I ever needed a quick answer, but he usually did make D's while Billy was more used to F's. On this test this day, Henry, stumped by an item on the test wrote, "I don't know the answer." Without missing a beat, Billy promptly wrote "me neither" on his own test paper for the same question. Miss Stern didn't identify the culprit the next day, but she did say "Me neither" was not a correct answer for the test question.

He should have been in seventh grade that year, and compared to us, seventh graders were pretty big and frightening, and we were scared to go down the hall to use the bathroom because if there were any junior high kids in there, they loved to hassle the elementary kids. One advantage we learned we had by helping Billy with tests is that he would be a bodyguard for us when we ventured down the hall into the junior high world, or out on the playground where sometimes older kids came over and hassled the younger ones. We even started to hang around with Billy some, and felt like we were pretty cool.

But he was also a bully in other places, and except for the ones who would help him in school (help him or die, we feared), others avoided him out of fear. One day I saw why. After lunch I was walking back towards the end of school for my next class when I noted a cluster of kids yelling and cheering. As I got closer I could see two people rolling around on the ground, punching and kicking each other.

One of them was Billy, bitterly fighting some high school kid much bigger than he was. I didn't see it start and didn't know what it was about, but it was violent. The other guy had Billy pinned down to the ground with his knee in Billy's stomach and was about to land a punch to the face when Billy lurched and twisted and rolled out from under the other guy. He jumped up and before the other guy knew it, Billy charged into him and landed a hard fist squarely on the guy's face, knocking him backwards into the concrete steps. As the boy struggled to get up Billy ran over and kicked him hard in the stomach and then hit him again in the face with his fist. Blood spurted from his nose and the side of his face, and Billy was standing over him, fists doubled up, taunting him to get up and fight some more if he was so tough.

Suddenly everyone started to scatter; the principal had come out the door at the end of the hallway and was walking quickly towards the sandpit where the fight was. Like the dozens of other witnesses, I ran the other way so Mr. Fields wouldn't recognize me and call me in for an account, and then probably a swatting for standing there and cheering on the fighters.

But I wasn't really cheering on the fighters; I was more dumb-struck by the violence. It was the first time that I had seen a real fight where people bled and were hurt. That was different from the simple squabbles in my past – it was real and it was awful. Maybe more than anything else, seeing that fight probably eliminated my already low interest in fighting.

Billy didn't come back to school for two days and when he did no one ever mentioned the fight, and I never saw him in another fight, although he did continue to be a bully at times, and a friend at other times. Somewhere in early junior high he decided that he might as well try to learn something himself rather than depending on us younger, immature brats for his results, and he stayed with us the rest of the way, and even graduated. He was eligible for sports for one year (due to his age) and he went to the state track meet as a miler.

I saw him maybe 20 years later after we had graduated, and irony of ironies, after having graduated from college, he was working, quite successfully apparently, as a shop and building trades teacher at a local high school.

You just never know!

Peas, Punishment, But No Penance

One day in the seventh grade the teacher's math book with the answers in it turned up missing from her desk. When it was discovered missing, after a whispering huddle between our teacher and the principal, we were all directed to empty our desks. After that search, when it was apparent that we were all innocent, at least for the time being, we turned into helpers, searching every shelf and drawer and closet in the room for the book, in vain, it turned out.

Miss Newcastle, who must have been 95 at least when we had her, looked distraught at the end of the day, more so than usual.

The next morning the principal showed up in the classroom and spoke of the evil deed that had been done by one of us, of the crime one of us had committed by stealing the teacher's book. They had determined, he said, that the thief was one of the seventh graders presently in the room, and just punishment was imminent. The guilty party was invited to confess on the spot and receive a reduced sentence, most likely only eight instead of ten swats with the principal's big paddle.

The guilty party didn't rush down the aisle in a remorseful confession. Two, then three minutes passed. The principal's eyes and the teacher's eyes were both scanning the room like searchlight beams, looking deeply into our eyes to catch the thief in a weak moment. Five minutes of silence and the principal could take it no more. "All right," he said, "since we know it's one of you and you won't do the right thing and confess, you will all have to stay in after class for one hour every day until you decide to confess."

"Maybe that will make you think about what you did," he said. Then he turned and left.

So there we found ourselves, suddenly criminal suspects again. This was not the first stay-in-after-school experience for some of us, though this time it seemed more serious. But this time we had more company. The ones who hadn't had the opportunity before to stay in after school were pretty nervous and jittery, imagining various means of torture and beatings. Our first time, we had expected beatings at least, and were greatly relieved when all we had to do was write 200 times, "I will not misbehave in school again." What a deal that was!

And after writing that 200 times quickly (nothing was said about legibility, which would have kept us there twice as long), we handed the paper over to the teacher who then told us we could go home, less than half an hour into what was supposed to be an hour-long punishment.

The first time didn't take long, so the second time it took us a little longer to write 350 more times something like "I will not flip peas in the cafeteria with my spoon again." More words and more times kept us there more than half an hour that time, but when we were finished writing we could go.

The third time we assumed it would be 500 times saying, "I will not throw rocks at cars passing by again." However, tired I guess of even looking at the scribble we turned in, this time we weren't asked to write anything. When we asked if we could go, after about five minutes of silence, the answer was no, you are going to stay here for an hour with your mouths shut and your brains working. Do your homework for tomorrow right now. You have an hour. And with that she picked up a book and began to read, ignoring the three of us completely. We knew better than to talk, and to overcome eventual boredom, we began to do our homework.

So we knew from experience that staying in after school wasn't that bad. But Shirley Jenkins, the straight-A student and teacher's pet, who for the first time in her life, found herself being punished in school, and for something she no doubt did not do, anticipated the worst. At lunch it was said that she was found crying in the bathroom, fearing for her life.

We, on the other hand, were quite pleased that she, and the others in the class, including all the girls, had to stay in, too. For once, we were all equal; no teacher's pet here, just a room full of common criminals. We veterans of staying in after school sharpened our pencils and prepared to write maybe 100 times, "I will not steal the teacher's math book."

But not this time. Miss Newcastle looked us over slowly, her eyes searching each of us as if she had X-ray vision that could see the guilty party inside. She finally said, "I am so disappointed in you all," and that was all. Our pens were poised to write, but the signal never came. That was all she said. We knew we probably shouldn't talk or else it might remind her that we were supposed to be writing. So, pretty soon, we got our books and started our homework. Before long, others took our cue and started doing their homework too. And, ironically, here was a whole class, made to stay in after school as punishment, all doing their homework quietly and efficiently.

That went on for a week. Each day after school Miss Newcastle would ask if anyone was ready to confess, and when no one was, she sat back down at her desk, still looking distraught, and we all quietly set about doing our homework. During our week of incarceration, no doubt more homework was done than in the previous two months.

We assumed we would have to stay in after school for the rest of the year, or maybe the rest of our lives, if the book didn't turn up. But on the next Monday we had a substitute teacher who knew nothing about keeping us after school, so we escaped. When she returned two days later, Miss Newcastle apparently had forgotten about it also, and since she said nothing about seeing us after school, we didn't ask, and so it ended. Perhaps there had been complaints from parents of children who could hardly be suspects, about the blanket accusation and punishment before being proven guilty. I don't know.

I don't remember if the book ever showed up or not, but that was the last of my stay-in-after-school experiences. Even though the reality wasn't so bad, the idea was a stigma and an embarrassment for getting caught doing whatever we had done. And this time we were innocent (or at least all but one person) of the crime, so it seemed especially unfair.

It was a lesson of sorts, a glimpse into a world where life is not always fair, but where it's important to overcome and keep going.

It's Only Words

No doubt I would have made better grades in high school algebra if the class had been in a different room, preferably the history room whose view out of the large windows was the back of the cafeteria, and so, not very interesting. As it was, out of the math room windows we could see across the street to the front of the fairly new gym and beyond to the football field behind the gym. There was nothing especially esthetic about any of this, it just provided a visual diversion from $a + b = c$.

But it was neither the gym nor the football field that became my source of diversion in algebra class. For while the girl who sat two rows over and one row up from me was a lot more interesting than algebra, her lack of interest in me soon caused her to give way to the utility pole across the street from the classroom window, and to the right of the gym. There was nothing special about this pole; it was just the one in my line of vision.

One day when we'd gone way past $a + b = c$, and I was feeling lost and hopeless, I was looking out the window and just noticed the pole. For some reason I started wondering why it was called a telephone pole. I couldn't think of a new name that could replace it.

Later I learned that is the nature of words. Once something gains a widely recognizable and accepted name, like cat or baseball bat, or horse, we all recognize it, and we're also stuck with it. Pole, in fact, has stood for a long, relatively slender, and generally rounded piece of wood, or other material for more than 500 years (in English), so we're pretty used to it by now.

Words that stand for specific things, like pole or cat, or tree or hamburger, are less likely to be confusing than words which stand for ideas or feelings, like democracy or peace, or love.

We express our thoughts and feelings by the use of words (and tone and body language), and we interpret what others mean by their use of words (and tone and body language) in our attempt to understand what they are trying to say. Sometimes they are easy to understand. "Dad, I'm hungry," is pretty clear, coming from a teenage boy. We depend on tone and body language to accompany some words of phrases such as "I love you," or "You did it again," or "That certainly was fun," or "We need to talk," for example, to help us feel more secure about the speaker's meaning.

But when we read something, we see only the words without the body language and tone of voice. When we read, we depend on our interpretation of the words on the page or screen. And that's where we have to be careful, for unfortunately, clear thinking and honest language are not universal goals of all speakers and writers.

"Insincerity," wrote George Orwell, "is the great enemy of clear language." It's easy to choose words that are clear and honest, and it's also easy to choose words that deceive, mislead, distort, or otherwise attempt to hide reality. Examples abound from all professions of people who choose their words carefully, but whose words and facts don't always agree.

What did he mean, for example, when a U.S. Senator said, "Capital punishment is our society's recognition of the sanctity of human life?" Or an administration spokesman speaking of a "period of accelerated negative growth" to describe what others may call an "economic recession." Or a medical report of a "negative patient care outcome," meaning the patient died. What is the difference between a "pre-owned" and a "used" car, other than a higher price?

We must supply our own meanings when words don't stand for obvious, clear, concrete objects (tree, baseball bat, cell phone). How many of us mean the same thing when we use or hear abstract words such as "liberal," "freedom," "human rights," or "the sanctity of life," etc.? What is the "American way of life" that our politicians are so fond of protecting for us? Do we all agree on what that means? Do we all live it? Is it the same for us all?

The Patriot Act is worth a comment. Names and labels influence us or arouse us or lull us to sleep. We learn not to question things associated with patriotism, but a quick examination of the Patriot Act reveals a number of our civil liberties that have been conceded. Because of its carefully chosen, misleading name, we trust it, at our peril.

And is it really a good sign of our "progress," as we are told, that is causing more and more suicide bombings in Baghdad? Do we share a common meaning of the word "progress" in post-war Iraq for example?

It's been a long time since I sat in algebra class and wondered about the name of a telephone pole, and I still can't think of another name for it other than "pole." Maybe because it's clear and simple and honest.

Strength For The Journey

Neither any of my classmates nor I were rich; in fact, many of us stared in the face at what many others would consider poverty. We were poor, but didn't know it. Our lifestyle was all that we knew, and it was one that we shared. There were no others around who had more or did more than we all had or did, together. So, it was the norm, as we knew it.

The struggle that each of our families realized and readily embraced was a common one in my community. Our fathers worked, our mothers stayed home and kept the family together, and we went to school. The struggle as blacks in a time when we were not welcome was also another shared struggle. We all had what we needed, and we went through our days with appreciation, coupled with the hopes of better tomorrows.

Our struggles were shared, with the mutual support of friends and family spread like the jam my mother put on our morning toast. It was a bond that kept us safe and focused. It also gave us strength for the day, and little did I then know, for the lives we were to face ahead.

Our teachers taught us the value of an education that may have been taken for granted. Our parents taught us self-love and respect for each other and ourselves. Our friends taught us to laugh, and our neighbors were further reinforcement for it all.

As time and life came and went, I found myself relying more and more upon the strength that had become a part of my character as a result of my youthful circumstances. I could not have told you what character building was if asked during my younger days, nor could I have cited how things then would help me later. But, as I look at my family, my life and my career choice of education, I realize these things were the fabric that helped to weave me into the man that I am today.

Had there been no effort, no need for struggle or mutual support, I might be without the values of life and love that I have today. Had education been given to us on a silver platter and without the civil fight, I may not have had the dedication and commitment to its excellence and availability for all that is now my mantra.

I learned most importantly that there is a lesson in the struggle, and a strength that emerges as a result. It's a strength that cannot be taught from a book, or as a lesson. It is a strength that is molded, created, baked and then enjoyed with one's self, and the others to whom you wish to impart happiness, a love, and a lesson.

Kindergarten's Life-Long Advantage

It has been said frequently that all you will ever need to know, you learn in kindergarten. And, as time continues, I find that to be truer than ever.

Just look around and you'll see both the good and not so good effects of what I choose to credit or blame on kindergarten. For those who are kind and thoughtful, courteous and sincere, I applaud the kindergarten teacher and lessons of days gone by. And, for those who are rude, thoughtless, ignorant in word and deed, I say shame on the kindergarten teacher and his or her apparently failed efforts.

I remember how rigorous the lessons seemed. Mrs. Smith seemed stern, almost mean in her demand for our class to behave and follow directions. Looking back, her requests were simple, and are now the obvious pattern for personal fulfillment. Things like not speaking while others were talking, saying please, and thank you were the constant requests imposed upon us. "Wow," I remember thinking, "this stuff is hard. If kindergarten is making these kinds of demands of me, what can I expect hereafter?" I wondered.

Little did I know, and not until much later did I completely understand that these were the basics upon which an easier, kinder, gentler and more respectful life could be built. These were, indeed, the building blocks of life.

Yesterday, they seemed insurmountable. Today, they seem almost too simple to carry the weight that they do. However, to those who embraced those simple lessons of life, there is a realization, appreciation, and respect that cannot be measured or described. Those who refused – either by choice or circumstance – to incorporate those lessons into their lives and being are forever shortchanged in all that they have and could be.

Everyone Loves The Fight

It was to be the event of the year, or at least the event of the day. Ronald – the bigger, more bully-like boy at our grade school, and Thomas – the studious and likeable one, were to meet for an old-school showdown on the playground after school. I cannot recall what happened to provoke this encounter, but by lunchtime, it was the talk of the school.

I still fail to see the fascination with watching a fight or any other negative encounter between supposedly intelligent beings, but as a child, it was the excitement that was fueled by the talk and excitement that swirled around the school.

The day's classes were over, and the time for the schoolyard showdown was now at hand. I didn't want to see this fight or whatever it was supposed to be, yet I didn't want to appear to be the only person in the school who wasn't a part of this headlining event.

The students had all gathered around the dirt playground, and anxiously awaited the arrival of Ronald and Thomas. Ronald arrived first, a testament to his bravado, however real or perceived. He showed up first; he wasn't afraid, and even seemed to welcome the opportunity to partake in unnecessary violence.

We all waited for Thomas to show up. And, we waited. After more than 20 minutes, it appeared as though he had something better to do than take the chance of getting his butt whipped by Ronald. His absence gave Ronald the opportunity to claim victory without a fight; to shout that he was the strongest and the bigger bully without the effort. Kids began to whisper that Thomas must have been scared, and ran home.

The more I thought about it, Thomas wasn't scared. He was simply smart. He was clearly the wiser and more intelligent of all of us who stood around waiting to see something that we'd all rather not be a part of. He was probably at home, having dinner or studying by now, doing what he was supposed to – and what we all should – have been doing.

He had won the fight!

Lunch Room Choices Mean Lifelong Returns

Nothing seemed longer, sometimes, than the line for lunch in our school lunchroom. It wasn't the number of students that made it seem so long. It was the choices that we were about to be faced with. Sure, there were jokes about the lunchroom lady, as well as the less than appetizing options that were available to us.

So, in anticipation of what was to come, the wait made the decision-making process all the more stressful. What we selected would dictate the rest of our day. A good selection meant that the rest of the day would, minimally, be pleasant. If we took the wrong selection, it could ruin our stomachs, and therefore the remainder of the day. It could bring bad thoughts, feelings, and influence attitudes and subsequent decisions and actions.

As I now sit and wait for my meals to be delivered to my table, whether breakfast, lunch or dinner, I reminisce about my wait in the lunch line. I think about the thought process that went into my lunch choices because of their apparent impact on my day. Yet, now I think about other choices and their impact.

My choice and decision to pursue education as my career, my choices in jobs, relationships, words and deed have all played a role and impacted my life. Where I am and who I am were all shaped by the simple act of choice.

For others, the choices were not so simple, or their returns as kind. I have learned of the fate of many classmates of days gone by who chose a different and more challenging road. Their end return was not, I am sure, what they were seeking, or desired in their selection. Yet, at the time, the choice seemed to bear minimal negative returns while seeming to offer more immediate gratification. In the end, such choices were wrong on both accounts.

To parallel life to the lunch line is more than fair; it's almost too accurate to bear. For as simple as the life choices we make from the options that we are presented, we realize the returns based solely on those decisions, good or bad. Once we have made a poor selection, it is up to us to refrain from duplicating that choice ever again, should we desire other results.

Sit back, look closely at the choices that life offers you; take them into consideration, as well as what they will bring to your day and your life. Make your decisions wisely, and stand tall after you have done so. Realize that life is, indeed, a smorgasbord that can make you happy and fulfilled, or bring you pain and grief based solely on what you have chosen.

Cultural Awareness Opens Minds To Many Possibilities

There are a lot of good reasons for taking college classes. Some people enroll in a program because they know a college degree will assure them a better job, higher pay, and more benefits. Some high school seniors go to college so they won't have to work all week for minimum wage, but their attention is often focused on making an impression, getting a date, partying, or just trying to figure out who they really are. Some drop out, but even for those who manage to apply themselves in their classes, getting a good grade may be just a means to an end – a degree and a better job.

After 12 years of compulsory schooling, they can't see college as an opportunity to learn. For them it still seems compulsory, and they put in only as much time and effort as they have to.

But along the way to the degree, students are offered all sorts of exciting new experiences, just by spending the day on a college campus. Colleges offer special programs, lectures, musical and sporting events and also programs on money management, health, fitness, and time and stress management. College counseling centers offer free counseling, information about careers, and the opportunity for students to test their interest, personality, and aptitudes.

Sitting in a class with people from another culture or people who live another lifestyle is a chance to stretch their understanding of differences. It also presents a setting where myths can be dispelled. One learns the importance of tolerance, which is just as important and useful as learning to factor equations or write complete sentences.

The status of expensive clothes or cars, and the stigma of wearing old, out-of-style clothes and cheap shoes, becomes less important than the ability to understand the lecture and do the homework.

Entering a college class is an opportunity to remember school as it used to be and notice the changes. Students sit a seat apart from each other, and rarely in the first or last row unless only a few seats are left. No one wants to appear too interested or too bored. Students usually sit in the same seat all semester, just like high school. But, unlike high school where everyone else is familiar, a college class is a group of new people waiting to be met. Students in the class may be complete strangers, but they are united in their efforts to figure out what the teacher wants and what the tests will be like. Meeting together two or three times a week for 16 weeks, students can find friends to study or eat lunch with, and these friendships can continue on after the class ends.

Sometimes employees are sent back to school to upgrade their job skills. Classes for them are usually sandwiched between a full day at work and home. They meet with other classmates who work, drive kids, rush to finish their homework, and try to maintain some sort of family life at the end of the day. They can learn a lot just by looking and listening to how other students manage their busy lives. Most returning students, convinced they can't think or remember things anymore, are often happily surprised. Although college can require more discipline than a senior high student can imagine, after working a full-time job and raising kids it seems manageable – even easy.

Somewhere between the senior high prom and the children's soccer games, college becomes an opportunity to learn. After years spent pleasing an employer, often for minimum wage, adults see college as a welcome choice to improve their own future. There are no parents to please with grades, but returning students must please themselves – a harder task. They are interested in the information presented in class, and ask thoughtful questions. They appreciate studying in the library or just reading a magazine or checking out the new books. They have invested their time and money in learning, in self-development, instead of choosing to be entertained by watching someone else perform on TV or in the movies. At the end of the semester they will have new knowledge and skills, and more confidence. People don't lose the ability to learn, but they can get out of practice, and convince themselves that learning is only for young kids.

Taking a college class is one of the best ways to find out that learning takes time and effort, but it pays back. Students benefit, not only by applying themselves, learning the material and succeeding in the course, but by learning how to expand their view of the world and the future opportunities it holds for them.

New Skills, New Life

I cannot think of a better illustration of the value and importance of having an employable skill than the following true story.

A 22-year-old man, John, recently lived at home with his parents. He worked just enough to keep himself stocked with beer, cigarettes, and tennis shoes. However, his bubble burst and he found himself out of the house, without a job and totally responsible for himself and his truck insurance. He thought for a minute about living in his truck, but decided to move in with some friends.

A couple of weeks later, his friends were arrested for theft. They had stolen cigarettes and beer from the corner service station. Being in the wrong place at the wrong time, John was taken down too. During his four-day county vacation, he had a lot of time to think and the $2,500 fine really helped reality set in. John decided to be responsible and get a job.

He had attended the local community college for two years while living with his parents. He earned several certificates in welding. He was appropriately humiliated when he told the foreman at a job interview that he did not have a lot of experience outside of the classroom, but he did know how to "run ahead." That was exactly what the foreman wanted, the rest he could teach him. John was hired at a beginning salary of $12 per hour. He worked eight hours his first day and 16 the next. Each day he would come home tired but proud because he had acquired some skills and now had an opportunity to put them to use.

It's been quite some time since I held a welding torch, probably not since high school, and I probably can't do it anymore. I can't repair my VCR or my computer, and let's not even talk about repairing my car, which is something I used to be able to do. My not being able to still do it today exemplifies the fast pace of technological advances as they apply to our specific needs, but that's another story.

How many of us, who are not medical technologists, know how to draw blood, run the blood analysis and read the results? Anyone who is not in the medical profession would face an impossible task if they attempted to do so. Now, what do all of the aforementioned skills have in common? I can think of at least three things.

First, millions of us depend, every day, on the people who are capable of performing these tasks. Imagine, if you will, an America without technologically competent people. Remember when the furnace went out and you couldn't find anyone to come fix it because the demand for skilled heating and air conditioning technicians was so high that there were just not enough of them to go around?

When our computer network crashes we immediately contact a qualified and competent computer technician, just as we would call an EMT if an individual was injured in an automobile accident.

Second, entry into these fields requires specific education and training. Sometimes we refer to this type of educational experience as "occupational" or "vocational" education. What we are really talking about is the development of specific skills, which can make us employable and competitive in today's world of work.

Our friend John couldn't have gotten the job that he landed if he didn't have the necessary skills for the position. Even though his skills were very basic, he had the basics down pat and enough common sense and the appropriate attitude to fit into the environment and grow with it.

John was fortunate in that he did make some sacrifices and had foresight from his past, which inspired him to attend the local community college and enroll in a program of interest to him.

Third, and maybe most importantly, many people tend to look down on these occupations, considering them "less worthy," "lower-class," or "less important." It has often been the stereotype and only the "best and brightest" go to college and that "those people"(I hate that expression) who are intellectually less fortunate attend trade or vocational schools. Whether or not that notion is true today, I don't know. But I do believe that a test of "those people's" economic competitiveness can be measured by the size of their paychecks. Considering that, in most instances, it took them only two years to acquire their skills while it took the so-called "best and brightest" four, eight, and sometimes even 12 years to acquire their skills. Even the skilled brain surgeon must take her car to the repair shop and pay upwards of $65 per hour for the services of this individual with only two years of education (beyond high school).

You know, you have got to be pretty smart to work on cars today. A computer of some sort controls almost every part, except the gas tank. So in addition to being an automobile repair specialist, they are also computer technicians and electricians as well.

You must also be pretty smart to understand the many functions of the human body, to understand how to operate on patients and understand how to interpret the results of "CAT scans," and "echo cardiograms," which are becoming so popular as a result of the many stressors in our lives today.

One defining advantage of individuals with specific skills, based on the trends of the local economy, is that there is always an opportunity for immediate employment. Remember John? He didn't have to spend sleepless nights working on his resume or spend weeks and months applying for positions and hoping for at least one positive response, as is sometimes the case with the traditional college graduate with a degree.

There is one valid concern regarding most career-oriented educational programs. That is the lack of a broad and diversified educational experience – the kind that we hope will expand our visions and vistas and prepare us to be life-long learners. Many students enter career-oriented programs for the specific purpose of getting a job that can help improve the quality of their lives or the lives of their loved ones.

Years ago, a great number of people sought university degrees because they thought "it will make me a better person," only to find out it made them an unemployed intellectual. That is not to say there isn't a legitimate need in career-oriented training programs for a broad-based education. We are challenged in this society to create a value for the long-term and often subtle effects that our educational experiences have in our lives beyond work and school.

We are challenged to find ways of encouraging and providing opportunities for a broader base of education in our occupational programs. This deficiency may be one of the reasons for the negative contemporary views on career-oriented training programs. However, as it stands, opportunities are abundant for the skilled individuals who come from occupational training programs and the pay is excellent. Even entry-level wages may be more than that of positions requiring a four-year degree. You also own those "occupational" skills and can take them with you wherever you go. The options are there for you to become employed, or to becoming an employer by establishing your own business.

Excellence Is Ripe For The Picking

Last week during an impromptu stop at the grocery store, two large boxes of watermelons caught my eye. It was hot outside and my mind drifted to the cool, pink melon that I envisioned on the other side of the thick green rind. The thoughts prompted me to turn my basket around. A good, ripe, cold watermelon would surely cool me off this day, so I decided to take one home.

A big problem for many is how to actually select a watermelon. I stood and stared at the more than 50 watermelons piled in the bins as though one would jump up and say, "Hey, pick me!"

They all looked the same, which made choosing what I thought would be the sweeter one a difficult task, so I casually thumped one or two. All my life, I have seen people (mostly men) thump watermelons during their selection process, yet I had not the slightest idea of what to listen for. What does a ripe watermelon sound like? How does it differ from one not yet ripe?

I kept thumping and quickly concluded that they all sounded alike. I stepped back to think of another method of choosing the best watermelon. While I was standing there scratching my chin, an elderly couple walked up and parked their basket at the edge of the watermelon bin and began a quiet discussion with each other. The man was small and wiry with short, thinning hair and walked with a stoop, the result of many years and circumstances, perhaps. He approached the bin deliberately and looked at the melons with the studied observation of a nuclear submarine inspector.

He stepped back from the bin to consult with his wife, who waited patiently behind him. He then stepped back to the melons and went to work. He thumped, then picked up one and held it to his ear. He thumped it again, shook it slightly, checked both ends then put it back into the bin.

He continued this pattern with at least 10 more melons, then stepped back to his wife for another consultation. By the third inspection, I was fascinated at his dedication and apparent confidence that he possessed the formula for selecting the perfect melon.

He again approached the bin and started the inspection process. I thought that this might continue for the rest of the day, I could therefore finish my shopping while he was still "looking and thumping." In a few minutes I was finished and returned to the bin of watermelons. The man was still there, in search of the perfect melon.

Since my departure to finish shopping, the man had moved to the second bin of watermelons and was still going strong. I could have stepped into the space he abandoned at the first bin, but that would create a problem. It was apparent that he knew, or at least acted as though he knew, more about picking watermelons. He had obviously rejected all the watermelons in the first bin. I would have felt odd searching through those. I would, after all, not want to take home a second-class watermelon. I didn't want to be seen in public by a watermelon expert – however real or perceived – selecting one of his rejects.

In spite of my long and careful observation of the gentleman's watermelon selecting tactics, I still lacked the confidence to select a perfect watermelon. Even if I thumped one, as he had done, and pretended to know what to listen for, it still would not match the thoroughness and intensity of this elderly man who was, by now, surely checking his 50th melon. Besides, I didn't want to imitate him by shaking and holding them to my ear, especially since the application of such a method to select a watermelon made no sense to me anyway.

At this point, I began questioning my want for this evasive, but alluringly perfect watermelon. Yet, if I were going to do this, I had to take some action. At this point I noted that the elderly gentleman had apparently made his choice. He finally took one over to his wife, who gave it her nod of approval. He set it in their basket and moved on.

Now it was my turn. Nervous and sheepish, I stepped up to the melons, looking around first to make sure that the old man wasn't watching me with disapproval. I randomly thumped three or four and even picked up a couple and examined their ends. I still don't know what I was listening or looking for. Heck, I even shook one, then put it in my basket and quickly headed for the checkout lane hoping to avoid the watermelon expert who might quickly look into my basket and judge my whole life and character simply by my watermelon selection.

In spite of the time spent, I did not learn who this man was or what he does for a living, nor did he learn that of me. The supermarket is an equalizer of sorts – everyone is a shopper, nothing more, nothing less. The experience of watching this man reminded me of the many small, perhaps seemingly insignificant talents and skills that it takes to get through life. While we can't master them all, we each have our own abilities that stand out to others. Therefore, we should never feel bad that we can't do everything like an expert.

If we have the will to succeed and seek to learn and do what we must with excellence, we should be happy and find some level of satisfaction with our talents. Now if I could only choose the perfect watermelon with confidence I would, indeed, be happy.

The Lessons Of Life And Time

It has been some time since I was in the sixth grade, but the memories are still clear. One of my classmates, Johnny, was a nice and friendly young man who was a genius with his hands. He could take an abandoned wagon wheel and turn it into a marvelous and working plaything. But, he never learned to read and appeared a bit slower than the others. He sought and reached out to me in friendship, but I did not reciprocate.

Youth selects on whim, perception or popularity and moves on. Only later, often when we approach what we anticipate as mid-life, do we sometimes pause to reflect on what we have done. If we're careful and honest, we can find things to alter or self-correct to guide us into more satisfying years remaining.

I have thought about Johnny and how he was mostly ignored by us in favor of others more popular, or capable. There were kids, too, who were ostracized or ignored because they were different or just didn't fit in.

We can't have the benefit of wisdom of years without living through those years. But, if I could re-do some things in my life, I would start by responding to Johnny. The truth is, I barely knew him and didn't give him – or myself – a chance. I wonder now if he may have been someone with whom I could have developed a lasting friendship. Perhaps I might have encouraged him to learn to read, and in turn he may have taught me the art of turning junk into jewels.

My grandfather, who lived to be 107, gave me ample time to get to know him. Yet, I regretfully never took full advantage of the wisdom and first-hand history that he presented. I simply did not realize the value of his presence and failed to take the time to spend with him as I should, and now wish that I had.

Modern society doesn't make it easy to slow down and visit. There are too many distractions that seem more interesting at the moment, so we put some things off. Someday – we say.

While my children seem fine, well adjusted and doing well, it is I that carry the baggage of feeling as though I could have spent more time with them in their youth. It was work, travel and more work. I saw my work and success as an investment in my family, yet I now wonder how much I missed by simply not doing anything with them, at least some of the time. I can't go back and make that up; they came and grew so fast. If only I'd known.

No missed opportunity looms greater than the one with my mother. In spite of the time shared and memories created, it wasn't enough to carry me through the years that I must now bear without her. Her encouragement to me to learn her recipe for beans and cornbread or her fried peach pies fell on deaf ears.

A strong woman, she always encouraged a strong belief in people, regardless of their actions. This was hard to comprehend as a child through tears brought on by the neighborhood bully. I couldn't understand how I could believe in someone who taunted me so that it ached inside. "You've got to love them," she would say. Only now do I realize the value and power of her words, as they carry me through situations that would otherwise cause me grief. It enables me to deal with those both for and against me. I hear you now, Mom.

I now recognize our inability to duplicate times and opportunities, chance and occasion. We can't go back and do it differently – whether making a friend, listening to a loved one or simply spending more time with a child, spouse or friend. I look back in reflection as life begins to change its colors and show a different side of things. At the same time, I look ahead and, I do so with promise.

Of all the things that I would not change, one is my role as an educator, to which I am firmly and wholeheartedly committed. I know that education is the key to many of the challenges that we all face in life. Yet, as I look back on all that I have learned, I ponder my legacy and impact on the lives of others. If I were blessed with another 50-plus years, I know now the differences that I would incorporate into my life, and those different choices that I would make.

I would be kinder to more people, and take the time to make new friends and cherish old ones. I would do the things that seemed boring as a child, but that now are voids in my adult life. I would get closer to nature, where we all live. I'd try to do less busywork, and take time to do more interesting and different things. I'd take more small risks, having learned over time that failure is only as damaging as we let it be, but our fear of failure can be devastating. I'd travel more and earlier, as seeing other places and people and ways of life is more valuable than I ever realized.

These are the lessons of life and time. Only by living and learning are we able to realize the value of that which we overlooked earlier. While I cannot relive those years, I can continue to create what I hope will be a path of self-realization and actualization, to help others be the best that they can be, and get the most from their lives. While I may have missed out on Johnny's friendship, real-life history lessons from my grandfather and mom's beans and cornbread and fried peach pies, I will try harder in the next half of my life not to miss any more opportunities of life and love.

Handicaps Are What You Allow Them To Be

I noticed a van, always parked in the same handicap space, several times without much reaction. I saw the van on a regular basis, but paid it very little attention. I couldn't even tell you if it had the appropriate stickers and certifications to be there. It was a rather non-descript vehicle – old, blue and plain.

But I eventually saw one characteristic, which struck me. It was the sticker in the back window that said "Just Do It!" along with the Nike logo with which the slogan is associated. It was then I started to pay closer attention to the vehicle, and subconsciously to seek out the person to whom it belonged.

Walking past the handicap parking spaces for me is kind of a reminder and opportunity for thankfulness. It is a renewal of appreciation for the abilities I still possess. I find myself wondering about those who are in these vehicles. Are they driving themselves? Is their handicap temporary? Is someone responsible for getting them to their daily obligations and desires? It is a stark reminder to be thankful for much of what many take for granted. Walking. Speaking. Driving.

I sometimes, albeit briefly, ponder the thought of what would I do if faced with a physical challenge. Would I be able to adapt to being dependent on someone else for that which I was accustomed to doing for myself? Could I handle it? What would I do? How do others handle such challenges?

In all honesty, I expected the blue van to belong to someone who had no physical handicap, but rather just the handicap of inconsideration for those for whom this space was designed. While it is not a good thing, it's a real thing, where those who have no real need for a handicap parking space take full advantage of its privileges. It was always real, but never more so until the day I watched as a specially equipped van circled in frustration searching for a handicap space. There were none.

The van eventually settled on the next closest space, and I watched as this woman struggled to get a young adult from the van and into a wheelchair. The young person had a lot of apparent physical limitations, and the poor woman struggled with all her might to make the transition from van to wheelchair a smooth one. I looked around as the vehicles that were occupying those spaces and tried to guess just how many of them were truly in need of the spot for convenience while this woman and young person were in need of it by necessity?

It was some time later, but I finally saw a person who drives this mystery van. I saw her as she was exiting the van. Yes, she was confined in a wheelchair. When she looked up, it became evident as to why she had this encouraging and spirited message on the back of her van. She was a young lady, college aged and a spirit found only in youth. Her eyes and smile were bright, and her voice was joyful as she said good morning to a stranger. She maneuvered her chair with skill and determination. She looked up, not down as she traveled from her van to her destination.

While I wondered what the condition was that put her in a wheelchair, it was evident that she had no handicap at all. I don't know her circumstances, name or anything else. But, her spirit is so illuminating, that if I were to write her story, it would be one of promise. Apparently, she isn't angry or bitter about her circumstances, and is not held back by any limitations she may be able to otherwise use as an excuse not to do something. In this young woman I see an encouraging reminder of how our so-called handicaps are only what we allow them to be. I would suggest that there are tons of people walking around without assistance every day who allow themselves to be held back by controllable factors and circumstances. Our handicaps are only what we allow them to be. Taking mobility and other characteristics of freedom for granted prevents appreciation. We forget that we are not entitled to be blessed with such amenities.

Just because a person cannot move as freely or quickly, or perhaps requires some assistance is not a handicap. It is only one if they allow it to be, unlike the young lady driving the van. They may face different challenges, but the rewards of achievement can be that much sweeter and more appreciated. All we have to do, too, is just do it.

There Is Nothing To Fear But Fear Itself

In one of my quiet moments, it occurred to me that if people would just take time to think, they could reconstruct their lives by remembering times when they felt strong emotions.

When we've lived long enough, most adults can come to understand the wisdom in these calming words: "The only thing we have to fear is fear itself." They admonish us to not give in to fears, but to use our God-given ability to go forth and overcome adversity. If we're fortunate, we learn we do have some control over our fears, and we learn how to deal with the situations that create our fears, to overcome and reduce them to manageable levels.

Many of our adult fears are rational, and with distance, time out, and perhaps help from our friends, we can view them as such and begin to work on ways to avoid the consequences of our fears, which can otherwise paralyze and terrify us.

But often childhood fears are not rational, not the result of a realistic appraisal of the situation, and, therefore, less easily overcome or explained away. The most terrified I've ever been in my life was after I saw *The Creature with the Atom Brain* when I was 10 years old. The creature had zipper track-like stitches all around his head where a mad scientist had captured a man randomly off the streets, cut off his head and replaced his brain with some gizmo that allowed the scientist to direct the creature's actions from a remote control box nearby.

Nothing my mother could say could erase that zippered forehead image from my mind. No amount of reasoning, praying, or her explaining that it was just a movie and there was really no such creature could help. Rational explanations don't usually work on irrational fears.

My friend's wife had an absolute terror of swimming pool drains as a child. She feared being sucked through the grate and into the underground world of pipes and sewers, and feared that she'd spend the rest of her life trapped down there with the rats and sludge.

It kept her from completing swimming lessons for years, because she was afraid to swim from the deep end, where the drain was, to the shallow end in order to complete her test. No matter how often her mother assured her that she could not be sucked through the grate like cheddar cheese through a grater, she could not overcome that fear.

There are more rational fears, of course, that probably most of us experience as children. I feared, for instance, that my parents would die in a car crash nearly every time they went together somewhere without me.

When I began to learn about the stars and heavens in school, I feared the sun would explode sooner than predicted, imagining myself frying one day like bacon in a pan. For a while I was afraid that gravity would give out and I'd go floating off into space, gone forever.

The air raid drills in my elementary school, to prepare for the atomic bombs the Russians were going to drop on us any day, made me afraid that I'd never reach adulthood, a fear that has only subsided since the fall of the Iron Curtain. Calming words go only so far, and they can never guarantee freedom from death in a car wreck or from an atomic bomb.

I feared integration. My high school class was the last to attend my segregated school, and I remember we feared having to give up the identity and security we knew in our school, for the unknown, for someone else's school.

Childhood fears that we sometimes tend to make light of, especially the irrational ones that often seem silly to parents – creatures with atom brains, swimming pool drains – can be devastating to a child. Our youthful fears often limit us in ways we are not aware of, strangling us, keeping us hidden beneath our covers, keeping us afraid of life outside.

During this graduation season, we are all thinking about moving forward in life. Academic struggles may have led us to believe graduation was impossible. We may have hesitated to take courses similar to ones where we did not perform well because we did not want to fail. Graduation is here, and those who made it know you have to try some things that you are afraid to do. Yes, the fears will be there, but we have to let our focus on ultimate goals overpower them. If we remember times when we conquered fears to reach our goals, we can gain strength to conquer new fears and improve our lives.

Time To Live Our Dreams

The events this country experienced in September 2001 have taken an emotional, financial and political toll. They changed the way America exists, perhaps forever.

What we have now more than anything is uncertainty. Uncertainty for those whose loved ones are missing, our economic climate, international relationships and for some, even day-to-day existence.

For me, this uncertainty stands as a reminder of how important and precious time is in our lives, how tomorrow is not promised and that clocks cannot be put on hold. Rather than allow the question of our tomorrows to loom as a dark cloud over our collective heads, we should allow it to serve as an inspiration to do that which is in our hearts.

I think often of the late comic Robin Harris. He had worked long and hard for many years to break into the comedy arena of the entertainment industry. Just as he began to realize the success of which he had long dreamed, he suffered a fatal heart attack. However, his dream was something that he did realize.

I think of how many people walk around with their dreams tucked in their pockets, waiting for the right time to pursue them. If nothing else, let me be the first to say that this is, indeed, the right time. Many today know not the fear and shackles of war, and even challenge the reality of it ever occurring. But times are indeed changing. Not just by the year, but by the minute.

The threat of war or continued strained, international relations is a real thing, yet one that eludes the mental grasp of many.

Now is the time to dust off your dreams, hopes and plans for doing what you want, saying what you feel, and really living your life to the fullest. The time to venture into life's uncharted waters is never ideal, but you may never know the ease of its navigation, or the rewards of the trip if you never venture from the dock.

People who realize their dreams sometimes speak of "life-changing" experiences that pushed them to the point of doing something. Well, wait no longer. Let the climate of our country be your inspiration. People now go about their days, nicer and more appreciative of their lives, which is a good thing. It makes everyone's days better. Yet, that same formula can also be used for personal achievement.

Arm yourself with the appreciation of yesterday and the uncertainty of tomorrow. It is, indeed, the best protection from going through life with the regret of never having, at least, tried to realize your dreams, whatever they may be. Whether it is going back to school, starting a garden, changing careers, being a better spouse or parent, or any of hundreds of other things, let today really be the first day of the rest of your life.

Procrastination is a funny thing. It allows false comfort for those who want to put off what really could and should be done today. The real tragedy is that they often never know what they missed.

Instant Karma

There are a lot of things during the holiday season that help me to think about the Golden Rule. There is the angel tree in the mall, the Salvation Army bell ringers in front of every store, the collection boxes for food at schools and churches, and the reminders in church sermons to help those who have less. Sometimes these requests for time and money are draining. Thanksgiving and Christmas seem to require endless giving and not necessarily something we really want in return.

After a day of giving – or shopping for loved ones and those relatives we don't really love that much – the Golden Rule can be clouded over by a haze of exhaustion and emptiness. It's difficult to visualize the connection between the dollar we slipped into the Salvation Army bucket, and the happy face of a four-year-old unwrapping a new winter hat. But just because we don't have the time to think about the many people who benefit from our gifts, or the opportunity to see their smiling faces, doesn't mean that our gifts are insignificant.

I remember when I was around seven and my mother first told me about the Golden Rule. I asked her what happened if the other children didn't know it, and even though I asked them to play at my house after school many times, they didn't ask me over to their homes.

She explained that sometimes the good feelings we give out don't always return to us in exactly the same way. And sometimes it's at a different time so we don't even notice it. But she told me that the Golden Rule was something that I could rely on throughout my life. If I gave out positive, friendly thoughts and actions, people would respond positively, and I would be a happier person.

Unfortunately, although many people say they also believe in the Golden Rule, or karma, or "whatever goes around, comes around," they don't seem to practice it in their daily lives. Maybe it's that little fear that no matter how much I give, I'll probably never get anything, so why give. That's a little like the feeling kids have when they decide they won't try salad because they are sure they won't like it. It's easy to watch all the commercials on TV for things we don't have and begin to think that other people are happier because they have a lot more things than we do. We rarely see the faces and lives of the homeless or elderly who live alone, or the children in the school backpack programs, who don't have anything to eat on the weekends.

Driving around the parts of town where we don't want to live is often a quick lesson on how good our lives really are. Even watching children who have no gloves or boots playing in the snow can motivate us to put another dollar in the Salvation Army bucket, or donate a turkey to a homeless shelter. And our instant reward is knowing that we did what we would hope someone would do for us if we, or our kids, didn't have enough to eat or warm clothes to wear.

Even after the Christmas season, there are small ways to spread what we used to call in the 70s—"good vibrations." Although many of us work in suburbia or high-rise office buildings, far from the faces of hungry children in their homes, there are many people, including our families, who could use a pleasant smile every day.

I recently spoke to the daughter of a friend about her job as a checker in a Wal-Mart store. She said that very few people spoke to her even after she greeted them as a checker is supposed to. She told me how much she and her co-workers liked to be recognized with a smile and a friendly "hello" and "thank you" from the customers they were serving.

Maybe the idea is so simple that it doesn't seem as if it could make much difference. However, frequently during the holidays, salespeople and customers are often disinterested, or worse, they are even rude.

Business transactions are much smoother when both parties are friendly and considerate. Being courteous takes conscious effort at first, but after a little practice it becomes more natural. If the Golden Rule works, this courtesy should come back to the people giving it out.

It's always nice to find ourselves in situations where people are positive and kind to each other, so we need to take the responsibility for making that happen – on the job, at home, and everywhere we go. If we really believe in the Golden Rule, we can take the chance of smiling or offering a hand to shake first, knowing that down the road this simple gesture will come back in some form to help make our lives richer.

Lessons About Learning

Through personal experience, I discovered that there is a value to public education that goes beyond what can be learned in books or on a blackboard. It is awareness of the poor and disposed – who increasingly populate our urban schools – who need and suffer the most. Regrettably, their needs are not being met.

During my generation, adults who benefited from the civil rights movement and from the expansion of the American public school system after World War II replaced the older generation of blacks who grew up before schooling was widely available for them. The intervening years were filled with major breakthroughs and educational progress. I, too, was swept up in a wave of attainment.

Then, there was no great mystery about education. Once everyone was afforded access, public schools in America worked just fine. Learning required hard work, common sense and a willingness to accept personal responsibility for our achievements – or lack of them. But during the 1960s and 1970s, America thought it was wise enough to redefine education.

The educational gurus of the day set out to make it more relevant, more attractive to teachers, more efficient for administrators, more palatable to all. They sought to transform the time-honored formula for the public school system that relied on heavy public support for schools in return for meritocracy, in which excellence was the watchword.

In this new educational order, everybody would succeed and

nobody would be allowed to fail. Children's inherent creativeness was to replace the educational drudgery of old. As educational excellence gave way to the feel-good lesson plans, and multiple-choice questions, support for public education steadily waned.

Public education, though, remains particularly vital to urban education. It receives so much attention from policy makers because black and brown students are more likely to make low grades and to drop out of school than their white counterparts. It is also a place where young people learn about each other and begin to share the civil virtues that make wholesome communities possible. It is the traditional pathway to success. It is the only social program that makes people independent instead of dependent. So if those who come to school aren't encouraged to make the most of the opportunities afforded them, all of society suffers.

There is more than a little truth to teacher and school administrator complaints that they are being made to answer for wider social problems among poor and minority students. The roots of these problems are linked to socioeconomic factors outside school that get in the way of urban kids performing well.

School is no substitute for the parent who gives his or her child a head start in reading with bedtime stories, and later cracks the whip on homework. Caring teachers can't stand in for missing fathers. Metal detectors can't send messages to youngsters about the value of self-control.

That said, our schools could and should be doing far better than they are. There is no excuse for graduating students who can barely read or compute. There is no excuse for schools that turn out kids who lack the competence or self-discipline to hold down entry-level jobs. There is no excuse for schools that are considered so bad by their own teachers that many send their own children to private schools. That's why a thoroughly aroused public is demanding tangible changes.

There are those who would scrap our schools and start over. I am not willing to go that far. It's important not to overstate the situation. Most of the kids attending city schools are there to learn. Compared with some of the neighborhoods around them, the schools they attend may be islands of tranquility. Yet any temptation to simply throw more money at the problem should be tempered and firmly tied to reform.

America has always put great faith in education. If public education is to maintain the public trust, however, it must be willing to look at itself honestly and adapt to change. With every crisis comes an opportunity. In today's environment, we must run faster just to stay in the same place. In asking more of our schools, we will really be asking more of ourselves.

We must start from the premise that there are still no great secrets about how to teach our kids what they need to know. What's needed are better execution of the basics, accountability, some decent management, and the fortitude to boldly act.

My own favored path to reform consists less of new educational programs, and more of removing barriers to the natural thirst for knowledge and betterment that exists in most children.

Love On A One-Way Street

I remember the year Coach Thompson came to our junior high football team. He was young and athletic, and it was probably his first coaching job out of college. We were a pretty bad team so he had a difficult experience coaching a team that lost most of its games. I assume the trouble was we were not a very good team, not merely his lack of coaching experience and ability. It was my first year to play and he was my first coach, so I didn't have anything to compare.

I remember him being young enough to go out and run with us sometimes, and he could always beat us. He was likeable, but not overly friendly. He taught something in high school, but I don't remember the subject he taught.

But what I do remember more about Coach Thompson was Mrs. Thompson. She was the second grade teacher, while he was a high school teacher and assistant football coach. They were newly wed, as I recall, and until she came to our school, I didn't know that teachers could be young and beautiful. So far the ones I'd had as my teachers were mostly old and, well, not as attractive as Mrs. Thompson.

She must have been in her mid 20s, but she looked even younger. She was slender with a good figure and had bright, friendly eyes and smile. It didn't take long for me to fall in love with this gorgeous woman. I suddenly developed an interest in the elementary wing of the school again. Under normal circumstances once you moved to junior high, you were never caught dead again down in the "little kid's wing" of the school.

But these were no longer normal circumstances. It wasn't long before I'd stroll down to the first and second grade wing, way out of my way to the lunchroom. I would slow down and look in at Mrs. Thompson teaching her students and drool the rest of the way to the lunchroom. Not because of the good food awaiting me there either. I found I could ignore pretty easily the fact that she was newly married to my football coach, and was probably twice my age. Such details did not get in the way of my infatuation with her.

Realistically, I couldn't figure out any way to take Mrs. Thompson to the after-football season dance. My biggest concern was that I didn't have a car, and therefore couldn't pick her up for a date. Since I never could figure out how to solve that problem, I didn't have to worry about what Coach Thompson might say if I were to ask if I could borrow his wife for the evening (it seemed more plausible at that time than it does now that she might even consider such an offer).

We spent the year strolling by her room and peeking in (I wasn't the only young male at the school who thought she was beautiful, so some days there were several of us strolling by, peeking in her door). I guess coaching a losing team and then having the team walk by and gawk at your wife every day was enough to encourage them to move somewhere else the next year. So as quickly as she entered my life, she disappeared.

Accepting and dealing with the harsh reality that my first love failed, but not one to stay down for long, I thought it would be good to look around for a replacement. There was a pretty girl in my biology class that seemed worthy of my time and affection. But it turned out when I asked her to meet me after school one day that she said she was interested in this guy in her math class, who had a lot more class than I did (her words). But he was interested in this other girl in his history class, and she was interested in the guy that dropped out of school and worked at the gas station. Probably because he was the only one who had any money.

I sometimes thought and reflected about this phenomenon of

one-way interests. I can remember at times throughout high school that I'd be interested in a girl, who was interested in someone else, and in turn, there were girls from time to time interested in me that I was not interested in. It was probably a good thing at that time, to reduce the number of us getting too serious too soon, or thinking we had found our soul mate too early. Since a lot of the interest was physical, one-way interests no doubt prevented some problems that occur when two people get together for the wrong reasons, including accidental pregnancies.

It was to my long-term benefit that Mrs. Thompson didn't find me as attractive and irresistible as I found her. If she had decided to leave Coach Thompson for me, I would have had to drop out of eighth grade and get a job to support her, and would probably not have had the opportunity later to meet the one who was to become my soul mate, for all the right reasons.

Have Hot Dogs For Breakfast

Early one morning, I walked into a small diner while visiting a small city on a recent business trip. I had never been into this diner, and for the most part was unfamiliar with the area, its people and practices.

I sat down and waited to be served. While waiting, I looked around, trying to take in the sights and smells that made this place so different. Different in my never having been here before, and different in its own right to be unique.

I noticed people who moved a lot slower than the people at home. The pace was deliberate, intentional and seemingly with much thought. Nothing seemed haphazard, and even time seemed to move slowly. The waitress came over, and very courteously took my order – a cup of coffee, water, dry toast, and oatmeal. Nothing special, but it was breakfast as I was accustomed. I continued to wait, and continued my close examination of my surroundings. It was a simple place, nothing special, but clean and comfortable. People were friendly, and most seemed to know each other.

An older gentleman sat at the table next to me. He looked, nodded with a smile and went about his business of getting situated in his seat and preparing for his meal. I wasn't really trying to listen, but couldn't help but overhear him as he placed his order. At first I thought that I heard him incorrectly. Then I thought about it and recalled what I thought I had heard, and realized that I did hear him right the first time. This gentleman ordered hot dogs for breakfast. Two of them.

Now, I realize that one does not have to eat traditional "breakfast" foods for their first meal of the day, but I was so entrenched in the traditionalism of this little town and restaurant, that his order threw me for a loop. Feeling that there was more, I wanted to know what was behind his order. I looked over hoping to catch his eye. When I did, I smiled. He smiled back, and I began a conversation. "So the hot dogs must be good here," I said. As though he knew what I was thinking or had been asked this before, he began explaining his reasoning behind his order.

He began by saying how people have such rigid expectations and parameters for their behavior. He talked about how people conformed their lives to expectations, rather than preferences. He continued by saying that ordering hot dogs for breakfast was his way of reminding himself – and others – that the joy of life is in the choices that we have. And that the greater joy is in exercising our right to enjoy those choices.

We finished what turned out to be a wonderfully enlightening conversation, and our respective meals. We exchanged goodbyes, and went our separate ways. I took with me, though, a new reminder of the freedom of choice that I enjoy and sometimes take for granted. I also took with me the observation that simple decisions and choices that we can exercise can make all the difference – in our lives and the world.

Winning Truly Takes A Team

I have happened upon a middle school boys' basketball game now for two weeks in a row. I watched as the young men anxiously awaited their opportunity to be the show's star...to steal the ball...to make a basket. The pace sometimes seemed so fast that I, in passing, had difficulty keeping up with what was actually going on. It was a well-mannered and apparently disciplined group of young men, yet the excitement was overwhelming. You could feel the anxiety in the air as it seemingly contributed to the haphazardness of the game.

Young men were running around, shouting, referees were sweating, cheerleaders were cheering. Yet, the team was losing. You would think that with this much energy, there would, at least, be some points on the board. But, there weren't. And when there were, there were not many. So what was the problem, I wondered? It seemed that each young man was bringing something to the team. One was quick, the other had passing skills and another could shoot.

This question became my project. And I made it my business to really pay close attention to this game and its players. I watched, and I wondered. I watched a little longer, and then wondered no more. The reason they were deficient on the scoreboard was obvious. Even though they were all good players, they played lousy as a team. Everyone was a ball hog. There was no teamwork on the floor. Everyone was trying to be a superstar, at the unsuspecting expense of the team and the game.

I hear the adage that it takes a village to raise a child, and that teamwork wins. Nowhere was it more apparent to me than at this basketball game. It was crucial that each person make a contribution to the success that all would enjoy. If each of these young men would recognize and respect their differences, in talent and ability, and then allow each of those things to work in unison rather than conflict, the team would be fine. And they would win.

But as long as they each sought to realize their own individual accomplishment without regard for the overall goal, or for the others involved – they were, and would forever remain losers.

This same principle must be applied to all that we seek to change.

We either do it together, or fail alone.

The Young & The Restless

Last week I talked to a good friend whose grandson is in first grade in another state.

He told me that the schoolchildren there had to give up recess a few years ago. Now, beginning in the first grade, they go to school all day long. They do get to go outside for a few minutes if they eat their lunches quickly and quietly enough before the next period begins. Otherwise, they spend the day working in school.

Shocking isn't it?

Who doesn't remember a time when we as schoolchildren would occasionally daydream the morning away waiting for that morning recess bell to ring? Our minds were invigorated with thoughts of fresh air, sun and some fun. It was a chance to make as much noise as possible without fear of punishment.

And if it was raining, indoor hijinks could satisfy us with a game of eraser tag or doing the Hokey Pokey. The goal was just to get moving fast enough so our young minds would be ready to soak up information in class.

The point about recess is that we should all remember is that we had fun, but we also learned about social interaction. Whether we liked them or not, every other kid on the block was out playing, too. We played with our friends and fought with, avoided or somehow learned to compromise with those we didn't like. Some kids were generous, but others took more than their share. Some were kind, but others were bullies, always eager to call names or start arguments.

We learned that it was sometimes OK to get angry, but it wasn't OK to hit first. If we made another kid cry, the bigger kids would jump in to save him and punish us. If anyone really got out of line, the other kids would tell their parents, and they would tell our parents, and we would be in trouble. This fear of a spanking or being grounded kept most of us out of trouble long enough, until the give and take of playing together everyday taught us that being friends, or at least getting along together, was more fun than starting fights.

These "playground lessons" were just as important as the math and reading we were doing at our desks, but unfortunately, children now have to learn them somewhere else. Most parents work, and many children go to after school care programs. Others go home alone and are entertained by the television and computer.

Parents and children are often nervous about their children playing outside or walking around their neighborhoods. Many neighborhoods are not safe for adults or children. The end result of these changes in our lives is that children no longer get as much exercise as they once did, and they miss out on social interaction, too. Once or twice a week physical education classes can't make up for that.

The statistics tell us that childhood obesity is a serious problem. And heavier children usually grow into heavier adults. We can see this result as more businesses cater to plus size customers, and more adults are suffering from diabetes while teenage girls struggle with eating disorders.

Medical research, doctors, health advocates, self-help books and current magazine articles all tell us that exercise is a key to health – for children and adults. Studies suggest exercise might also help to ease depression and help control hyperactivity.

Unfortunately, at the end of a long, stressful day, relaxing in front of a television with a bowl of ice cream or a bag of chips is a lot more inviting than going to the spa, jogging around the block or getting on a treadmill. But for school-aged children, play is exercise and it's too bad that their opportunities to play at recess have also been taken away.

It's true that kids have more to learn in school than ever before, but experts tell us that learning is facilitated by taking breaks between lessons.

Corporations believe that productivity – from secretaries to executives – will increase if they will break the long hours at their desks with trips to the restroom, or just stand up, swing their arms and walk around their desks. Our kids need that chance to move around, too. Who knows – maybe running around on the playground would, in the end, help them learn more and get better grades.

Part II
Communication: The Key To Life and Love

"Communication is not only the essence of being human, but a vital property of life"

John A. Pierce

Words do matter. Talk is not cheap. Words of encouragement and praise uplift and encourage us, help us grow in self-confidence and self-awareness. Words of destructive criticism cause us to retreat, to shrink to less than we are capable of being. Yes, words do matter, and so do other forms of communication. Every gesture, every mood, every non-verbal cue communicates messages of approval or disapproval to others.

In their research on emotional intelligence, Daniel Goleman, Richard Boyatzis, and Annie McKee concluded that our moods have a direct impact on others. Those with a high level of emotional intelligence are adept at perceiving how their moods impact the moods of those around them, and have learned to manage their moods so that they do not negatively impact others during times that they do not feel upbeat and optimistic.

While I speak of communication, I do not rely on any theory of communications, but rather on my own grassroots, firing line and day-to-day experiences. I have learned that every communication offers a choice, a choice of the form of communication (verbal, written, visual, or physical), a choice of what to say and what to leave unsaid, a choice of the timing and a choice of who will receive the communication. Each of those choices has consequences for good or for ill.

I have experienced communications from and with a wide variety of people from President Bill Clinton to homeless persons in a soup kitchen line. In all these situations, I am amazed at how alert I have *become to the verbal and non-verbal cues communicated to me, and how much they influence me. I know as well how much my verbal and non-verbal cues influence those around me. That is why communication is the lifeblood of an organization.*

Communication is visual, aural and physical, encompassing all our senses on a continuous basis. Communication is the primary currency for getting the work done, building a common spirit within an organization, and nurturing relationships. In the stories that follow, I share what I have learned about how communication can help, harm or heal. I share what I have learned about good communication – how it can build trust and support for change, and how poor communication can cause misunderstandings, unnecessary risks, and discouragement.

Do we realize the importance of our actions and our words? Do we realize the importance of communication and the choices that result from positive or negative interaction? These passages speak of the importance of communication.

Communication Is An Art Form

Communication today is like music. Anyone with e-mail can send a message and it will appear on the screen of computers anywhere in the world, within seconds. Documents can be faxed and received in minutes. Letters sent through the post office have become "snail-mail," even if they arrive the next day.

Communicating electronically is fun, and some people spend hours every day on their computers, sending and receiving messages to and from people they have never met. Instead of leaving our comfortable offices and walking to another office to speak to a colleague in person, we call and give a message, or we send e-mail. Children would rather play video games than play with each other. Many homes have enough televisions so that everybody can watch his or her favorite show on their own individual TV.

Unfortunately, the technology developed to facilitate distance communication has the opposite effect on communication between people who see each other every day. After spending the day communicating with a computer or a television screen, there isn't any real desire to practice face-to-face communication.

Communication is a skill. Most skills are developed through practice and revision, but we assume anyone can communicate just by opening his or her mouth and saying what they think. This is like playing catch by throwing a ball and hoping someone will catch it. To play catch, we have to think about the catcher and throw the ball to him or her at the right speed. To communicate, we have to think about the person we are speaking to and how he or she will receive the message.

Most communication involves relaying information to someone. But the speaker's emotions and relationship to the listener can distort the message or make it unpleasant. If the speaker is in a position of authority – a teacher, parent or boss – he or she can give the message as an order. Orders enforce the superiority of the speaker and the inferiority of the listener. We assume the person in power does not need to consider the relationship, but the listener appreciates being treated as an equal. By explaining the order, the speaker can put himself on an equal power level with the listener. As equals, the speaker assumes the listener has integrity, can understand the reason for the request and is willing to do what is needed.

The listener completes the job because he or she chooses to be responsible, not because the speaker's power threatens.

Sometimes communicating as equals does not work. The listener might not be responsible or the speaker might enjoy the feeling of power. It's possible to get used to speaking from a position of power and assume this is the only way to get the job done. We have all heard parents yelling at children. When this happens on a regular basis, children don't respond unless the person yells or hits them. Parents continue to fear they might lose control, and the children learn to judge adults by how much they can get away with.

In a work situation we assume the boss does not need to consider how he gives orders to his organization's workers. But if he treats them as inferiors, they may never become self-motivated and proud of their contributions to the organization.

In addition to skill, communication takes energy. It is much easier to send a written message than to have a face-to-face conversation. To hear the other person's opinion immediately and reply in a considerate and intelligent manner requires attention and sensitivity. Even a thank you, or a wave requires awareness and energy. Although you'll probably never see that person again, saying thank you makes him or her more likely to allow someone to take cuts in line, hold a door or offer a seat on a bus the next time the situation arises. Receiving consideration also has a ripple effect, making the receiver more likely to do a favor for someone else.

Communicating is like putting out a product; it is a statement of who we are. We often modify the statement, considering the audience and the purpose for writing, and we organize and check for clarity, whether the writing is an e-mail message, a letter of application, a journal article, or a note to our children's teacher. We should apply the same care and thought to our spoken word.

Communication is more effective if we consider the effect our message might have on the person who receives it, before we speak or write.

Written Communication Skills Cut By Television Time

Are our children watching too much television? Federal education researchers are now reporting that children who watch more than six hours of television each day are those with the weakest writing skills.

Children typically spend as much time viewing television as they do going to school.

Well, after about 30 seconds of reflection, it seems to all add up. Television requires very little cognition; just flip the switch to "ON" and the rest is easy.

On the other hand, writing requires the activation of at least three of four brain cells. Writing puts the brain to work while television puts it to sleep.

It has been noted that many people with severe brain disorders, with no idea of what is going on, will sit quietly before the television screen for hours.

In 1992, the National Assessment of Educational Progress, a somewhat invisible unit of the U.S. Department of Education, tested 30,000 youngsters in the fourth, eighth, and twelfth grades for a "Writing Report Card."

The report says, "To become good writers, students need expert instruction, frequent practice and constructive feedback."

While some improvements have been noted since the earlier assessment, many students at each grade level continue to have difficulty in producing effective informative, persuasive or narrative writing.

From one perspective there is no reason to believe that the situation will change. Writing is no longer essential to the exchange of information.

Without a doubt, many of us continue to read newspapers and magazines, but our primary sources of information and entertainment involve electronic technology.

As I write this column, it occurs to me that we don't write nearly the number of letters we used to write to friends and relatives. Now, we simply pick up the telephone.

Thus, our ability to communicate surely has been altered or impeded by television. My friends who make a living helping people understand the power of communication tell me that television has reduced even the spoken word to a minimum.

The spoken word now plays second fiddle to pictures. And vocabulary is reduced to the lowest common level. But much worse, we are also told that we are losing our ability to present ideas, because we are so used to visual communication instead of verbal.

"American business has been taking it on the chin lately, with one of the most crippling ailments…poor writing," says author, William Zinsser in his book, *On Writing Well*.

"I am not talking about professional writers, but all the ways that people communicate in the workplace every day, the memos, business letters, the explanations and instructions of how a product works, or even the explanation of health insurance benefits."

Television watching is a symptom, not a cause, as pointed out in an *Atlantic Monthly* article. "It is a symptom that children have been blocked, somehow, in their more imaginative play, and turn to television in frustration as a kind of quick fix."

Just imagine, if we could somehow bring young people from a very early age, to the understanding that writing is an enchantment that can touch any and every aspect of their whole lives. Flip the switch off.

What I Learned About Writing

I have a good friend who has been teaching college students to write for almost 20 years. Not only is he an excellent teacher of writing, he is an excellent writer himself.

While I have always enjoyed writing and reading the works of those I consider craftsmen of their trade, I have never considered myself a good writer, mostly because I didn't always know that writing is hard work. I have never had a problem with hard work; it was just a matter of knowing that writers don't always start as good writers, but must work hard to become good. Writing is hard work, and not something at which a lazy person is likely to excel.

Well, anyway, my friend the writer/teacher, after lengthy discussion about the newspaper columns I had been doing for a while, quizzed me about my newfound appreciation for writing. He was fascinated with my evolution and development as a writer.

I had been writing a weekly column for about eight months for five different daily and weekly newspapers and found writing newspaper columns to be at once the greatest challenge and the greatest pleasure I had experienced in a long while.

I told my friend that in the process of becoming a better writer, I discovered that basically I had to unlearn a lot of what I had learned about writing. I had to learn to give myself permission to write something down, even if it did not make much sense. Discovering that not everything that is put on paper the first time has to make perfect sense has given me a new sense of freedom to think and write without fear of being wrong. I can always go back and revise what I said until it feels right to me.

I believe there is much more to writing than grammar and mechanics. There was a time when I was so worried about appropriate punctuation that I never got beyond the first paragraph. Our eighth grade English course still haunts many of us. Unless we were unusually fortunate, our early attempts at writing were not supported by a nurturing environment. It seems that some teachers were and are so concerned with rules that they don't allow students to get their thoughts on paper. We become obsessed with the mechanics of writing, rather than permitting ourselves a free flow of expression. Correctness and rules are important, of course, but writing is more than spelling and punctuation.

I said to my friend that writing is like playing golf. In order to do it well, you must be committed and willing to do it frequently. It is a process much like working on your golf swing. You do it over and over until you get it right. It's also like the discovery process, I went on to say. You learn something new every time you write. Unless you have the determination to practice, which improves your work through the pure act of repetition, you probably won't improve your writing skills.

There is some unmasking involved in transferring thoughts to writing. Once this happens, people are free to dissect your innermost thoughts. My wife is among the first to read my column and is always concerned that I might be sharing too much about who I am. Because I'm told that we either consciously or unconsciously seek approval when we write, we make ourselves vulnerable. Writing is risky; we expose ourselves to criticism, disagreement, and the real possibility of failure, all without our normal social defense mechanisms to protect us. When it's on paper, it's unretractable, sitting there for all to see.

There is also something mesmerizing and compelling about sharing one's thoughts in writing. It is an emotional experience for me as well as a function of my personality. What I read, think and feel is a reflection of my individuality. Ideas flow freely when I write from my own experience. I find that it is practically impossible not to tell the truth when writing about a topic that comes out of my own experience. People are always asking: "Are you sure you want to say that? What will people think?"

Barbara Tuchman – an historian and two-time winner of the Pulitzer Prize – put it eloquently: "Nothing is more satisfying than to write a good sentence. It is no fun to write limpidly or dull, in prose the reader must plod through like wet sand. But it is a pleasure to achieve, if one can, a clear running prose that is simple yet full of surprises. This does not just happen. It requires skill, hard work, a good ear, and continued practice."

Unfortunately, some people enjoy catching others making an error. Therefore, when I ask someone to criticize what I have written, I know to put his or her comments in proper perspective. Furthermore, often people I ask for advice will be too generous or too critical.

Vividly, I remember the first column I wrote. Just coming up with an idea was one of the most trying processes I have experienced recently. Finally, out of desperation, I just decided to put something on paper, no matter how ridiculous it sounded. It worked, and I still practice this. This works for me because it at least gives me something to play with.

Once I have started to write, I have learned not to interrupt the process constantly by reading what I have already written, changing words or spending a lot of time with one sentence. There is ample opportunity to go back and address word choice and sentence structure. For example, if I use a word with which I am initially uncomfortable, I will underline the word and continue to write, knowing that when I revise what I have written, the underlined word will be my clue to make a better word choice. When I have an opportunity to give advice to students working on a writing project, I tell them not to be immobilized by a word, a phrase, or a sentence.

I don't get too hung up with sequence when I write, thinking I have to write an introduction first. If the idea for a good introduction is not there when I begin to write, I proceed with my writing, knowing that

I can always go back and develop the introduction. I do the same with paragraph transition. If I'm not comfortable with the transition at the time, I don't allow myself to get writer's block. I simply make a note like "work on transition" and move on.

I have always been an avid reader, but now that I write columns, I find that I read more than ever. Not only do I read in order to gain factual information that is absolutely necessary, but also I read in an effort to observe different writing styles.

There is an abundance of books dealing with writing techniques and strategies. Excellent writers, such as my friend, are standing in the wings, ready to help; however, in the end, we learn to write by doing it over and over again.

I feel a special kinship to those who teach writing. I understand now, more than ever, that writing should be taught as something more than a set of rules to follow. Students often don't learn well with a negative approach of focusing on mistakes; many do better by encouragement from writing teachers. Writing has many uses. It is a means of learning and exploring an idea, or thought, or feeling, or belief. Writing requires freedom from worrying about mistakes. It is writing for one's self which allows us to clarify and verbalize our thoughts.

Writing is also important as a means of communicating our thoughts and ideas with others. This requires a different thought process about writing. We have to consider the reader, and also the conventions of written English.

Both kinds of writing are important; writing for self-discovery and writing to explain to others. Both are valuable. Both are necessary.

As a writer of newspaper columns, I realize more than ever the importance of writing both in the college curriculum, as well as outside the classroom or workplace.

The Real Answer To Trusting

At the end of the 60s one of the slogans, designed to unite the younger, more rebellious generation against figures of authority was "Don't trust anyone over 30." That generation smiled and winked as they turned 30 and pushed the limits of trust to 40. Now most of them are around 50, and many wouldn't trust anyone under 30, including their own children. What makes us decide that some people deserve our trust because they have integrity and others don't?

A longtime friend was recently promoted from division chair to dean. He had always related well to his faculty, praising their intellectual ability, hard work and dedication to the students. However, six months after he became a dean, he began to see the faculty, including his former division colleagues, as lacking in integrity, wasting time, and worse – as trying to slough off their responsibilities.

On the other hand, the faculty, which had always thought of him as a division chair who supported them and had their best interest at heart, began to think of him as the company man, promoting long range administrative plans with little concern for the faculty who would carry them out.

Although the people stayed the same, the change in position of power caused a shift in trust. So lack of trust can also be a problem between politicians and their constituencies, between policemen and the public and even between parents and their children.

Trust is also a problem between rich and poor. Those who can't afford to wear stylish clothes or live in a house in a "good" part of town – poorer people – may gripe about richer people trying to take advantage of them – paying low salaries for hard work. They fear downsizing, in which lower level employees often lose jobs or take salary cuts so the company can maintain its profit margin. Those who are comfortably well off tend to stereotype poorer people as dishonest, and worry that welfare fraud is ruining the economy.

It is unlikely that one perception is correct and the other is wrong. In most situations, individuals try to do the best they can. They may be misguided, or underestimate how much they can achieve, but most offer honest effort, not premeditated cheating. Integrity is one personality trait that does not depend on power and wealth.

Criticizing someone for being lazy or self centered is understandable, but assuming an individual is purposely sloughing off his responsibilities is a character judgment. Even people with integrity can make mistakes.

It seems easier to question the integrity of someone who is far away from our position in life. Maybe that is because we are so familiar with the trials and hassles we have to deal with in our own situation. But because we are less aware of other people's problems, the lives of those who are even less fortunate can seem easier.

I have overheard mothers describing a baby too young to sit up as "spoiled." They go on to suggest that the baby is crying to purposely manipulate the mother into picking it up when it has already been fed and changed. Some people accuse teenagers of getting pregnant on purpose, just to get a government check. These kinds of hostile judgments increase the distance and distrust between people.

The best way to increase trust between people is communication. The effort it takes to communicate with someone implies that person is worth your time and energy. This is a great start. Sometimes the message is unpleasant, but most people would rather be warned about a bad situation before they are suddenly faced with it. Communication brings people closer together so even people with very different views or lifestyles can begin to understand and respect each other.

We all know those times when we failed to live up to our principles, but we'd still like others to think we have the integrity to be trusted. The people we live and work with probably feel the same way.

One interesting example of trust is driving. Driving through crowded city streets, or facing high-speed oncoming traffic on a highway, we all trust each other to follow the rules. But most drivers go beyond the rules to be courteous – to consider the other guy's situation, to follow at a distance, dim lights on time, keep moving at the same speed after passing, allow people to cut in if their lane ends. On the streets all people are equal: red and green lights apply to us all, and think about how many of us – rich and poor alike – obey them every day. In our cars, we also have the power to destroy, but we assume from each other the integrity not to purposely misuse this power.

If people on opposite sides of any situation can communicate, they can develop trust and learn to work together for mutual benefit.

Misunderstanding Can Begin With Simple Words, End With Dire Results

Some time ago, during the part of a church service when special needs were being addressed, one parishioner stood and asked the congregation to remember Travis Terry (not his real name) in prayer as he had been diagnosed with cancer that week. I was sitting next to an elderly couple on a pew several rows back from the speaker. As the speaker sat down and another stood to request a prayer for something else, the woman next to me turned to her husband and asked, "What'd she say?"

In a voice loud enough for her, as well as those of us around them to hear, he answered, "She said that Travis Berry died of cancer this week."

"Oh," she said, apparently satisfied with the information. For the mother of Travis, "diagnosed" is much better than "died," no matter how frightening a cancer diagnosis may still be.

For the man who misunderstood the speaker, it probably mattered little since he apparently didn't know Travis "Berry." He, of course, innocently passed on to someone else information that was incorrect. I assume in this case that the misunderstanding, which led to misinformation for these two people, didn't cause any particular or lasting problem.

Unfortunately, not all misunderstandings of words are so benign.

Some weeks ago, in Washington, D.C., an aide to the mayor resigned from his job after using a word that sounded like another word, which offended some of the people who heard it.

Now, any communication between two people can so easily go awry despite our best intentions – ask any husband or wife. There is a speaker, a listener and a word or idea to convey. The speaker may mispronounce a word or the listener may misunderstand the word and mistake it for another, as in the case of the couple in church.

The listener may also misinterpret the meaning of a word or apply a different meaning than the speaker intended, leading again to misunderstanding.

Sometimes such misunderstanding has little negative effect, but when race is at issue, even the slightest misperception can have serious consequences, as in the case of the Washington aide. In a conversation with city colleagues (who are black) the aide (who is white) said the city would have to be "niggardly" with its budget (niggardly, stingy, meager, scanty, miserly) as financial resources were scarce.

But there is also the context for communication, including a speaker, a listener, a reason for the communication and the situation. We speak differently in different situations. Each new occasion calls for an appropriate, specific and insightful response.

For example, while it is both illegal and unethical to shout "fire" in a crowded theater, there may be situations where shouting "fire" to your heart's delight results in no inappropriate responses by others.

Or we use euphemisms to soften reality. Most of us might use the words "passed away" instead of "died" in the company of someone whose loved one has recently died. We do so out of respect for how our words may impact on the listener. In other contexts, we can feel perfectly free to use the word "died" rather than its euphemism.

It is the situational context that the Washington aide failed to consider which resulted in his subsequent resignation. While the word in question is quite suitable for the job he employed it to do, the speaker ignored the situation and used a word that sounds so much like the racial epithet that most listeners would hear the wrong word, and so hearing, react accordingly.

That is one of the dangers of words. They can inspire us, and they can fry us when misused or when misunderstood.

There are two issues here. One, the speaker demonstrated an insensitivity to the situational context by his choice of words. So, even though "niggardly" is a valid and useful word, it is not always the best word to use for all contexts in which it is uttered.

The other issue here is the reaction of the listeners. Since "niggardly" is not exactly a common household word, many listeners when hearing the word, might easily "hear" the wrong one and take immediate offense. Objectivity on their part is also necessary if misunderstandings are to be corrected, if truth is to prevail. Overreaction against the speaker is an injustice more serious than his unfortunate use of a word.

When we were kids, we heard the phrase, "Sticks and stones may break my bones, but words will never hurt me," which we learned all too soon to be a lie. Words can soothe and words can rankle. They can bring great hope or great despair. Being sensitive to words, to their meaning and to the context in which we speak is critically important to fostering effective communication and understanding between people.

So is giving someone the benefit of the doubt because we understand that their choice of words may be careless, but not intended to do harm.

The Most Important Pronoun

I can't remember where it was that I heard it, or who the speaker was, but I remember being surprised at this answer to his own question: "What's the most important pronoun a young child learns?"

Probably my age and experience as a parent and an educator led me to anticipate the word, so I was unprepared when the speaker said, "The most important pronoun a child learns is ME," his confident voice reflecting his assurance that he was right. He went on to explain that it's important for a child to discover that he is a "me" separate from other "me's." One's increasing consciousness that he or she is no longer attached by the original umbilical cord, nor bound by the many symbolic ones that follow in the early relationship between parents and young child, helps develop the independence of thought and action necessary for a successful and independent life.

That was OK, and it made some sense. But the pronoun I was listening for was YOU, when a child discovers that there is someone else in the world besides him or her.

Sometimes it is an older child who finally comes to terms with the fact that we are not alone, that the world was not created for our sole benefit, that our parents were not put here merely to buy us toys and serve us, that we cannot (or should not) always get all that we can think of to want. It sometimes takes a while to accept that we are in fact one of many, too many and too diverse to begin to comprehend. Sometimes we never learn, or accept, the necessity in a civil social setting to balance the need for "me" with the equal need to consider "you."

Prisons are filled with people who put themselves first in disregard to others. In cemeteries lie the remains of lives ended early, unable or unwilling to make the sometimes unhappy but necessary social and personal compromise. In cemeteries also lie victims of those who caved in to hatred and violence and selfishness, who put "me" before "you" without regard to the consequences.

When I come to recognize that you also exist, that you also have feelings, needs, joys and sorrows, that you get hungry and thirsty too, that you don't like cleaning the dirty toilet any more than I do, that music can make you feel happy or sad too, that you also like the smell of roses and the taste of wine. When I come to realize, in other words, that you are a lot like me in some pretty important as well as mundane ways, it can change something. For one thing, it makes me think of you as lot more equal to me. As a consequence of that, it makes it harder for me to want to harm you.

Expanding beyond the singular me and you, it makes it harder to go to war. One of the things we must do in war propaganda is cast our "enemy" as someone vastly different than we, whose lives differ from our way of life, whose values or cultural practices are far different and by implication inferior to our American values and traditions. We emphasize the differences, and only when we come to see our "enemy" as sufficiently different from us can we allow ourselves to go without guilt and kill him.

One way we redefine our adversary is by labels. Derogatory labels stereotype, distort, distract and demean the group – whether it is a country, a race, a religion or a political belief. Words lead to thoughts and soon to deeds; before long in our minds and coffee shop conversations the distortion and mystery of labels become our working reality. We are often wrong, though. For example, during the Cold War, the people of the former Communist countries of eastern Europe were lumped together with the Soviets, as Commies, Reds, Pinkos, etc., dismissed en masse by a simple word.

How many schoolyard or barroom fights either begin, or at least escalate, when racial or ethnic slurs are used? The label abstracts the humanity from the person, reducing him to a list of stereotypical generalities and therefore not a unique human being. He is no longer a "you" but a blurred, mythical "them," not one of "us." So the one obvious difference is exaggerated and all our similarities ignored.

Some differences trigger quick and heavy responses. How many millions and millions of people the world over have died unnecessarily in wars, uprisings, revolutions or purges? How many were killed in the name of someone's god, country, race, ethnic group, tribe, gang or even sports team? This can result when we allow our few differences to override our many similarities.

Don't Fear, Change Is Inevitable

"**My**, you haven't changed a bit since I saw you last." "My, look how you've changed since I saw you last."

Which is the compliment and which is the curse? It depends. When the comment refers to our physical appearance or growth, the older we get the less we want to change, i.e., look older. When we're young, we can't wait to get bigger, so we beam when Aunt Suzy gushes over how much we've grown.

However, when the change refers to our outlook, our attitudes, beliefs, or feelings about things rather than our physical appearance, the matter is more complicated.

As we age, we get more set in our ways, and not only in matters of behavior, but also of thinking.

We tend to adopt policies, beliefs or creeds without really questioning their validity, and then we are more likely to defend our position than listen to new reasons why we should "change our minds" about something.

Again, we are more likely to see such a change as a weakness, as an admission that we were wrong, which we don't do easily.

We often fear change, fear the unknown, and so will let our old patterns and habits pull us through life quite comfortably.

Few of us question where we are, or where we are going, or entertain big changes that might alter our lives in any substantial way.

We'd also rather keep a scoundrel in office whom we know to

be a scoundrel, than take a chance on the change that might occur with a replacement.

We often fear new ideas and the new truths that science discovers, because of their potential threat to the established social, religious or political order.

A new truth ought to cause realignment in the way we think or believe, but in fact, the comfortable, established old truth dies hard.

And we are not always kind to the messenger who makes the discovery, often preferring to silence the new truth along with the teller of the truth in order to avoid dealing with the new consequences.

Countries also get set in their ways of thinking about things and can't seem to dislodge or alter their view.

When things don't work as promised, we simply do more of the same, instead of stepping back and re-evaluating the situation.

The war on drugs is an example of following the same mind-set on how to approach the drug problem, which we seem no closer to winning than when we started 25 years ago, despite the billions of dollars expended and the half million men imprisoned. We're even afraid to talk about changing our approach.

Yet, according to Wendell Johnson, "No other fact so unrelentingly shapes and reshapes our lives as this: that reality, in the broadest sense, continually changes."

He tells about the ancient Greek philosopher Heraclitus who contended that we cannot step in the same river twice.

Not only does the river flow and change, but we also change, so that we are not the same person that stepped into the river earlier.

No event is ever exactly repeated. Woodstock II was not the same as Woodstock I.

This year's family reunion is not exactly the same as last year's family reunion. The child who comes home from college this spring is not the same son or daughter we sent away last fall.

And the home the child returns to is not exactly the same as the home he or she left last fall.

A few days ago I saw a young man in Wal-Mart pushing a cart

with a baby inside a little carrier; he was following his wife around as she shopped for clothes, and he showed all the signs of impatience with shopping and pride in his infant that I once showed many years ago as I was pushing my baby around in a basket in Wal-Mart.

There I was 15 years ago; I'm still me now, but a different me. I'm at a different place in life now than he is, having moved beyond those years to here, yet realizing that someday I'll be somewhere else.

That lesson, that things change, has been one of the hardest for me to really learn, and I don't always act like I know it even yet. It's easier to notice changes in children when we see them behaving in new ways we don't like. We call the new behavior a "phase" which they'll soon grow out of, we hope.

We sometimes tolerate the transition period, or at least minimize the struggle, hoping they'll soon move on to other stages in their development.

Adults may also go through phases, though they may be less noticeable or regular or predictable than children.

Whether in church participation, civic group participation, gardening or lawn care, etc., our level of involvement or interest can change over time.

Our situations change; kids get older and their needs change, from diapers to soccer practice and piano lessons. Our health changes, our work conditions may change, and all these changes affect us in various ways.

A pillar in our church or community this generation might have been a bum a decade or two ago, or may become one a decade from now. That's why "IS" is such a deceiving little verb.

Friendships change, even as adults. Our interests change. Our lives change. What unites us all more than race or gender or religion is the stages through which we all imperceptibly move.

When asked by a Chinese emperor to prepare a statement that might be appropriate for any occasion, his wise philosopher spoke these words: "And this too shall pass away."

Despite our fear of change and differences, we can be comforted in times of trouble or despair by knowing that "this too shall pass."

And, lest we get too cocky or confident in ourselves, no matter how far we rise, realizing that "this too shall pass" might help make us more humble.

Computer Age Brings Changes

Computers have proven to be so fascinating and useful that we tacitly assume everything having to do with computers is modern, efficient, and professional and therefore, better. When it comes to processing data, that assumption is probably true. But there are many other factors involved in the efficient running of an institution, business, or home – for example, personal communication.

Computers have shifted the focus of communication from a face-to-face approach to a long distance, impersonal point of view. Instead of physically speaking to someone, we send e-mail messages. E-mail can have a lot of advantages for both parties. Instead of walking into someone's office and surprising him or her with an emotional complaint or a difficult decision, using the computer allows the writer to express his message without emotion, and the reader has time to think about the problem before making a decision. If the response is negative, the sender does not have to cope with the disappointment or anger of the person who receives it.

However, when we are not sitting alone at the computer, we are often dealing with other people. In face-to-face conversations, we need to learn how to express ourselves, how to respond to others, and how to anticipate their reaction to our message on the spot, without the advantage of composing a logical e-mail response at our leisure. Judging by the turmoil within our communities, differences in opinion can easily escalate into physical violence or even murder. In a drive-by shooting or road rage, often this anger is expressed toward someone the murderer doesn't even know. In fact, shooting someone at a distance is much easier than trading punches and bloody noses. In the same way, it is much easier to send notices about downsizing or cuts in pay via computer than to walk into someone's office and tell him face to face that he will not be getting a raise, he needs to begin working Saturday mornings, or his job is over.

Computers are the hottest new toys on the block. Walk into any institution, from schools to hospitals to department stores, and almost every desk has a computer on it with a document in process.

Typing this article on the keyboard at my desk seems to be the most practical, efficient way to write. However, I remember what writing with a pencil and paper or typewriter was like before we were launched, or in some cases, dragged, into the computer age. Many of us, who resisted the initial waves of computerization, vowing that pencil and paper has always worked, have learned to use a word processing program. Some of us have purchased home computers with the latest technology. Others have discovered the fun of surfing the web and the convenience of e-mail. Many have adapted to using computers just to keep their jobs.

As more and more institutions have become computerized, it's obvious that computer literacy has become an important factor for success in the world of work. Schools are filled with students taking computer classes and using the skills they learn to boost their performance in other classes as well.

One reason computers have become so popular is they can process information quickly and efficiently, and with the addition of e-mail and fax capabilities, the information can be sent long distance in mere minutes.

With the addition of a modem, we have access to the Internet and its vast systems of information. We can research science papers, listen to songs in foreign languages, look up how to care for a pet rabbit, check the weather forecast, and order books without ever leaving our desks. We have more information available than we have time to read it. Even hackers must sometimes feel overwhelmed.

And for those of us who are challenged by organizing data, the computer offers us spell check and grammar check as well as spreadsheets and bookmarks and address books and e-mail folders and computer help lines to answer questions when we can't figure out how to make a program work.

Deciphering Meaning From Language Can Be Subjective

A short time ago I happened to see a distance learning class in which a linguist was explaining how a definition often reflects an attitude or bias toward the subject being defined. We usually think of a definition of something as the final answer, as the "way it really is" and few of us dispute what the dictionary says.

But we should not be so quick to accept without question such tidy statements that appear as the force of fact. I was interested in watching him illustrate to his students how the choice of words used to define something determines how we think about and respond to it. He used Ebonics as an example to show how to create a reasonable definition that fosters a positive attitude toward it.

A typical definition usually starts with the word and has an is, as in "A dog is…" So he started with, "Ebonics is…" That was the easy part. Next, he had to try to explain or describe it accurately and clearly in such a way as to make it meaningful. That's the difficult part, and the part where the definer's attitude comes into play.

"I like Ebonics," he admitted… "and I am a linguist, so I can say that." He said he was going to start with the word "code." "That will give it dignity," he said. "Ebonics is a code," it now read.

He went back to the board and added "systematic" in front of code, making it sound even more complicated and organized. Surely a "code" of any kind that is "systematic" sounds legitimate, not haphazard or makeshift.

"Let's add 'linguistic' to narrow the class now," he added. His definition now became: "Ebonics is a systematic linguistic code."

That sounds pretty forthright, codified in concrete: it has credence and legitimacy. Based on the association and meaning of the words used to define Ebonics, you could substitute "English" or "Spanish" for "Ebonics" and the same words of description could apply.

"Now let's embellish it," he said, and he stepped back to the chalkboard and added "even elegant" to the description. The definition that he had just made up, not without reason and authority, became: "Ebonics is a systematic, even elegant, linguistic code."

The definition sounds positive, dignified, and favorable, because of the words chosen to describe Ebonics: systematic, elegant, linguistic, code. Who wouldn't like a code that is systematic and elegant? He may be right about all of those elements. I am not a linguist and not in a position to make an informed determination about the legitimacy of either Ebonics or his description of it.

But what he did next was instructive. He asked his students if any of them could write a definition that would sound legitimate, but reflect a negative attitude toward Ebonics. They scribbled away for a couple of minutes and then one of them said, "I don't really feel this way, but a severe critic could say "Ebonics is a non-systematic, non-elegant, non-linguistic pseudo-code."

The students laughed, and the professor pointed out the problems with defining something only by telling what it is not, but he also said that the definition nonetheless made a good illustration of his point. It had a similar ring of authority and finality that the first definition did, only leading its reader to an opposite conclusion about the same subject.

So which is Ebonics? The remaining point of this article is not to discuss its merits, but rather to call attention to the implication of words and language. Miscommunication results from misunderstanding, sometimes from deliberate attempts to deceive, sometimes by inconsiderate or thoughtless word choice, sometimes by tone of voice, or even body language.

One particularly dangerous little word that often creates

inaccurate statements is "is." As we saw with the definitions above, when you say that something "is" something, few people question the descriptors. And how powerful one simple, perhaps even unintended statement can be. When someone we trust says, "That is a good (or bad) place or book or movie, or class, or car," we tend to not question it, unless we have had a conflicting experience. We go to movies based on the recommendation of a friend who said, or implied, that it is a good movie. We trust his or her judgment to be true, that is, to agree with our sense of good.

But we should be especially careful about what we claim "is," for "is" sounds final and unchangeable, and it is much more difficult for us to change our perceptions or attitudes.

In one of the first classes I taught in college, I remember a student writing a short paper asking what I thought was a poignant question, "What is a criminal?" As I recall, he had served a short prison sentence, at age 17, for a fairly minor crime, and now that he was out of prison, he could not find work. No one would hire him, he said, because they said they didn't hire criminals. "I went to prison and paid for my crime," he wrote, "but will I always be a criminal to society? Everywhere I turn, people tell me, 'You're a criminal!' "

He was no longer a criminal because he did the things society required of him to make amends. However, he went on to say, in his own mind he was still a criminal. For him the distinction was critical.

For him, this label would be a life-long handicap. For the rest of us, it is important that we be aware of our words and their implications.

"Deciphering meaning from language can be subjective" is how I leave you.

The Other Digital Divide

No one is more aware of the division between people evolving with the constant growth of technology and communication than I. Both personally and professionally, I have been committed to and working toward leveling the computer-technology battleground. Those who know and have access to the Internet and the information that it offers, will be and possibly will remain further ahead than those without access. This is commonly known as the "digital divide" – creating even more space between the haves and have-nots, the knows and know-nots.

But as I watch the daily breakthroughs of computer technology that are supposed to enhance our lives, I wonder if anyone is noticing what is emerging as another digital divide.

It is caused by the things that are to make our lives easier, faster, more accurate and overall enhanced – the ATM machines, e-mail, faxes, Palm Pilots and electronic cashiers at the grocery stores. While they make our lives more comfortable, they are driving space between us as people, and may stand to ultimately drive us further away from each other, eliminating human contact.

Looking back, things like the mail system were supposed to keep us in touch, and e-mail was designed to enable us to communicate with others across the street as easily as across the globe. Yet, we resort to e-mailing rather than partaking in actual conversation. The telephone was supposed to help keep us in touch, but now the voice on the other end is an endless spill of electronic prompts, with no human to be found.

At a time when computer technology and artificial intelligence have brought the world closer together and made it more accessible, they also have driven people farther apart. Knowing how close we actually are should encourage closeness that bridges cultural and economic gaps. It should assist us in getting to know each other, and ourselves, better.

I remember reading that McDonald's was experimenting at one of its locations with a kiosk that would allow customers to place and pay for orders electronically. While this may save time, money and increase the accuracy of orders placed, it all but eliminates human interaction.

Communication is one of the most valuable tools that humans have. We speak, read, write, sign and hear. These tools of communication allow us to work to interpret messages from varying sources. They make us think, feel and grow. To eliminate these from our everyday lives would surely contribute to the demise of human encounters as we know them. What about a hug? Holding a hand? Sharing a smile or a "good morning" with a friend or a stranger?

It may appear challenging to utilize our new technological conveniences without letting them consume or replace our personal interactions or intimacies, but it's a challenge that must be embraced and faced head-on. Otherwise, we become victims of our own intelligence, without really understanding its impact. Our modern accomplishments, while appearing to enhance our existence, also seem to drive a wedge between our willingness and ability to engage in personal contact.

While dealing with each other can sometimes be time-consuming and even challenging, it is an irreplaceable act that should be treasured.

Put People First-
No Matter The Cost

Last week I cleaned out a bookshelf of old educational materials and browsed through a book published in the middle 70s, now almost 25 years old. Considering the changes we've experienced since 1977, many educators would consider the book obsolete. But a quote caught my attention.

"The democratic problem in education is not primarily a problem of training children; it is the problem of making a community within which children cannot help growing up to be democratic, intelligent, disciplined to freedom, reverent of the goods of life, and eager to share in the tasks of the age. A school cannot produce this result; nothing but a community can do so...consequently, we must have good communities."

Of course, this book was written during a time when task-oriented leaders considered educators who focused on solving problems of communication between people and their feelings a little too "touchy-feely" for their own good. And now, 25 years later, the "flower children" and the Vietnam veterans have grown up and we are dealing with the results of what we did or failed to do for our children and grandchildren.

Possibly as a backlash to the "make love, not war" era, we have become good at evaluating situations in terms of the hard, cold facts, and have learned to avoid being swayed by sentimental emotions. Unfortunately, this is often dangerous for us and for the people involved.

For example, in making the world safe for democracy in the

Balkans, we bombed and destroyed the bridges, roads and institutions necessary for everyday life. Now, a few years later we can see that our heavy-handed approach did little to solve the real problem – the longstanding disagreements – which created the war.

Closer to home, we build more prisons but seem to ignore whatever is causing the increase in crime. We put drug users in jail and confiscate millions of dollars of property, but do little to provide education or alternatives beyond teaching the catchy phrase "just say no." We pride ourselves on a tough approach to social problems but we don't seem to be able to prevent them. We work long hours to provide our children with the "things" they want, but we often ignore the time and attention they need to become happy, successful adults.

Part of the problem is that money is tangible. We can determine how much profit is made or lost as the result of a change in policy. People's feelings are not as easy to measure. When a company lays off workers, the company recognizes an immediate savings in its payroll. But it is harder to see the effect on those laid off, or the employees' loss of faith in the company or the increase in stress for those who have to absorb the extra work. Assuming there is no emotional fallout from layoffs or assuming they will promote company loyalty is another indication that money is more valuable than people.

There are many other situations where we can see people choosing to save money or make a profit without considering the effects on the people involved. Misleading the public by encouraging them to buy products which could be dangerous for their health is another indicator that profit has become more important than health. Sending a small child to day care for nine or 10 hours a day is an indication that a job is more important than a child. And paying day care workers minimum wage is an indication that we don't think the job they do is worth a higher salary.

Unfortunately, there are other sides to these problems which make a clear choice much more difficult. For example, if the company does not lay off a few people, it might be forced to close, laying off all its employees, perhaps hundreds or thousands. Many products, including some natural foods, can be dangerous to our health if consumed in excess. And it's better for a single mother to put her child in day care and get a job rather than risk losing her home and her children because she has no money to pay her bills and buy food.

In addition, instead of making clear choices after looking at the facts, we are often influenced by the stresses in our lives and how we feel at the moment.

However, we should look at the choices we make and evaluate whether we are choosing solutions that benefit people or whether we are choosing to make money at others' expense. Even children recognize hypocrisy, and most of us can see through people who say they are trying to help but are actually only working for their own profit. Those in power, our community leaders who can influence many people by their words and actions, have an even greater responsibility for choosing policies that will benefit a majority of people.

Children learn from role models so we must offer them the best possible examples of people-centered choices. Sometimes in order to create the community we want, we have to vote to put people first, no matter what it costs. If we can spend billions of dollars on military technology and space travel, we should be able to increase the small fraction of that money that we put into our schools and communities. Why not put more into schools, parks and community centers in the first place, to help people become self sufficient and keep them out of jail, instead of funding new jails, treatment programs and homeless shelters after it's already too late?

Speech Difficulty Shapes Outlook On Life And Others

Hello, my name is Curtis Ivery and I am a recovering stutterer. This is a part of my life that has not always been easy for me to talk about, but certainly one I have thought a lot about.

When I think about my childhood years as a stutterer old memories are resurrected, some painful, some warm, some funny.

I couldn't talk my way out of fights. Someone would walk up and want to fight me, and I couldn't make my words come out of my mouth to say, no, I don't want to fight, and so I ended up in fights I never wanted. I lost out on a lot of fun things in school when words didn't come out fast enough.

You learn to substitute quickly. When "two" won't come out quickly, switching to "a couple" works. Sometimes when asked how many you want, you can hold up five fingers when the word "five" won't come out.

Sometimes you can't do that, so you end up ordering more than you want simply because you can say "eight" but you can't say "five."

Telephones were probably the worst. Words beginning with "h," like "hello," or "hi" were among the hardest to say.

So whenever the phone rang and it was up to me to answer, I could feel my body tense up, my nerves and muscles preparing for the ordeal about to follow.

If it rang a third time, I felt duty bound to pick it up and try to answer.

I would build up courage, pump up my adrenaline, lift the receiver and try to blurt out "hello" with a quick burst of air.

Sometimes it worked, and a loud hello came out fast. But when it didn't, there was silence.

I would try hard to shape my lips and force out air correctly to make an "h" sound to start saying "hello" or "hi," and when it didn't work, only air would rush out, without the accompanying "h" sound.

My breathing rapidly increased, sweat oozed from my brow, I would exhale deeply, relax momentarily, then try again to push out air and force a sound so I could acknowledge a greeting, now in response to the person at the other end who would be saying "Hello? Hello? Is there anyone there?"

Making phone calls was even worse, especially in dating years when I'd have to call the girl and try to arrange plans.

The same problem faced me, except that I had to say "hello" pretty quickly, or after her third "hello" she would usually hang up, never knowing I was on the other end still trying to say "hello."

Sometimes I would try to call back in a few minutes, after trying to force myself to relax, hoping that this time it would work.

But sometimes I just couldn't bring myself to try again, after I had become so angry and frustrated over being unable to do such a simple thing as say "hello," and so I missed dates, missed opportunities, missed moments and situations that can never be recaptured.

The five-minute speech in my sophomore English class was every bit as horrid as I anticipated it would be.

I found myself in front the class with my hands shaking so badly that I kept dropping my note cards.

I stood there, looking out over the class of 23, sweat running down my forehead, trying quietly, desperately, unobtrusively, to make an "s" sound.

I would prepare forcing air into my lungs, then planning a burst of air out, but something kept going awry and it didn't work.

I would drop my cards, shuffle them, look around, heart pounding, hands sweating, trying, trying to say the "s" sound so I could get back into my seat where I could wallow privately in my own humiliation.

When it finally did come out, about five or six tries later, so much time had elapsed that the class thought I was being cute and they laughed at me.

That broke my flow of words, which often worked like a magnet to pull up other words – and so talking fast and non-stop sometimes worked.

I don't remember what I planned to say after the first word, but I remember standing there, wanting to cry, but because I was a 15-year-old boy, I couldn't.

It's a funny thing about someone who stutters: you can't tell it by looking. You don't see a white cane, you don't see a wheelchair, you don't see any obvious signs of anything amiss, and so you don't expect it when you greet someone who is at the moment unable to respond.

It's easy to think of that non-respondent as rude or ill-mannered, and if it happens to be someone of another race, it's easy to generalize and stereotype. It's easy not to be as friendly the next time, when all the while that person is bursting inside with frustration, wanting so desperately to say "hello" to you back, to be able to talk to you, to meet you, respond to you, to be your friend, but the tongue won't work; the words won't come, a chance is missed, and you'll never know why.

Without a doubt, stuttering as a youth influenced me and how I related to the world. Stuttering defined my limits and possibilities, more than any other single thing, more than God, more than my parents, more than my friends. More than anything else, the inability to communicate, to speak, limited my choices and my actions.

Despite the many unpleasant memories caused by my stuttering when I was younger, it has made me more aware of others, has made me less quick to judge them, has allowed me to be more tolerant of their own needs. It has made me painfully aware that all of us have pain and all of us have limitations.

Ageless Mind, Ageless Spirit

Yesterday, I ran into a colleague who had attended a conference with me. We began discussing a good speaker we had heard. He was an interesting man, I said. My colleague agreed and described him as well organized, persuasive, confident and self-assured. He did exhibit all of these desirable qualities.

But I explained that I found him even more interesting after a lunchtime conversation with him. I learned he was a veteran of the Vietnam War, raised four children and loved to play golf, dominos and chess, and had just moved into the city of Detroit.

There are many different uses of the word interesting and many points of view about what makes a person interesting. What impressed me most about this speaker was his varied interests. In addition to a full-time job and a large family, he had managed to find the time to play golf, dominos and chess, and now, nearing retirement age, he was committed to improving his golf game. He probably has the same 24-hour day allotted to all of us, but he has managed to stretch himself to find the time and motivation to develop new skills.

Shortly after the conference, I overheard a teacher complaining to his friend that he really wished his parents had made him take piano lessons and practice every day when he was young. Now it was just too late. Many people feel they are too old to try something they have never done before. Certainly, most of us aren't as physically fit as we were at 17, but just the basic abilities to walk, talk, and move our hands and feet are enough to begin swimming, playing the piano, singing, painting or learning a new language. We probably won't be able to dance as well as a ballerina at the start, but we could learn to dance well enough to have fun and enjoy the benefits of exercise and companionship. If physical ability is not holding us back, there must be other factors that keep us from branching out. Time and energy and the numerous things we must do every day limit us all. Many people, especially those with combinations of job, family, children or school, are too exhausted after their day has ended to want anything more than the entertainment of a short TV show or half a chapter of a book and sleep.

Another problem could be that people become discouraged before they start. After watching good actors, dancers and comedians on TV and hearing good music on the radio, it's easy and probably reasonable to assume that we'll never be as good as they are. But most people take tennis and music or art lessons to develop themselves and have fun, rather than to become professional and make money.

Often there is a certain amount of embarrassment in trying something for the first time like taking music lessons, learning to hit a baseball or trying to ride a bike or to roller-skate for the first time. No one wants to look or sound like that again.

On the other hand, realizing that every successful artist, writer, musician or athlete started with the same hesitant steps and made lots of mistakes along the way should encourage us. When I see people practicing new skills, I always admire their effort and patience. Most of all I admire their having overcome embarrassment and fear of failure and their having found the time to take that first step. If they enjoyed what they were doing, it was always easier to come back a second time.

A recent article suggested that learning new skills could help "age-proof" the mind. It suggested playing card games or board games, learning a new language, keeping a daily journal or learning how to play a musical instrument could improve reasoning and memory. Another benefit: as people try new activities, they also meet others who share their interests and offer enthusiasm and support.

Although it might seem to employers that outside interests can take time and energy away from concentration on the job, people who have outside interests and hobbies are often happier and more satisfied and happy at work. Satisfied people make better employees. Self-motivation and willingness to apply one's self to new situations are skills most employers are seeking.

So, in addition to contributing fun and friendship, pursuing new interests can enhance the way people carry out everyday responsibilities. More importantly, people can show themselves and the world that it's never too late to reach out for new experiences and to develop their own special talents.

Circumstances Yield Our Best

While it wasn't my intent, I couldn't help but overhear the conversation conducted at the table next to mine. Two young women were discussing the plans of one to buy a new house. It so happened that she and her husband were now buying a home after renting for many years, and only after their landlord doubled the rent on their Victorian-styled home. The other young woman stated rather matter-of-factly that perhaps these were the ideal circumstances, since they were not too old to own their own home and the situation was forcing them to do what they should have done many years ago.

How profound, I thought, though simplistic in its parameters. Sometimes, it is the worst of circumstances that makes us step up to the plate.

I searched my mind for other instances where circumstances that seemed negative and perhaps damaging could put one in the position to actually come out ahead.

I recalled friends who were experiencing challenges with their adult son. The son had received the best of education before entering the armed forces in the footsteps of the father. Thereafter, he returned to a blanket of security that prevented him from moving on in life on his own. It was a terrible struggle that the parents encountered. Not physical or abusive, as the son was the epitome of courtesy and respect. It was the internal struggle realized by parents when pondering the best thing for their child – give him the support that it outwardly appeared he needed, or use the tough-love approach and allow him to realize responsibility in the real sense on his own.

Well, they opted for the latter, and while it was hard, it was the best thing for everyone. Shortly after the proverbial rug was removed from under the son's feet, he began to stand on his own. He went on to a satisfying career, got married and began a family.

Another instance is one many of us experience – being fired or laid off. It is an abrupt realization of the dependency that we have on an employer for our livelihood. While most of us view being fired as an insult, a set-back or a negative view of our performance or ourselves, there are many who go on – albeit forcibly – to live their dream of returning to school or pursuing a career in whatever they really want to do, rather than doing something they feel they must for survival. It is the removal of a safety net that actually doubles as a noose.

When circumstances arise that appear to be detrimental to one's existence, growth or maintenance in life, they are simply opportunities disguised as setbacks. It is like a poorly wrapped second chance, if you will. Yet, it still requires us to take advantage of the moment, rather than allowing it to be overwhelming. Like the lady buying her house: without the greed or lack of consideration of her landlord, she and her husband would perhaps have gone on through life without ever knowing the comfort, security and investment of owning their own home.

So, next time opportunity masked as opposition knocks at your door, open the door and welcome the opportunity to be better, learn more, have more and be richer in your very existence. Don't curse the circumstances, but welcome them with open arms. Whether you immediately recognize it or not, it is, indeed, the chance you've been waiting for.

Needless Risk As Dangerous As No Risk

"Nothing ventured, nothing gained" is a well-used and even hackneyed expression. However, it probably reflects a deep-rooted value in American culture.

We value and reward successful risk-takers and respect those who apply themselves and sometimes fail. We have very little tolerance for timidity or for those who are unwilling to take risks. We have all grown up in a system and with a set of values that rewards risk taking.

Unfortunately, I'm not sure many of us know precisely what risk taking means. For sure, it has different meanings for different people. We are told at a very early age that if our life is going to get better, we have to take risks. We are also told that we must take chances to overcome obstacles.

Sometimes the obstacle we are trying to overcome is another person. Sometimes it's a set of social conventions. Often it's the influence others have on us or the restrictions that our own shallow expectations have on us.

No matter what we are breaking away from, the act of risking symbolizes the moment of truth – leaving the position we've grown accustomed to, forging ahead and confronting the unknown.

Take, for instance, a 48-year-old successful middle manager that has worked for the same company for 15 years and is suddenly laid off. He not only must find a new job, but he must also learn new skills.

He owns a home and is well established in the community. His reversals may also involve the trauma of being uprooted and separated from his family, friends and the support system that have provided a safe haven.

On another level involving risk, some of you may know of a young person who has been stricken with a debilitating disease. The media are often peppered with human-interest stories of young people who have courageously confronted such problems.

Success doesn't necessarily have to be part of the equation. What is important is that they didn't cower and succumb to their reversal.

However, there is another kind of risk taking that is foolish, dangerous and self-destructive. This kind of behavior has little to do with responsible growth and development. Yet it, too, may be a perverted reflection of our culture.

As I drove to work one morning recently, I noticed several kids standing on a corner at a bus stop in my neighborhood. Just as I approached the corner, a young girl, who looked to be around 14 or 15, dashed out in front of my car crossing the street, then just as suddenly, dashed across again. Needless to say, I was dumbfounded.

Later, another teenager told me that this was a recent passion among teenagers. They were mimicking a scene from the movie, *The Program*. The movie depicted a young boy playing chicken with an oncoming car while lying in the middle of the road.

A larger part of this risk taking can be linked to teenagers' strange sense of invulnerability. They just don't believe what they read or see on the movie screen will actually happen to them.

According to Frank Farley, Ph.D., a pioneer researcher of risk behavior, "between 10 and 30 percent of Americans are addicted to living life on the edge."

Joel Mangione, an 18-year-old, was typical. Two years ago, as the story was told in a prominent magazine, Joel and three friends drank and partied until the early morning hours. When Joel and a friend returned to their dorm, they decided to indulge in their most recent passion – elevator surfing.

They climbed atop one of the two elevator cabs that occupied the double shaft in their high-rise dorm. Then as Joel tried to jump from one cab to the other he slipped. For a few moments he was wedged between the cab and the shaft wall. Then he fell 16 stories to his death.

Many experts in the area of child psychology say that Joel's act was a matter of testing and expanding personal limits.

Dr. Adele Hofmann, former director of adolescent medicine at the University of California, Irvine, said, "As the thrill seeker tries to find his own star, he measures himself against his peers. It's a test of who's the biggest, who's the bravest, and who's the boldest."

A purposeful life is a life full of risks. We should not be mired in fear and indecision, which leads to depression and undermines our sense of self.

Nor should we engage in senseless self-destructive behavior where a person takes foolish chances. Risking everything over the wrong issue is as destructive as never risking at all.

Making Excuses Won't Bring About Success

Five years ago, my grandfather died at the ripe old age of 107. Up until just a few months before his death he read the newspaper daily and could debate politics with the best of us. He was strong and opinionated. He never hesitated to proclaim his allegiance to the Republican Party, often saying to me, "Boy, never forget it was Lincoln who freed the slaves and he was a Republican."

Papa, as we fondly called him, never wavered in his commitment to the Republican Party. I'm not sure he ever understood my infatuation with the Democratic Party in what one may call my more formative years.

He never allowed the trees to obscure his view of the forest. He always said things like "No excuse is good enough for not succeeding." Papa had a strong work ethic. He worked day and night to make ends meet. He and my father were my live role models.

In terms of material things, my grandfather did not have much to show for all his years. On the day he died I was summoned back home to help make financial arrangements for his burial. But he left us with a great legacy...one filled with wisdom and pride. He pioneered a trail blazed by passion and commitment. He taught us to understand that there is no shame in failing, provided we worked as hard as we could to achieve success, and that every day we should only accept the best as good enough. In fact, he would often say "Abraham Lincoln failed many times before eventually becoming President."

When I think of the stories Papa shared with me about growing up in a Jim Crow society where the challenge was, if you were black, to prove you were human, I'm reminded of the strong historical shoulders upon which this generation of young black people stand. He did not have to talk about the degradation of separate drinking fountains, the denial of voting rights, the persistence of legal segregation. I could see it in his eyes and hear it in his voice.

This brings me to an important point. We as black people must move beyond excuses. Sure, we as a race for a period of almost 200 years were subjected to one of the greatest tragedies known to mankind – slavery. But that's behind us now. We must now free ourselves to move forward and look back only to gain strength from where we have been. I can't count the number of young high school and college students who have said to me that the reason they're not succeeding is racism. Our experiences of suffering is but one among many. We should remember the suffering of the Ukrainian people under Stalin, or the Cambodian people under the Khmer Rouge or the Jewish experience of the Holocaust.

Aside from being ineffective as a solution to just about any problem I can think of, excuses such as racism only add to the disappointment and sense of helplessness. William Raspberry, a popular black columnist for the *Washington Post*, put it best when he said, "Forget the legacy of slavery argument; forget the entire range of arguments that attribute every black hardship to racism."

"We should not use past suffering as an excuse for failure, but rather to work harder than those who never had such handicaps to overcome. We must make brick without straw, lift ourselves by our bootstraps when we have no boots. The only thing left for a poor man to do to overcome poverty is to find a good job, work hard, and save," according to Dr. Benjamin E. Mays, the late President of Morehouse College in Atlanta, Georgia.

Again, we should not hold ourselves hostage to the past. The greatness of this generation of black people will be determined by how well we deal with the needs of the day in light of where we need to go as a people. We don't have to be rocket scientists to know that we are in trouble. Just read the paper, watch television or talk to friends. We are killing each other, our babies are having babies, and we have an unprecedented number of fatherless households. The list could go on and on.

I recently read that nationwide, blacks comprise about 50 percent of all males in state juvenile and adult correctional institutions. If that's not enough, let me share some statistics with you that will surely suggest that we must move and move fast. There is one white attorney for every 680 whites; one black attorney for every 4,000 blacks; one white physician for every 649 whites; one black physician for every 5,000 blacks; one white dentist for every 1,900 whites; one black dentist for every 8,400 blacks and less than one percent of all engineers are black. Granted, these statistics (taken from a speech I made in 1986) are many years old, but I would suggest that the numbers are still much the same.

Some are likely to read this chapter and say that I'm oblivious to the reality of racism and that I speak like an alien from another planet. Well, for those who may be inclined to think that, let me say that I know racism exists in this country as well as in every other country on this planet. But in spite of the ugliness of racism wherever it is found, people must see it as just one more obstacle to overcome. As Frederick Douglass stated so eloquently: "It's not so much the success that one achieves in life that is important, it's the obstacles that one has to overcome while succeeding that's important."

In the spirit of Frederick Douglass, Papa's legacy was evidenced by more than mere material success, for he demonstrated the kind of dignity and character that enabled him to overcome any obstacle. We owe it to the millions of people like Papa who preceded us to regain the moral strength, the courage and will to succeed, no matter the circumstances. No more excuses!

Country, Friends Suffer From Illiteracy

Thinking back, I really don't remember getting excited about reading much of anything until around the eighth grade.

I didn't grow up in an environment where books were all over my house. My parents encouraged my sisters and me as best they could; however, they both worked long and hard hours outside the home and had little time to read themselves.

In fact, my father can't read. My father and I have never discussed his reading problem even as I write these words.

Sure, I realized many years ago that he could not read, but because he never chose to share his affliction with me, I didn't see it as my place to offer the topic for discussion.

Anyway, it didn't seem to count. He loved and cared for my sisters and me in the most perfect way.

We did not get our first television until I was 10 years old. Given that we had no television during my early childhood years, reading probably should have been one of the family's main recreational activities…but it wasn't.

My best friend in grade school and many years later was in a curious way an enigma to me. He could not read.

However, in every other way, he was the smartest person I ever knew. He was admired and respected by every kid in the neighborhood for his ability to do almost anything better than the rest of us. His Achilles heel was only exposed in the classroom.

I never understood why the teachers continued to be unaware of his affliction.

As I look back, it was probably my best buddy's brilliance that kept our teachers unaware of his inability to read.

If someone gave him something to read, he would make believe he read it. We did his homework. When we went to the neighborhood grocery store, we read the candy wrappers for him. We did it all, not knowing that we, along with our beloved teachers, were victimizing the most popular guy in the neighborhood.

What happened to my best friend? Well, almost three decades later, he can't read, and stands on the busiest corner he can find in the same little neighborhood where we played together holding a sign that he can't read: "Homeless, will work for food."

This situation is not unique in the experience of my wife and me. One in eight Americans is functionally illiterate – 23 million people! That means they can spell out letters but can't fill out a driver's license or employment application.

There's an even more alarming statistic: there are 23 million more who read so poorly they can't function successfully on a day-to-day basis.

Together, these 46 million people represent more than one third of the entire adult population.

Today in a society saturated with communication, literacy is a hot topic.

We as Americans do not read as well as we should. Almost anyone we talk to informed on the subject of literacy will tell us that the standard of literacy required by modern society has been rising throughout the developed world, but American literacy rates have not risen to meet this standard.

Higher-level literacy abilities for all children must become a central goal of our schools.

However, the schools can't do it alone. Public policy should create opportunities for community agencies to focus on the issue of literacy. Adult literacy training can be done in collaboration with day care, or in libraries, or by "storefront" neighborhood organizations.

As I stated earlier, literacy in this country is a hot topic. We live in a world of the written word. Just to cross the street, we have to be able to read "Walk" and "Wait."

To get a license to drive a car, to apply for a job, to apply for welfare or Medicaid, to get Social Security benefits, to get credit or a bank loan, we have to be able to read questions and write answers to them. Illiteracy is a problem we can't talk enough about.

Revenge: Fight With Fist Or Brain Power?

A while ago, I read a brief comment in the paper from the Supreme Court, which expressed "a powerful and legitimate interest in punishing the guilty..."

Shortly thereafter, there was an article about a criminal who was granted a stay of execution. The article consoled the family of the victim, who would not have the "satisfaction of watching the criminal die."

Revenge, the old concept of "an eye for an eye," seems quite popular these days. It's surprising how many people feel better if they get revenge against someone who has wronged them. Possibly this is only a negative twist on the golden rule – many of us are quite happy to hurt others if we feel they hurt us first.

Revenge is not a new concept. It has motivated family feuds for centuries. Many of the ongoing conflicts in the world are fueled by revenge. There are often no new grounds for disagreement. The primary goal is to seek revenge for what happened in the past, often before the antagonists were born.

Sometimes the target of revenge is an institution. For example, students who disagree with the administration might vandalize a school. A store might be plagued by shoplifters, who feel no guilt about stealing from someone who is making a profit.

It is surprisingly easy to encourage others to forgive and forget. But when it happens to us, we want to seek revenge. Sometimes we call it seeking justice and often with someone who is younger or on a lower social stratum, we want to "teach that so-and-so a lesson."

When the person who has been wronged is a member of a group, for example a gang, the means for revenge expand. The argument is no longer between two individuals, but between two gangs, so the victim can seek revenge on anyone in the other group, including family members. As more innocent victims are hurt, each group becomes more loyal and more determined to seek revenge.

Many of the groups that started today's political, religious, racial and social conflicts around the world, continue to seek revenge today – for example, in Ireland, the Middle East, Africa and the Balkan countries. Each group tends to stereotype the other side so the conflict is fueled by emotion. Logic, including the original cause of the conflict, has been lost in the years of fighting. So one key to breaking the cycle of aggressive violence and revenge is to try to focus on logical reasoning.

A person seeking revenge should consider the consequences. Killing someone, even someone with a criminal record, will not bring his or her victim back to life. "Teaching someone a lesson," whether it means spanking a child, jailing a teenager, or shooting an adult, can backfire and produce a person filled with hate who starts another cycle of revenge.

On the other hand, criminal behavior must be stopped, and criminals – including vandals and shoplifters – must realize they are ultimately hurting themselves by their actions.

Violence and aggression can be curtailed with threats. For example, people will behave if they know the punishment for misbehaving is painful enough – be it jail or death. But the end result of threats is people who behave because they must, not because they want to. Maintaining this behavior requires constant supervision and control, and ultimately results in a type of police state.

Native Americans have a practice of "counting coup," in which touching an enemy is considered more impressive than killing him. In this way the winner shames his opponent with his greater skill and courage. In the same way, a victim who does not seek revenge can demonstrate maturity and strong self-control.

Some judges have sentenced shoplifters to standing outside the store they stole from, wearing a sandwich board explaining what they did. The shame and humiliation of this punishment is probably more effective in preventing further shoplifting.

Ultimately, people have to learn that acts of revenge, like the violence that prompted them, are really not beneficial to anyone. In fact, if it were possible for the drive-by shooter to see the grief on the face of the mother of the child he shot, or for the school vandal to understand how paying for repairs of the damage he did will keep the school from buying any new equipment for the year, they might be willing to stop their violence. Or at least, they might realize the people who are suffering are not the ones they wanted to harm.

In the long run, we should all model the behavior we would like our opponents to learn, and to turn away from fighting from a position of strength, instead of giving in to the desire for a violent victory, and perpetuating the need for revenge.

Written To Distraction

A while ago someone asked me why I write newspaper columns like those collected in this book. "Doesn't it take a lot of time?" he wondered. And they don't really have anything to do with your job, he added by implication.

He was right to think that it takes time to write, even something as brief as a column like this one. And many things that I write for the newspapers are not directly related to my job.

So why do it?

It's not that I had free time on my hands from work; in fact, almost the opposite is true. If I let it, my work could consume nearly all of my time and mental energy. There are times when the workload gets out of hand, when special projects require extra time and attention to the point of being overwhelming. During these situations I am less likely to have time to think and write something that is not directly related to the project at hand. Having one more thing to do that keeps me from being social or with my family is sometimes too much – and so writing gets delayed another day.

It's more difficult to write while other things that require focus and attention are weighing heavily on my mind. When I begin to write and find myself distracted, or staring too long at a blank page, it is a sign to go on and do whatever needs to be done. When I can achieve closure on something I have been working on, it frees up an extra space in my mind for something new, and that's the most likely time for me to sit and think and write. Between projects there is sometimes a little mental space that allows my mind to wander or an idea or memory that seems interesting to think about.

So why bother with the extra work and effort? Sometimes when I'm tired after a long, busy day, it's tempting to sit down and turn off my mind. But the act of thinking and writing is so interesting itself that it's worth the effort. Sometimes, in the middle of an idea, some insight, or an even better idea, pops out of nowhere and even surprises me.

Writing also requires discipline. Even with a clean idea or feeling about something, it takes reasoning and organization for it to make sense to other readers, and a sense of coherence, so that things seem to flow logically from one point to the next. All of this is more of a challenge than a problem, almost like a puzzle to be put together, one piece at a time.

Writing is still work, and time consuming. But it also puts me in touch with life and events that impact or influence all of us in one way or another. In my daily life at work, focus is more narrow and concentrated on the task at hand. If all I thought about were the things I face at work, I certainly would stay busy, but it would be a far less rich experience without writing – and the thinking that stands behind it.

Writing is a way to force myself to take some time to think about things, to look around and see other parts of life in our community or country.

Writing something for others to read is also humbling. Expressing a thought or opinion or idea about something exposes oneself to the world. Not everyone will agree with your view or conclusion, and sometimes critics can be quite blunt. Writing opens you up to criticism for beliefs, for perceived inconsistencies or errors in thinking. It's always possible to see something in a different light later, especially with different information, or to have a different opinion or belief that is not always popular. It is possible to say something that is confusing or misleading despite your efforts to check on clarity.

Despite the risks, writing does have rewards. Occasionally, someone will send a note of gratitude, reflection or appreciation for something; once someone told me that a column I had written made her rethink her relationship with her teenage son. Something I had said helped her see something differently, and it helped. And she took the time to let me know. In the long run, maybe that's why I continue to write.

Building A Good Vocabulary Versus Becoming Child Couch Potatoes

A few weeks ago *Time* magazine mentioned in its "numbers" column that in the 1950s American children had a vocabulary of 25,000 words, but by 1999, their vocabulary averaged only 10,000 words. This is shocking news, especially to educators who have been regularly teaching vocabulary skills for the last 40 years.

Among the general public, there could be many varied reactions to this information ranging from "so what?" to genuine concern that if vocabulary is a measure of intelligence, which has been suggested before, no matter how hard we try, our children are not getting smarter.

On the other hand, anyone who has seen a preschool child operate a remote control for the television set, use an answering machine, VCR, or computer will have to admit that now children master things that never existed for us in the 50s. With all the brain cells we supposedly don't even use, it seems reasonable to wonder why children can't learn how to master video games and, at the same time, build a good vocabulary. Assuming the studies that generated these numbers have given us valid and reliable results, there must be some cause for this effect.

Certainly, daily life has changed dramatically since the 50s. Many children are now living the kinds of lives we would have considered fairy tales back in those days when many families didn't even have black-and-white TVs, much less video games or computers. That was long before water parks and way before McDonald's had indoor play areas.

All of these entertaining activities take the place of what kids used to do with their free time.

Too many children have become couch potatoes, opting to surf the cable until they find something entertaining. On the other hand, most parents who try to play their children's video games would have to agree that it takes a high level of concentration, hand/eye coordination, memory, problem-solving skills and practice to defeat the enemy. Even children's sports, played primarily for recreation in the 50s, have become more competitive. Kids now practice before and after school to achieve higher levels of expertise. For example, child gymnasts now perform much more difficult routines than they had to master 50 years ago.

Of course, with the wide availability of TV, since many children have one of their own, it's much easier to find a show to watch than it is to pick up a book and read. So, many children view reading as something to sit through in school, rather than free-time entertainment. And parents, even those who used to read a lot, often give it up when responsibility for a job, home and family takes up most of their day. Although we find less time to read for entertainment, we are surprised and upset when our children follow our model. In addition to worrying about their vocabulary, we wonder if they will develop any creativity, thinking back to those rainy days when kids used to act out the stories they read, or make up new ones.

It's hard to know whether we are really in trouble, losing our vocabulary, creativity and even our motivation by letting ourselves be entertained the easy way. Or, as we age and life changes, often the way we used to do it seems better. So are we only reacting with alarm to change?

Thinking back about changes over the last 30 years, we are not only getting used to new appliances and buying new technology for the computer age, but we're looking at life a little differently. We make a lot of choices about how we spend our time and money, and therefore, what we consider important. With today's array of choices, reading is only one of many ways of getting information.

And many people who used to read books have switched to reading the Internet. Maybe we don't learn the vocabulary from the Internet that we would get from the classics. But it might be more important to worry less about how people get information and more about what they do with it.

Kids learn how to process information and remember it for future use. They also have to learn how to choose which information is useful and which is potentially dangerous. It is an uphill battle to convince a child that a page of black and white print is as exciting as a screen full of multi-colored moving objects with a sound track. Maybe kids do need a little work on their vocabulary, but more importantly, they need to know how to choose those activities which help them learn and grow.

If we worry less about their choice of TV and videos, and more about spending time with them and helping them make a comparison between life on the screen and "real life" at home, we might, in the long run, be accomplishing our goal of teaching those kids how to have more happy, successful, productive lives.

Part III
Ethics and Morality

"Everyone has a right to his own course of action."

Moliere

From my "in-the-arena" perspective, ethics is simply doing the right thing, no matter what the consequences, for situations in the home, at work, and in other settings. A personal code of ethics and morality is one's safe harbor from the storms of life. A code of conduct serves as a moral compass, or governor, to help one find true north even in periods of extreme pressure and confusion.

I remember being told as a child that the test of morality is what you do when no one is looking. It has also been said that it is easy to do the right thing; the difficult part is knowing what the right thing is. So, on what basis do we determine what is ethical? Stephen Covey, after years of research, concluded that there is a set of universal principles to guide ethical conduct that have been tried and tested over many centuries. He calls them the "laws of the universe": fairness, equity, justice, integrity, honesty, and trust.

Who has the ultimate authority to determine what is ethical or not? Have we become a nation that increasingly hides under the cloak of "ethics" to avoid meaningful discourse?

In an organization, employees hunger for leaders with integrity and credibility in whom they can put their trust. That is why organizations seek to place in key leadership positions mature, experienced, and ethical individuals who have demonstrated good judgment and can maintain a posture of calmness in difficult situations. Lee Bolman and Terrance Deal, in their book Leading with Soul, stated that "leadership is an ethic, a gift of oneself to a common cause, a higher calling. It is offering oneself and one's spirit – gifts of love, shared power, and significance."

In the following stories or passages, I explore what I have learned from my own efforts to live according to a personal code of ethics that is based on proven theories of moral philosophy, lessons learned personally over the years, and from the ethical and unethical behavior I have observed in others.

Ethics And Attitudes

There is something about middle age that causes most of us to take a personal inventory from time to time about what we believe, what we value, and the principles that guide how we conduct our lives.

Every person, regardless of age, acts upon what he believes to be the fundamentally correct way to act. Every day of our lives we make many decisions that test our own ethical dilemmas.

It is here that we see that our ethics are not mere abstractions. Our values show up in the way we treat our friends, enemies, spouse, children and colleagues. The bottom line is that ethics are the attitudes and rules we follow in dealing with one another.

Recently I shared a story about the time a young lady gave me back too much change at a fast food restaurant. Frankly, I did not recognize the fact that my trip to pick up a couple of hamburgers rewarded me so handsomely until I returned home. I had received almost $20 more than I should have. At the risk of sounding like a goody-two-shoes or Mr. Ethics, I will tell you that I did return the money. However, to this day, I'm not sure I did it for the right reason.

As a parent I have watched as some Little League football coaches teach 9 and 10 year olds to hold while attempting to block, which is clearly illegal. I have seen baseball coaches teach kids to cheat and basically do everything necessary to gain the competitive edge.

I am old enough to remember watching the television show *I Love Lucy* when two beds were required for bedroom scenes that showed

Lucy and Desi tucked away for the night. But now, in our salad bowl ethical environment where everyone does what is right in their own eyes, as long as it "doesn't hurt anyone else," contemporary television sitcoms make no effort to come to terms with ethics and morality.

The highest value is tolerance, at all costs, even when our entertainment and much of our literature appear to be corrupting influences. Honest people can honestly disagree on what is honest and ethical. The problem I find with trying to discuss ethics is the many differing shades of gray.

For example, my wife and I have had a 20-year debate about whether we should open each other's mail when it has been specifically addressed to one of us. I have never felt it was a big deal, thus the shades of ethical gray. She does believe it is a big deal.

Many choices on how to talk with our children reflect the gravity of our choice of ethics. I have a friend who has strong religious convictions, and he was trying to guide his three teenage daughters during a period where hormones and peer pressure apparently had greater influence than his fatherly counsel. He suspected that one daughter was sexually active. He was perplexed and caught in a quagmire.

His deep religious convictions prohibited even the thought of suggesting that his daughter should avail herself to some type of birth control. For him, abstinence is the only ethical alternative. Should he set aside his convictions and yield to "reality" and try to ensure that his daughter protects herself, or should he stand by his values? He made a choice. By the way, he eventually found out his daughter was pregnant.

Daily the media portray a crisis of ethics. Politicians are being indicted for criminal conduct; singers are being accused of child molestation; lawyers violating the laws and going to jail; and the list is endless.

As we slowly work our way back to the notion that ethics matter, we should hold ourselves accountable for the things we allow ourselves to do. We must practice what we preach and incorporate ethics into every decision we make.

Actions Reflect Ethics

It's not just what you say, it's what you do that matters – is a dressed up version of the adage, "Actions speak louder than words," if you will. And, so goes our ethical make-up. Everyone acts upon what they believe to be good, just and right, based upon what they interpret to be the same. Yet, our daily existences include on-going challenges to those beliefs, presenting the true test of allowing our practices to match our presentations.

Our true values reveal themselves in how we treat our friends, families, strangers and enemies. The bottom line, therefore, is that ethics are the attitudes and rules we follow when we deal with each other.

I watch when parents teach kids to cheat or cut corners in order to gain a competitive edge. I watch when adults are the beneficiaries of another's mistake, and walk away without acknowledging the mistake.

How many of us have witnessed someone getting too much change, and watched as the recipient gleefully walked away as though they won some sort of prize?

One of America's favorite pastimes is watching television. Yet, the programming makes no effort to come to terms with any degree of ethics or morality. Kids curse their parents, the language rivals that of some bar, and the acts are nothing short of lewd. Gone are the days of Lucy and Ricky as they ventured good nights in their own separate beds, or the Cleavers who were never shown going to bed at all.

What about music, or better yet, the music videos? I have a hard time figuring out what it is that they are selling. Is it the song, or the human element?

Yet, in the wake of challenges that our entertainment sources present, tolerance emerges as the highest value. Tolerance must be maintained at all costs, even when our entertainment and literature appear to be corrupting influences.

Honest people can honestly disagree on what is honest and ethical. The problem arises in the differing shades of gray. In the final analysis, however, we must hold ourselves accountable for our actions, be they actions of commission or omission. As I have often said, we all should practice the test of looking at the person in the mirror. Can we look that person directly in the eye? By all means, practice what you preach.

The Dichotomy Of Defining Morality

The headlines accusing President Clinton of sexual involvement with someone other than his wife gave us another opportunity to wonder how strong the moral fiber of the country really is. Some people seem to enjoy lamenting that things are so much worse now than when they were kids. Many of these people think America was doing fine, morally, during the 50s, but the free love and attraction of sex, drugs, and rock and roll of the late 60s began a downward slide to our current lack of morality.

It's true that sexual promiscuity, teenage pregnancies and drug use have escalated since the hippie days of Woodstock. But, on the other hand, the hippies marched for racial equality, advocated non-violence, encouraged ecological awareness and went to jail for refusing to fight in Vietnam. Today, Americans are still divided on the moral basis of these same issues.

One problem is, who decides what's moral and what isn't? For some people, the Bible, the Ten Commandments and their church define morality. However, many others justify their own position by labeling it as moral. Unfortunately, it's easier to take a moral stand than to actually fix the problem. For example, it's easier to argue against abortion than it is to accept the expense and long-term commitment of raising a child. We acknowledge the moral response to drug use as "just say no," but it's much harder to focus on other ways to deal with the stresses of life in our culture.

Many moral issues have several factors which conflict with each other. For example, doctors are considered morally responsible when they prescribe mood-altering drugs to adults to alleviate depression, but young men are spending years in prison for smoking what used to be a backyard weed. Another example is greed. Commercials encourage us to be greedy. When we want more, we support the cycle of supply and demand that fuels our economy. On the one hand, we should not covet what our neighbor has, but on the other, we should try to keep up with the Joneses.

Other moral issues are decided by one group which then enforces its opinion on others. An example is the moral conflict associated with assisted suicide. Although the patient expresses a wish to die, others think it's morally right to keep him alive, even in extreme pain.

On the other hand, sexual morality, which used to be dictated by the church and enforced by the family, now seems to be defined by personal choice. The freedom to accept all kinds of sexual expression has opened our eyes to the possibility that some people have unusual, even dangerous sexual habits. Children often get mixed messages – most parents encourage their children to refrain from sexual activity as long as possible, but they understand when hormones are raging, accidents can happen.

However, the children are influenced by what they see in magazines and on TV and the movies. Sex sells, and advertisers use sex to make a profit. Movies incorporate sex to hold viewers' attention, and many singers, actors, dancers and TV personalities use sex to promote themselves. It's not surprising when teenagers copy what they see. Although they are physically able to make babies, most teenagers aren't emotionally or financially ready to commit to marriage and raising a family. We consider their behavior immoral when they become sexually active, but many also think it's immoral to offer sex education classes in school and parents are often too embarrassed to explain the facts of life to their own kids.

Our culture's preoccupation with sex has made it an issue in almost all relationships. We worry about sexual harassment at work, sexual relationships between teachers and children and sexual abuse in the home. We even worry about a brief kiss between elementary school children, wondering if this means kids are becoming sexually active at an even earlier age.

Fortunately, most children, before puberty, have little or no interest in sex. Boys don't even want to hang around with girls and vice versa. If reproduction is explained to them, they are often amazed that their parents were willing to go through such a "yucky" act just to have a baby. Even though Barbie dolls have shaped what little girls think they should look like, they don't spend much time dreaming about sexy teenagers. Their parents should still be responsible for the clothes they buy and the image they project. It might be "cute" to dress a preteen girl in short, tight, sexy clothing, but how will it influence her image of herself?

We consider alcohol and cigarettes too dangerous to distribute to children; we could also limit children's involvement with sex. Evaluating the outcomes of our attitudes and behaviors, and choosing to be morally responsible could resolve many moral issues. If we don't want our children sexually involved or pregnant, we need to tell them the truth about reproduction and how much energy, time and money it takes to raise a baby.

We need to encourage our kids to make the most of their interests and skills first, and tell them that there will be plenty of time to explore their sexual interests at a later, more appropriate date.

It may be impossible to enforce moral behavior simply because it is a religious teaching, but if we look at the results of what we do, it is easy to recognize that moral responsibility provides the best outcome for everyone.

Role Models Are Chosen, Not Necessarily By The Role Models Themselves

I've always thought of my personal and professional accomplishments as the direct result of the lessons learned from the steady hands and firm voices of my mother and father, and also from the mentors who surrounded me throughout the years.

And as a result of the accolades I've received through my work and other endeavors – which I greatly appreciate – people sometimes refer to me as a "role model," a term that makes me feel uncomfortable.

Who or what exactly decides a role model?

For a myriad of reasons, I think the term has become contrived and clichéd. It used to be that a role model was a person who evolved naturally in their surroundings – an organic creation if you will. It used to be that a role model wasn't "manufactured" to shill cereal, toys, candy, etc., but instead offered positive characteristics to be emulated not from a sense of duty, but from a sense of self-preservation and self-responsibility. I don't believe a person should be held up as an arbiter of morality when it is forced on them out of misdirection and a lack of foresight by others who may seek to find what they are lacking within themselves through the deeds and words of others.

A perfect example of the apprehension of being a role model can be found in baseball legend Mickey Mantle, whom I saw on a television interview years before his death. He had it all -- riches, fame, and the unyielding devotion of fans whose behavior veered toward blind worship, and it made him uncomfortable.

Mantle, it seems, just wanted to play baseball. He found the spotlight disturbing and the pedestal on which fans placed him difficult to sit on. Mantle thought of himself as an average Joe who got lucky. There were others, in far more difficult situations who he thought were more worthy of admiration: single parents, factory workers, doctors, etc. As I watched the interview, I couldn't help but notice the sadness that surrounded him. There were so many kids, including myself, who envisioned what it must be like to be the greatest hitter in baseball. Who knew that this role model didn't consider himself as such – and didn't want the pressure of having to live up to those responsibilities.

Mantle is among the many people who have attained "godly" status in the eyes of many impressionable youngsters and adults. But he is only partially right about who the real role models should be. We don't choose to be role models; we are chosen. The only choice involved is whether to be a good role model or a bad one.

You don't have to be an athlete soaring down a football field or hitting home runs or dunking the basketball to be a role model. It doesn't matter that an athlete has a gambling problem or that he's been promiscuous. We'll overlook those shortcomings as society continues to push or sell the athlete as a role model.

The athlete's accomplishments are admirable, but youngsters need to know that they all won't make it into the major leagues. Making the big leagues is a dream that is attainable for some, but others will have to reach their goals in other professions.

I remember my father talking about the athletic feats of Willie Mays, Satchel Paige and Mickey Mantle. It was as though he was lost in time when he recounted some of the stories he had been told by others about his heroes.

His eyes would bulge, and his voice would get louder as we talked about how he would have accomplished as much if he had a few breaks. But role models don't have to have millions. And they don't have to have fame to qualify for the title.

The real role models are the many people in our lives who teach individuality, morality and a sense of independence to those around them. They are the true guiding light for everyday reality. And my father, who sometimes spoke of what "could have been," turned out to be the ultimate role model for me through his work ethic, moral code and dedication to his family, but I don't think he ever realized the effect his actions had on those who surrounded him.

Thanks, Dad!

Negative Ads Come From Negative People

You can usually tell who's trailing in a political campaign by which candidate starts negative attack campaign ads. The theory must be that if you can't sway voters on the merits of your own ideas and charm, then you have no resort left but to tear down your opponent.

That's sort of like a football team that can't win on its own talents so it tries to injure opposing players in order to win at all costs. Unfortunately in America today, our elections have become too much like sporting contests whose outcomes matter little the next day to most people except serious gamblers and Washington lobbyists.

Watching negative campaign ads, one wonders what kind of person so willfully pays money to engage in dirt and deceit to beat a fellow American who simply has a different vision for America. Why isn't the character issue raised by voters right there? It's much easier to keep a scoundrel out at the beginning than it is to dislodge him once he gets entrenched in power.

If campaign behavior and advertising reflect a candidate's indifference to truth and decency, can we assume that indifference will carry over to the office? Can we assume that what we see on TV is what we will get? That the values and attitudes portrayed there will carry over to the elected office? Does the candidate give us any reason to worry about what he/she might do to the rest of us once elected?

Negative ads are the refuge of the hapless and immoral. They typically deal with outright lies at worst, or deception and distortion at best. They usually focus voter attention on a perceived worst element about a candidate, no matter how petty or irrelevant to the issues of the day, no matter how distorted or out of context the statement might be.

I wish voters would someday in mass and in unison scream out: "No more lies, no more tricks, and no more deception." I wish voters would unite and reject any candidate who engages in any negative campaigning whatsoever. If both candidates resort to negativity, then neither should get one vote, and the office can be left empty for a term. We may discover we don't need that office holder anyway.

Or a future candidate might get the message that what voters want is truth, honesty, a clear idea of a plan, and to know where someone stands on the important issues. Candidates also should know that we don't believe a word they say about their opponents, that we expect it to be distorted or abject lies. In fact, when they spend time blasting their opponent, they waste an opportunity to tell us something about themselves. They should persuade us to vote for them rather than trying to scare us into not voting for someone else.

I also wonder why candidates are always interested in fighting (rather than working)? "Elect me to Congress (or dog catcher) and I will fight for you." And why do they always talk about how tough they will be, but never about how smart, or compassionate or reasonable or understanding? I would love to see a contest someday where both candidates try to demonstrate their creative and intelligent proposals to problem solving rather than their toughness or meanness.

While negative ads provide no useful or reliable information on which a voter may make a reasoned and informed choice, other ads can give a sense of a candidate's values and thinking. In a campaign ad that wasn't negative towards an opponent, one candidate placed a nonetheless negative ad in a newspaper with the headline: *To Save a Generation of Young People...We Must Teach Them There Will be Bad Consequences for Bad Behavior.*

My concern here is his negative approach to solving a problem in the name of sounding tough. The candidate sounded far more interested in punishing juveniles for bad things they do than in providing solutions and opportunities that will help prevent those juveniles from doing bad things in the first place. It's the philosophy of after-the-fact punishment rather than before-the-act prevention, typical jails-over-schools approach to our social problems.

I worry that we rely so much on the legal and court system to deal with problems, instead of using our social systems and educational programs to provide guidance and opportunities that offer our youth hope and encouragement in a world that can look pretty scary to them. An ounce of prevention can indeed be worth a pound of cure, and prevention is usually much cheaper (and more loving) than punishment.

Living By Golden Rule Lifts Society With Value System

The people who study how and why people acquire their value systems suggest that we don't value the things we have plenty of as much as we value what we have little of. Unfortunately, this seems true. We have plenty of people. In fact our cities suffer from over-crowding. We are living in a time when a child's life is worth the price of a jacket or a pair of shoes. Children in gangs shoot other children without remorse. They say that killing another person doesn't have much meaning for them.

Today, a lot of children grow up in day-care. Even two-week-old babies go to day-care. These kids are dropped off on the way to work, often as early as 6:30 or 7 a.m., and picked up after work as late as 6:30 p.m. These kids put in a 12-hour day. People who are often overworked and may never have had the opportunity for professional training care for our must valuable possessions, our hope for the future, all day. For many daycare workers, raising other people's children is not a long-term career choice, it's just a way to earn money like any other minimum wage job.

When kids get old enough for school, many come home to an empty house. They learn to microwave dinner and eat alone, struggle with homework alone, and watch TV alone. Children who go to after-school care are still watched by people working for minimum wage. Many see their parents only a few hours a day.

After high school, teenagers hope to find a job, but there are too many people who want to work, and not enough jobs. College graduates and people with masters or doctorate degrees often accept low wage jobs because there are no openings in the fields they have prepared for. Some companies have laid off full-time employees who have worked conscientiously for the company for 15 or 20 years, and replaced them with part-time employees who receive no benefits. Youthful college graduates often replace older employees just before retirement.

Older retirees are placed in nursing homes. Many sit alone all day watching TV, hoping that someone will come to bathe, change, or feed them. Some wait for weeks or months for a relative to visit. The staff, often making minimum wage, provide basic care at best, and at worst, ignore them or treat them with disgust.

Providing care for our own relatives would require someone to stay at home and to give up a professional career, or work part-time for a much lower salary with no benefits. For single parents, this is impossible; for most of us, less income would mean lowering our standard of living – among the highest in the world.

How can we make an adequate living and still take care of our children and elders? How can we teach children to treat others with kindness and consideration? How can we stop the flood of homeless families, violent crimes, and abused children? How can we teach ourselves to see people as equals with the same feelings we have instead of as tools for making a profit?

Because the media present these problems on a national scale, it is easy to feel helpless. No individual is powerful or wealthy enough to solve national problems, but all of us can learn to treat family members, colleagues at work, and strangers on the street with the same kindness and respect we would like to receive. If someone smiles at me, the warm feeling it gives me helps me pass on the smile to the next person I meet. If I praise someone, that person feels good about himself and is more likely to work harder than when I give out only critical comments. There are times when only criticism is deserved, but too many people criticize when things go wrong, and never encourage or praise when they go smoothly. A smile or word of praise will not solve our problem of hate, but it does have a ripple effect.

All people need to feel valued. If the experts are correct we must make a conscious effort to reach out to the people we meet to show them they are worthwhile. We must learn to treat our children, colleagues, students, workers, bosses, and elders as individuals who matter in our lives.

Are Churchgoers More Moral?

Driving to work recently, I tuned in to a National Public Radio program discussing the appointment of John Ashcroft as attorney general. There was a report on the protests by pro-choice groups against Ashcroft's more stringent position on abortion. One member of an anti-abortion group stated that when she sat next to a pro-choice speaker, she felt the urge to lunge across the table and violently attack him. Only her Bible by her side restrained her from doing him serious harm – even possibly taking his life.

Abortion is obviously a powerful and emotional issue in this country. It is an issue that is difficult for many people to discuss without emotion. It is easy to get upset when someone is arguing against our deepest beliefs, and at those times it is easy to say things that conflict with our values. There is an unfortunate irony here. Would this woman's strong belief in protecting life – and avoiding violence – apply to any age, not just to the unborn, including those with whom she disagrees?

As a churchgoer, I have heard a lifetime of messages urging parishioners to follow the strong morals preached in church and the Bible. I also get the tacit reminder that people who go to church are more moral than people who don't. Sometimes that message was refined into the idea that morality correlated with frequency of church attendance.

This underlying notion seems reasonable for a nation with the motto, "In God We Trust." And it might be somewhat true. Most church attendees do not stay out Saturday night and sleep in Sunday morning. They probably spend more time listening to sermons about doing better. However, becoming a moral person depends a lot more on what is in the heart than which church one belongs to, or how often one attends.

And, there is also the question of moral judgments: Who is correct when conflicts of opinion arise? Killing is one of the morals our society is in conflict over. Despite the commandment that we should not kill, many people lean toward the "eye for an eye and tooth for a tooth" position. Capital punishment has become popular, probably as much to satisfy our notion of just revenge, as to reduce the expense of lifetime imprisonment. Is saving taxpayers money a moral basis for killing someone?

Abortion is certainly treated as a moral issue by many groups in this country. There is much concern over the killing of unwanted babies, and the new president (George W. Bush) has already taken his moral stand on the issue of cutting off funds in other countries who discuss it as a means of birth control. But who speaks for or will take care of the helpless newborn, possibly with abusive parents who may not want the child? Is there no moral issue about what to do with the unwanted life?

On the other hand, hospitals save the lives of patients, some of whom are in constant and severe pain, by continuing to keep them on life support even when there is no hope for recovery. And at the same time, Dr. Jack Kevorkian and other doctors are arrested for helping patients who want to die.

People tend to take a strong stand on these issues, feeling that their position is moral and the other person's is not. However, people on both sides have given much time and thought to their positions. There are usually strong moral justifications for both sides of most conflicts.

There is also a wide range of moral judgments about violence in the media and its effect on children. Many people think killing is justifiable in movies if the good guy wins. Some people think it's OK if only a few people die, and others enjoy watching hundreds get sprayed with machine gun fire. Most people feel that watching people get killed in movies doesn't affect them, although many think it might not be good for their children. Beyond the question of a moral decision which is good for "me" but not for "you" is the reality of the millions of dollars spent on TV commercials, and the many people who maintain that they remain unaffected by what they see.

The question of morality extends to all nations, even to those that are not primarily Christian. For example, when the government closed the churches in communist countries, morality did not disappear. Moral behavior was just as important, although its source was no longer attributed to the church. In fact, in many countries where church doesn't play as important a role as it does in the United States, some of our most troublesome problems – crime, murder and teenage pregnancy – occur at a much lower rate. I'm sure many have questioned why in a country where church is so strong we have such a love for violence and sex. Is it possible that the idea that churchgoers make moral decisions and that there is no hope for others somehow diminishes the responsibility for those who sleep in on Sunday to act morally? If so, we need to focus on moral individuals rather than moral churchgoers. Whether or not someone gets dressed up and goes to hear a sermon on Sunday, he or she should be taught moral behavior and the consequences of immoral choices – not only the possible influence on "judgment day," but the real everyday effects of good behavior.

We all have the responsibility to make moral choices not only for ourselves, but for the benefit of everyone else in our society now and future generations.

Can't They Stop Killing For Christmas?

It's funny, but when we look back on a year it is often marked, not by our achievements and progress, but by the deaths and tragedies, both personal and public, that remind us again of our mortality and the unpredictability of life. The 20th century will be marked more by its many world, regional, and civil wars with their staggering death tolls and destruction than for its major achievements in medicine or science or basic living conditions, or even race relations.

So, as I look back on 1997, what I come to first, of course, and perhaps what touches most Detroiters, is the recent death of Coleman A. Young. One of America's first major city black mayors, he was a warrior, and he embodied for many people the new Spirit of Detroit. He integrated the police and fire departments, and spurred downtown development. For 30 years, he led Detroit and he died leaving the city struggling to continue his legacy of service and commitment to improve the lives of all Detroit's citizens.

Although I never met him, at his funeral, I sensed what it might have been like to know him. From the words spoken in memory, I came to better know his legacy. I could see the pain and grief in the eyes and faces of so many people who came to pay him their respects, and I could understand better what he has meant to this city. I regret that I did not have the opportunity to meet him.

Tragedy struck recently in Kentucky with the shooting of several students in their school while huddled in prayer. It is meaningless to call the murders senseless when all murders are senseless. But killings such as these represent the kind of crime we fear most – the unexplainable, the random, the brutal. We need a rational motive for murder in order for us to be content, for it to make sense. In this era of wanton violence becoming more and more prevalent, we are all potential victims of thrill seekers.

What is the source of such violence? It's easy to point to examples: violent movies and television shows so often portray violence and mayhem as ordinary; tough and mean and intolerant are glorified, while wit and reason and compassion are thought to be uninteresting and so are simply missing as movie topics or themes.

Where are the movies and television programs that counter the onslaught of trauma, that provide a balance, that present experiences and situations and stories in ways that will honor life and respect the social values and code of behavior necessary for a successful social community, that reject wanton violence as either solution or mere experiment?

It's also easy to point to race as an apparent motivating factor in some of our violence, providing a constant reminder that although we are a pluralistic nation of immigrants of diverse origins and interests and talents, we still have not learned how to live together in peace and mutual respect. We still have a long way to go to overcome the things we allow to divide us.

You can rarely solve a major problem with a tainted solution. That's how affirmative action has come to be viewed, and this year saw successful challenges to the legitimacy of affirmative action as a means of ensuring equality of opportunity. A satisfactory and lasting solution to this impasse can only come when in our hearts and minds, we can overcome our own prejudices and intolerances and limited knowledge of given situations and put our cancerous racial barriers beyond us. We must at last relegate racial tensions and animosities to the scrap heap of 20th century history. But until that elusive day, what do we do?

One small but positive thing is to make sure that people in position of authority or fame – whether politicians or sports stars – are sensitive to the nature of their responsibility and influence. Sports stars, for instance, who inevitably become heroes and role models, sometimes make their own egos and antics more important than their team. Dennis Rodman and Latrell Sprewell, for example, are millionaire athletes known as much for their antisocial behavior as for their talents on the court. The NBA was right to suspend Sprewell for attacking his coach and Rodman for kicking a photographer.

Both are acts of aggressive violence and such behavior can't be tolerated in a civil society. They send the wrong message to our impressionable youth looking for heroes. That message says if you don't like what someone is doing, violence is the answer. We cannot let that go unchallenged.

A striking and obvious contrast is presented by Princess Diana and Mother Teresa, connected by their meeting in June in a New York slum, and their subsequent deaths, one shocking, one expected, both mourned by the world. One can find few things they had in common, other than their generosity of helping those in need, each in her own very different way.

It's unfair to compare the two women, for the one lived barely a third as long as the other and fate took them down very different paths. Casting harsh judgment on the Princess's life and work when she barely had time to begin seems premature. It was, in retrospect, interesting to observe the treatment of their deaths in the press. The Princess, of course, died early and tragically, and for that she gained our sympathies. Mother Teresa's death was less shocking, and thus apparently less newsworthy. If the coverage of each person's death reflects what we value as a society, it's time for a national dialogue on what really matters.

While writing this column, I was given the tragic news that the son of one of my colleagues was killed last night in a drive-by shooting.

Suddenly this becomes even more real, even more frightening, as it gets closer to home. What do we do? I feel so helpless and outraged, what can I say to her? Nothing will bring her son back, that's all that matters. No words, no comfort, no rage will bring him back to her. As a friend of the family, I grieve for them. And as a parent of teenagers I cringe; it could have been my son or daughter. Here we were, the last week of the semester, one week before Christmas. Can't they even stop for Christmas? Can't they even stop killing at Christmas?

Detroit is known as the Renaissance City. We are on the move. We are revitalizing downtown Detroit. But folks, unless we rebuild a bridge to our youth, there can be no renaissance. We must assure them of decent jobs and real hope for a secure future, or there can be no renaissance. Unless we can get a grip on crime, on violence, on senseless killing, on hate, on racial and social injustice, there will be no renaissance.

I leave this year disillusioned, and right now, horrified and outraged and feeling absolutely helpless. It is my sense, and I hope I'm wrong, that in our efforts to achieve a color-blind society, we are slipping backwards. In our efforts to achieve peace and security, we are slipping backwards. Murders are up in Detroit this year; more than 454 compared to 428 last year.

I wanted to end this on a happier note. I wanted to say that despite all the horrors of this year, hearing Christmas music, seeing Christmas lights in the evening, pausing to reflect on the meaning of the season and on the good will that often comes out during this time gives me hope and joy and encouragement to carry on. I hope I feel that way tomorrow, but right now it is the most recent tragedy that haunts my soul.

Violent Criminals Must Pay For Their Crimes Against Society

Just talk to anyone considered a member of the baby-boom generation or the generation that preceded them on the subject of crime, punishment, right or wrong and you are likely to hear some compelling childhood stories about the consequences of straying off the beaten path.

We knew that when we did wrong anywhere in the community someone would be there to take matters into their hands, and in this instance, I speak literally. My father did not need to be present when I broke the rules.

Practically any adult in the community had permission to correct my behavior using appropriate encouragement, which would occasionally mean a good country spanking.

Then, when I got home, my father was there waiting to add his two cents. The reinforcement went further. Most of us had an uncle or aunt living with us, or not more than a block or two away. We were neighborhood people. All the neighbors knew all the kids and helped to keep us out of trouble. That's what we called community.

We didn't have to be counseled about the value of life; we understood it inherently. I was about 12 years old when I climbed a tree in my back yard and deliberately destroyed a nest of bird eggs, only to discover that I had taken away the prized possessions of a mother bird that reluctantly scurried away as I recklessly invaded her home and ravaged her soon-to-be family.

How could I have been so cruel?

Later that afternoon, my conscience dictated that I share this terrible act of ruthlessness with my mother. Surely God or someone would ask me to pay a price for this act. Perhaps to some, my reaction was a little idiotic. But back then we valued life in any form.

Our definition of a gang war was neighborhood kids meeting on the nearest vacant lot to play tackle football without anything remotely resembling protective equipment.

Getting into trouble at school meant running down the hallways, chewing gum, throwing spitballs or talking out loud in class.

Guns and drugs were as foreign to us as UFOs. We went to church on Sundays, which often proved to be an all-day event. And if we were really lucky, Mama didn't invite the preacher over for supper, meaning plenty of fried chicken for me and my sisters.

Anyway, we understood clearly that there were cause and effect relationships. If we violated the law, we would likely go to jail. If we took someone's life, we would surely have ours taken in return, which brings me to the motivation for writing this column.

I was absolutely appalled, some years back, to read that an 18-year career criminal, who shot to death a gas station attendant during a robbery, was given a sentence of life in prison. I'm not quite sure what I expected, but I know that there's no such thing as life in prison in this country. This individual will be back on our streets someday, only to take another innocent life.

If ever there was a case that begged for something more than so-called life in prison, then surely this was it. The entire insidious, cold-blooded act was captured on videotape. Millions of people, both young and old, who were repulsed at such a senseless and brutal act, waited breathlessly for our criminal justice system to deliver a message. But once again, the message that it sent was one of tolerance.

The robber had us figured out long before an innocent gas station attendant lay drowning in his own blood on a cold concrete floor.

In a time when the average citizen is afraid to leave home after sunset, when children are shooting children, and when crime knows no boundaries, why is it so difficult for us to send the message that crime and punishment go hand in hand – that the commission of a crime inevitably means punishment?

Whatever you are operating, if you are attempting to control behavior, you do it by: number one, establishing ground rules, and number two, setting up a procedure to determine when the ground rules are violated.

In other words, try them. Are they guilty or innocent? And if they are guilty and they violate the ground rules, punish them. That is the way we were raised as children. That is the way we should handle dangerous violent criminals.

Now I'm going to introduce, albeit reluctantly, the issue of race into this discussion. I have a wife and two children who often believe that I have been somewhat preoccupied with race in more than a few of my columns. I think they believe the idea of a color-blind society should start with me. I truly commend them as well as many others for an unjaundiced view of the world. However, here are some issues we should confront head on.

One monumental issue is this. We as African Americans have a generation of young people at risk.

Nationwide, blacks comprise about 50 percent of all males in state juvenile and adult correctional institutions. Young black males under the age of 18 are entering juvenile correctional facilities faster than they are graduating from high school.

The overall homicide rate for black males is 60 per 100,000 – higher than that of white males, white females and black females combined! Furthermore, a black male homicide victim is most likely to be killed by another black male.

The Rev. Jesse Jackson poignantly underscored the corroded conditions of law and order in black America. "As I was walking down these isolated streets and heard footsteps rapidly approaching from behind, I was relieved when I turned around to discover that the people following me were white," he said.

Few people could get away with the above statement, but Jesse Jackson possesses a lot of political capital in the black community. What he said may jar our sensibilities, but it ought to stir every member of the black community to action.

We must re-establish a sense of community, a community that not only encompasses the nuclear family, but includes our tradition of the extended family as well. Mothers, fathers, sisters, brothers, grandparents, aunts, uncles, cousins, all working together to foster the desired community.

Guns Can't Protect Us From Fear

Television news is full of reports on children and guns, following the shooting of four children and their teacher in Jonesboro, Arkansas. There have been several shootings of children by other children in the news recently, and although we all share the same sense of surprise and horror, people have different ideas about what is causing the problem and how to solve it.

The shock of a child shooting a classmate and, in the case of Jonesboro, planning an ambush, is overwhelming. How could something this awful happen in a small southern town?

Many people blame our culture which offers children and adults violent movies, videos, and video games that encourage the child to participate in shooting, stabbing, punching, and if those aren't enough, blowing up an enemy, even if it is a cartoon foe.

Others criticize the lack of gun education courses to teach children and adults how to handle guns safely. However, this recent tragedy was planned and carried out by a child who knew a lot about guns and had experience shooting guns with his family.

Many people who don't own a gun think the answer is to severely restrict or ban guns as many European countries have done. Many others who own guns and have used them safely for years point out that the real problem is violence between people.

It does seem that violence has increased. There are articles on road rage, full-page pictures of random shooting sprees, and newspapers, news magazines and TV news programs carrying daily stories of violent crimes around the world as well as in neighboring communities. So, whether or not there has been a big increase in violent crime, there has been improvement in the ability of the media to bring us up-to-date news and pictures of violence. This kind of news is exciting, but, unfortunately, it leaves us with the impression that violent crimes are an everyday occurrence in our communities.

Unfortunately, violence on the news has the same effect on people as violent movies or video games. The more we watch people getting beat up or killed, the less shocking each incident seems. So, after the hundreds or even thousands of murders most high school kids have witnessed, each death seems a little more mundane. In fact that is exactly why shows become more violent – to hold the attention of the audience.

On the other hand, gun enthusiasts are technically right when they say guns don't kill, people kill. People who are frustrated, or hurt, or feel life is unjust get angry. They want to hurt the people who made them angry. In a fight with fists or knives they must approach the person they hate, and face more anger. They could lose the fight, or get badly hurt or die trying to win. Often, the fear of losing or getting hurt is strong enough to change their minds about fighting. However, if a gun is handy, they can kill from a distance, without fear of being hurt themselves. In fact, we've all heard of shooting sprees in which a gunman is just getting rid of anger and frustration, shooting anyone who happens to be in his way.

Even in our highly technical society with all our material goods, people are still frustrated and angry, and more and more of them own guns. It's impossible to eliminate the hassles of everyday life and the anger they cause, but we could eliminate the easiest and most deadly way of expressing that anger – by giving up our love of guns. This doesn't mean no more hunting with guns, or no more target shooting. It means instead of glorifying guns, we should look at guns as the deadly weapons that they are.

The slogans, "If we are armed we are safe," and "If we outlaw guns only criminals will have guns" don't seem to be working. We are all free to carry concealed weapons now and we can own as many guns as we want, but we don't feel safer. Our guns can't protect us from the anger and frustration that causes the killing.

Our society is concerned about preserving our health and safety as well as our constitutional rights. We have banned or restricted smoking, drugs, pornography, and some types of guns.

So far, we are more concerned about the right to own and use guns than we are about the growing number of Americans who have been murdered with them. However, as more and more people buy and use guns, more and more innocent victims will be shot. We have banned cigarettes from public institutions, public transportation, restaurants, stores, movie theaters and even some parks to protect the lives of smokers and protect nonsmokers from second-hand smoke. Maybe someday we will consider the threat of gunshot wounds to be as dangerous as second-hand smoke, and restrict and control the possession and use of guns.

Ending Crime Starts At Home

"This makes me not want to ever be around my own kind. It makes me not want to live in my own community. It makes me not want to invest my dollars in my community. I'm sick of every time that you look around someone's whipped on a woman or whipped on a college student," she said. "We have to strive to be something."

I meditated on the words from this outraged black woman whose son was beaten in a carjacking. Unfortunately the newscast on which she appeared was one with striking familiarity.

There is nothing new about this story. A lot of black people fall victim to black hoodlums. In fact, blacks are the principal victims of black criminals.

As was once stated by a prominent individual, "For too long, treatment of the subject of black-on-black crime could be likened to the emotionally challenged child of a family in years past. In public he was spoken of in whispers and tolerated by his family as a cross to bear."

Finally, we learned to deal with issues of this nature honestly and openly and as a result we all developed and progressed. In many ways, black-on-black crime beckons the same response.

Why do we tolerate lawlessness? Why do crimes go unreported in an area where crime is a major problem for citizens? Why is it that police can know about a drug marketplace and yet find it almost impossible to obtain witnesses and complainants in illicit transactions? In the matter of drug trafficking, whose children are buying the junk?

Why do we as a community tolerate undisciplined children? Do we really believe that the children who commit murder, robbery, rape and burglary are someone else's?

This is in no way to suggest that other groups and communities are not without problems. However, for the moment my focus is on the African- American community.

The African-American community has real opportunity and obligation today. Both opportunity and obligation are in our own hands. It is time to exercise whatever influence and power we have to move toward a solution.

One way we can do that is by relinquishing the naysaying position held by many of our leaders, by ending the temporary expediency of explaining away the lawlessness of some of our own people. It is time for us to recognize that the man who steals our money, the man who maims our family, the man who sells our children drugs is not our "brother." One who is worthy of being called brother is one who lives in peace with all men, who does no harm to others. He is a man who does his best not to become a parasite on mankind. He is a man who lives responsibility and sees to it that his children live responsibly in his community.

One of the ways a man lives responsibly is to take responsibility for himself and his family. Few of us will argue that this is asking too much. Concerning some people in the black community, we should look at the truth without blinking. Something is very wrong.

We, as African Americans, must take responsibility for what is happening in the community. It is time for those of us who care about the good of the black community to step up, be heard and make a difference.

However, let us not forget that the teaching of civility first and foremost starts at home. If few think we have troubles now with rape, robbery, murders, carjacking, etc., think of what we will be facing in the next decade when a new army of children deprived of family and community guidance is out on the streets. It's a sobering prospect to contemplate.

Once again, the solemn words of the disheartened black mother summons all of us who care to step forward: "Where is your mama? Where is your daddy? That is all I want to know. Where is your grandma? What did they teach you? What did you learn in school? Did you ever go?"

We must save our communities. If we don't, who will? As the comic strip character Pogo once said, "We have met the enemy and it is us."

Study Of Human Sexuality Shows Need For Change

I have spent a lot of time thinking about sex the past 72 hours. Wait a minute. Don't rush to any conclusion about some obsession you think I might have before letting me explain.

My wife and I spent the weekend helping our daughter do research for a paper she is writing. The topic just happened to be "The Changing Attitude Toward Sex in America."

To further influence my thoughts on the topic, last week both *Time* and *U.S. News and World Report* had as their cover stories a discussion of a national study on human sexuality, which presented a portrait of sex in America.

The survey designed by academics at the University of Chicago's National Opinion Research Center, asked 210 pages worth of questions to 3,432 Americans. I hope this helps explain my most recent preoccupation.

It's funny and at the same time sad how my wife and I reacted to some of the graphic materials we reviewed. She spoke out loud while I wondered silently about the unabashed approach used in the majority of the documentation to explain the issues related to human sexuality.

My wife questioned if it would be appropriate for our daughter to read and write about what many would consider x-rated material.

I had to remind my spouse that our daughter is a college freshman, and that education is about considering every point of view.

Further, the issue of sex is not going away anytime soon. Sexuality has been a major preoccupation for people all over the world for all of recorded history.

Sexual suggestions can be observed in ancient art; they can be read about in literature representing almost every established religion. In fact, much of our portrayal of sexuality comes from art and literature.

It seems that often we are confused and at times even in a state of denial when confronted about our attitudes toward sex.

Our society's changing beliefs about love and sex, and the right or wrong way of making and maintaining a loving relationship with another person is especially perplexing for young people as they face complicated decisions regarding sexual relationships for the first time.

Things are changing. Philip Elmer-Dewitt in an article in *Time* in the early 1990s pointed out as much. "Kids do have sex earlier now. Half of all kids have done it by the age of 17. The percentage of adults who have racked up 21 or more sexual partners is significantly higher in the 40-something boomers than other Americans."

Messages about sexual behavior that prevailed in the first half of the century now appear to be changing. The experts are telling us essentially what we already know: the loosening of gender stereotypes; greater openness about sexuality; and the growing acceptance of recreational sex as opposed to reproductive sex.

And AIDS must also be thrown into the equation here: 76 percent of those who have had five or more partners in the past year say they have changed their sexual behavior.

One cannot prophesy where we will be in the years ahead, but we should be clear that sexual behavior, which lies at the center of human experience, will only change for the better when our values and environment change.

Law Can't Deal With Euthanasia

It is difficult these days to read a newspaper, magazine, listen to a news program or even chat casually with a friend without the name of Dr. Jack Kevorkian being mentioned.

The 69-year-old retired pathologist admits to assisting 80-100 people die since he began his doctor-assisted suicide crusade in 1990.

"First we tell them they are dying," said Dr. Kevorkian. "We do tell them the diagnosis, but we don't tell them the prognosis. We tell them they have cancer. We don't tell them that no matter what we do it's almost certain that you are going to die soon. Up to 90 percent of patients die in too much pain in the final days, some people want death, and I am going to give it to them."

No stranger to controversy, Dr. Kevorkian is widely criticized for his latest assisted suicide. Mainly because the patient, Roosevelt Dawson, was not known to have a terminal illness. Dawson is the first known African American and the youngest person every to seek Kevorkian's services. This 21-year-old college student at Oakland University was suddenly and mysteriously stricken in January 1997 with a viral infection which left him paralyzed. According to Kevorkian, Dawson had more than a year to think about his condition and the quality of life without the use of his arms and legs and breathing only with the aid of a ventilator. Dawson won a court battle against opponents who tried to have him declared incompetent. With Dr. Kevorkian's aid, his death came recently in his mother's apartment with her at his side.

Although the roles are reversed, this recent assisted suicide brings back vivid memories of my own mother's battle with terminal cancer – a mother and a young son not knowing what would happen next, fearing that life's most precious bond would be broken.

In the case of my mother, I remember walking through the hospital corridors approaching room 447. I had been told that my mother was very sick and would not recover. Not knowing what to expect, I was not prepared for what I was about to see. She was only 49 years old, but there she was moribund and wrestling in pain. For me, it was so undignified. I was overcome with anguish and a sense of helplessness. If there was only some way to ease my mother's suffering.

During her last days, I was so often reminded of what a strong and dignified life she had led, how shameful and painful her final hours of life had become.

This experience is repeated daily in the rooms of terminally ill patients and often, as loved ones, including doctors, we stand watching and wondering when enough is enough. How much pain must one endure before we pull the plug? But when it comes to federal and state sanctioned euthanasia, we can't be guided by gut-wrenching anecdotal experiences. It's common knowledge that thousands of doctors have been practicing passive and in some instances active euthanasia for years. Most of these people have been guided by underlying commitment to the sanctity of life. No one knows how often doctors write the prescription or verbalize the formula for a lethal overdose. A survey conducted by *Newsweek* a few years ago found that one in five internists say that they have helped cause the death of a patient.

Why should we want to take such an intimate experience and move it to the impersonal morass of our legal system? Frank Zimmering, professor of law at the University of Chicago, put the matter succinctly in reference to the proper place decisions of this kind should be made: "Some decisions are beyond the law's competence to make with any vigor or confidence to be right."

The Michigan Supreme Court has issued guidelines where doctor-assisted suicide may be legally permissible under a specific provision of the constitution. These so-called guidelines are fraught with peril. The potential for mischief is great. Who will make these decisions? At what point in the process and under what conditions do we discontinue life?

It has been suggested that legalization of doctor-assisted suicide will have just the opposite effect intended by principal opponents. For example, once we establish legal prescription, doctors will be more vulnerable to lawsuits.

Betty Rollin, respected author, probably put it best when she said, "It's hard to imagine the kind of suffering that makes people beg to die. These are not people you normally see…unless they are someone you love."

Political Correctness Should Not Become A Stumbling Block

Mea culpa, but I'm just a little confused these days. In a recent meeting with a predominantly black organization some of the people there were perplexed by my reference to the term "Black American."

It appears that the expression is no longer in vogue. The new catchword used to refer to members of my race is now Afro-American. Evidently, unbeknownst to me, the term "black" still carries vestiges of an era long-since dead in which people were conveniently classified by color. But now the term Afro-American emphasizes our African heritage. Like European Americans, African Americans can look with pride at an ancient tradition of civilization, a cornucopia of cultures and a glorious tapestry of art, music and literature.

Well, I suppose they had a point, but I still felt uneasy. After all, I have just gotten used to the term Black American and now I have to adjust to a new politically correct term. I would certainly not suggest that we should pay obeisance to the status quo, but I would like to think that we are not allowing ourselves to be defined by two or three self-anointed leaders.

My daughter and her friends as well as my wife are the language police in my household when discussing gender. They recently suggested to me that the correct way to spell women is really "womyn." This is one I had to think about for a while. Seriously, over the years, I believe I have had my consciousness raised and have become more sensitive to language that intensifies animosity between ethnic groups and gender.

To be sure there are some words that are meant to hurt or somehow diminish an individual or group. When we are told that our choice of words hurts, knowingly or unknowingly, we should be prepared to back off. For example, when Native Americans say to the Washington Redskins organization, "Your choice of Redskins as a mascot is offensive and hurtful," the organization should listen with intense seriousness and find a way to compromise.

What pains me is how unfair some of the political-correctness charges are. Often when in a casual conversation with some of my friends and associates who happen to be something other than black, I can sense their concern for choosing the right words so as not to offend.

During the 1992 presidential campaign, Ross Perot used the term "you people" while addressing the national NAACP Convention, and consequently came under intense criticism. I remember thinking that perhaps Mr. Perot should, as a national candidate for the presidency, seek to be more aware of code words that certain groups find offensive; however, it never occurred to me to judge him for his untimely breach of etiquette.

If we ask the person speaking to do a computer search for offensive code words before uttering a sound, we should consider that speech becomes intelligible only when it conveys what the speaker is really thinking or wanting to discuss. With people being so easily criticized for what some consider inappropriate word choice, it is little wonder that often what people say in public is not the same as what they believe in private. Perhaps it should be said that silence corrupts language.

I have talked with many people, both black and white, who choose not to be involved in conversations for fear of not being politically correct. Many have questions about affirmative action, abortion, multi-culturalism, and several other rather sensitive topics, but are afraid that their choice of words may cause others to categorize them as bigot, racist, sexist or worse.

Non-minorities do not have a monopoly on this kind of behavior.

I often find that I tend to be overly cautious when referencing certain topics and people. However, I must acknowledge, I probably feel less inhibited than my white counterparts in expressing my thoughts without being overwhelmingly concerned for word appropriateness. After all, only white men can be racist…so I'm told.

Families Without Fathers

We all know change is a constant in our lives and society, and the wise accept and adapt to change. However, degeneration in our social and family structure has to be recognized, fought and reversed – more so, when it involves the future of a child and the stability of the family unit. The increasingly common trend of families trying to function without fathers is not change; it is degeneration and another step towards the dismantling of the family support system.

Gone are the days when almost every child could count on his or her father to be the breadwinner and totally engaged and committed to the well-being of the family. Nearly forgotten is the time when most every child knew that dad would be there with them during thick and thin. Also lost to a bygone era is when almost every father understood how critical his presence was to a child.

The traditional face of fatherhood has changed dramatically. For too many of our children, when asked, "Who's your daddy?" the answer is "I don't have one."

There is no more disturbing social trend than the explosion of father absent families. Over the last 40 years, the total number of children living in single parent homes tripled to almost 20 million. More than one-third of America's children reside in one home and their biological fathers reside elsewhere. Half of children living absent their dads have never set foot in their father's home. By some estimates, two-thirds of all children born this decade will spend part of their childhood in a home without dad. More than any time in American history, the average child will live a significant slice of life in a fatherless home. In black communities, the problem is multiplied.

As shocking as these numbers are, they do not include the increasing rate of children who experience father flight before birth. The percentage of children born to unwed mothers nationally is above 30 percent. For blacks, the rate is more than double that figure. In some of our urban areas, it hovers around 80 percent.

The mushrooming absent father family structure isn't merely the latest evolutionary phase with little or no consequences for children. Anyone who makes that claim is intellectually dishonest. To the contrary, communities composed primarily of children in female headed, single-parent families tend to perform poorly in school, are vulnerable to all sorts of behavior problems, are prone to sexual promiscuity and fail to establish lasting relationships.

Thus the inevitable conclusion is that if the plight of America's children is going to improve, we must first reduce the number of missing fathers. This won't be easy. Reversing the trend means first embracing the idea that fathers make exceptional contributions to children, not the least of which is stability and discipline. When fathers are out of touch, children suffer greatly. Secondly, if a woman desires a committed father for her child, she must insist that he come to parenthood with a wedding ring.

Next, we have to change our views about divorce. One upon a time, it was righteous to stay together for the "sake of the kids." Nowadays, divorce is recklessly sold as a magic formula for women trapped in bad relationships. The conventional wisdom is that it is better to get a divorce than stay in an unhappy marriage - "for the sake of the kids." But with so many single mothers trapped in poverty, and their children acting out, a good case can be made that children are better off with married parents – even if the partnership involves compromise – than with their parents split.

Studies clearly validate that children with involved, loving fathers do better in school, have a good self-esteem and avoid risky behaviors such as drug use, truancy, and criminality compared to children disconnected from their fathers.

So if responsible fathers are the desired models, we must once again advocate, value and support responsible fatherhood. Every community and religious organization must make marriage promotion a nonnegotiable priority. We must all act as catalysts to help transform our society into one that believes in, advocates and furthers the institution of marriage. There is no substitute for good parenting and we should all note parenting is a gender-inclusive term. Children and families need responsible fathers. Period.

Without Honesty, Social Interaction Becomes Impossible

Why is it so difficult to be honest? Honesty has little meaning in isolation; it's a social value and as such it requires a positive response from the person(s) involved in some kind of interaction. It requires that one person recognize and reward the great difficulty another person may have in deciding to overcome the temptation not to be honest – especially when there are potentially negative consequences.

Let's say you notice a dent in your car one morning. Your teenage son drove it the night before. You ask him about the dent. Now if he knows about the dent and if he has had some part in creating the dent, he faces a dilemma. He has to decide quickly whether or not to admit what he knows about it.

He also realizes that you are upset and if he admits to creating the dent, you may then invoke negative consequences on him. He can, of course, deny knowing anything about the dent, and if he is a good liar, may get away with no consequences. What's his payoff for being honest? It's this situation where we, as adults or authorities, play a big role in helping a person make a decision, and in helping a person learn how to think about honesty.

If we insist on the truth, on being honest, and the person admits to doing the action we object to, then if our next step is to punish the person for having done the deed, we are setting him up for the next time to be less honest. After all, a simple lie might have worked and saved a lot of grief.

So do we punish the behavior, or reward the honesty of admitting it? That's a difficult decision, but we must keep in mind the future consequences of what we do in a situation such as this. There are many people with whom we face the dilemma of whether or not to be honest, or more likely, how honest to be. We spend enormous amounts of every year presenting an image of ourselves to the world.

Or we remain silent sometimes so we don't reveal that we disagree with a position, fearing somehow that if we're truly honest, others won't like the "real" us. So what about honesty? How do we achieve it, how do we promote it, how can we enforce it? And why should we? Is it worth all the effort? I say yes it is worth all the effort, and more, and that no matter what the cost of practicing honesty, without it we are doomed. Let's not forget the moral implications associated with the idea of honesty. Honesty is the glue that bonds friends and family and society together; honesty gives us some comfort in knowing that there are really 16 ounces of cereal in the box, and not only 15.

Honesty is what makes most of us pay our income taxes every year and file reasonably accurate returns. It allows us to meet someone halfway, to show up at the appointed hour, assuming you'll keep your part of the agreement. Honesty allows us to trust each other.

So trust is one of the major benefits of honesty. We rarely trust someone whom we suspect of being less than honest (other than politicians). It used to be a high compliment to someone to say that "he keeps his word." That's another form of being honest, of doing what we say we'll do, of being dependable.

Honesty is also associated with truth and the reputation for being honest, and telling the truth is often greatly envied, if not always admired.

Our first duty is to be honest with ourselves – then with our loved ones, our friends, our acquaintances, the shopkeeper, and finally other members of the family of man. Honesty is not a black or white issue, not a male or female issue, not a young-versus-old issue. It's a pillar of human relations or interpersonal relations, of social relations, without which the world we know would be radically different. It's ultimately imperative that each of us comes to recognize the immense value and importance of being honest, not only with others, but with ourselves.

Thus we come to value honesty for its own sake, for the inherent "rightness" of doing to others what we hope they will do to us. That is, to be honest and truthful.

But how people respond to our honesty will lay the groundwork for how honest we learn to be.

Dishonesty can begin like cancer, and grow with success.

Trust: The Center Of It All

A lot of people are angry at the United States these days. Some of these people live in other countries, but many of them live here. There is heated debate over the war in Iraq, and the resulting economic and social problems and increasing questions about when that war will be resolved. There are complaints about the economy, the environment, cronyism, and the loss of our personal rights.

Yet, whether one wants to reelect Bush for another term in 2004, or would vote for any politician who has a chance of winning, the U.S. is still a pretty good place to live. There are plenty of people willing to risk arrest and deportation for a chance to work in our chicken plants. There are lots of others willing to leave their spouses and children in Asia, South America, or Mexico, for the chance to work and send money back home so their families will have enough to eat, and the children have money for school tuition. They are willing to wait the five years until they can apply to become citizens so they can sponsor their families, or to work seven days a week for as long as it takes to save enough money for all the airline tickets and application fees. Life in America without one's family may be hard, but it's better than life in a country where there are no jobs, and no hope.

One of the nice things about living here that we often take for granted is trust. Although tourist books warn of pickpockets and scam artists in big cities, we Americans tend to trust people. Our very way of life is built on trust. Every service transaction is based on trust. We trust the mechanic to change the oil and install a new filter in our cars. We trust the waitress to bring us clean food, and she trusts us to pay our bill, especially when we leave the money on the table and walk out before she can pick it up. Those of us who can't repair our own computers, VCR's, car engines, washers, dryers, and air conditioners, etc., have to trust the repairmen we choose. We need to believe that they are able to fix the appliance and won't overcharge us.

When we buy things from the Internet, we have to trust people who live a thousand miles or more away. We give them our credit card numbers, hoping they won't charge us for thousands of dollars more than we are buying. And they trust us to give them a valid address, and the credit card number for an account that is not overdrawn.

We also take trust for granted. We assume it's safe to eat in a restaurant, or drink in a bar without fear of a suicide bombing. Despite the shock of 9/11, we trust pilots and bus drivers to get us to our destinations safely, and on time. When a burglar breaks into our home, or someone threatens us on the street, we assume that the police will offer help and if we have to go to court, the law will be upheld.

In fact, we take it for granted that people are to be trusted, and we are surprised and angry if they are dishonest. However, in many countries, honesty is not the norm, and people do not expect to be treated fairly. Here, we think small town standards should be the universal law. That is, people should be able to leave their homes and cars unlocked and expect to be safe. We still believe that no one should need three locks on the door in an inner city apartment, even though we know it's often absolutely necessary. And we deplore the kinds of extortion that permeate daily life in many other countries, where there are constant threats to personal safety, even in small towns, and many people routinely pay for protection.

It would be hard for us to imagine paying for protection because we believe that is a job for the police that we already pay for in our taxes. When we feel threatened, we trust that we can call 911 for help (and there will be a speedy response). The police also believe that it's their responsibility to protect citizens. And within the limits of human nature and the stress of the job, they do. We are quick to criticize when people we trust don't do their jobs.

Maybe we are better able to trust because fewer people here go to bed hungry every day. Living on food stamps or worse, in a homeless shelter, is not the ideal for anyone. But living in a country where there are no good jobs, and no food when the husband gets sick or dies, is even worse. Hungry people will steal or even kill for food for themselves and their families. As a result, in places where people are poor and have many needs, there is less opportunity for trust.

Fortunately, people in America, for the most part, still feel that it is good to trust, and treat as equals, people from different countries, who speak different languages, have different colored skin and hair texture, and different religions.

Second Chances

I recently watched an evening news program which included a segment showing a room full of prisoners watching a video. The film explained the various extra punishments inmates would receive if they committed additional crimes after they were released. The narrator stressed that the punishment would be much more severe the second time around. The film ended as the narrator explained that several states are starting to use these kinds of programs to cut down on recidivism for inmates who could be released at any time .

On the surface, it's amazing that any criminal who had served time would commit a crime again. But the facts are that many criminals do commit further crimes once they are released. And if they were determined enough to break the law the first time, threatening them with stronger punishment afterwards may not make much of an impression. Those words of advice might help to keep people who have never been in jail from committing a crime, which would send them there in the first instance. But there are definite differences between those people who are in jail, and those who are not. One of the big differences is poverty.

There are some criminals who have important, well paying jobs, but the majority of inmates are poor. Many of them come from families who didn't have enough money to meet their physical needs when they were younger. Some probably never had enough food or warm clothes and shoes, or a clean, safe house to live in. Just the everyday stress of work, family, and appointments are plenty for most people. But the added worry about how to get enough money to live on, pay the rent, and heat the house is enough to make life dangerously stressful.

Usually, even the poorest homes have at least one television set, with never ending commercials about beautiful people driving new cars, wearing designer clothes, and living in nice houses. For poor families, there must be the follow-up of wondering why their lives are so different from what they see on TV. This would be easy to translate into a general feeling of low self-esteem, and questions about why life seems so unfair.

It would be easy to suggest that education is the way out of this deep hole of poverty. After all, it's free for everyone. However it's hard to teach a hungry child. And it's also hard to teach a child who was kept awake all night by his parents arguing, or the sounds of gunshots and police sirens, or worse, the threat of physical violence. When teenagers who come from warm, loving homes find reasons to drop out of school, take drugs, or get pregnant, how can we expect students who come to school hungry, tired and worried about problems at home to be diligent, successful learners? Without family support, these students often drop out of school, which also results in low self-esteem.

Without a high school diploma, it's much harder to get a good job – one that pays more than minimum wage. Lack of a source of income encourages some people to think about stealing money, or committing other crimes to get rich, or just to pay the rent.

Without a successful, loving role model, kids may never learn how to deal with life. They may never realize that their feelings of frustration, which are very valid, could be eased in more positive ways. Without loving, helpful people in their lives, they may never learn that people are more important than money. And, it might become easy for them to return to crime, or gangs, or drugs to fulfill their physical and emotional needs.

And after spending time in jail/prison, they are back on the streets with only a warning against further criminal acts. Although they served the time for the crime, it's impossible for them to get even a minimum wage job after a jail sentence. Most go back to the same unsupportive, or even dangerous lives that led to their crimes in the first place.

Although a warning about the punishment for future crime couldn't hurt, why not offer inmates something, which might go further toward preventing them from committing a second crime. They need some assurance of getting a job, and they need to get their GEDs and they need to learn to look at their feelings, and set some realistic goals for themselves. And they need help in doing this.

Why couldn't a little more money be invested in helping inmates to prepare for a more positive, successful life after prison? Why couldn't employers be encouraged to give them a chance?

Don't Be So Quick To Judge

It was a cold, brisk morning. The sun was shining, but the temperature served as a stark reminder that fall would soon be replaced by winter. I was watching as parents from a local private school were preparing to board their chartered bus for a class trip. I happened to have a meeting nearby and coincidentally became a witness to this activity. I noticed an associate whose children attended this school. We spoke briefly and continued on our way.

As she began to walk away, I overheard another parent comment on how she was walking. The lady said that she was walking like an old lady. It did not appear that the comments were meant to be harmful or vicious. They were probably just made to pass the time and occupy the silence of the waiting parents. The parent that I knew just kind of shrugged and made no real response to the comments, but I knew what she was thinking and only imagined how she felt.

What the other parent did not know was that this lady was diagnosed more than a year ago with multiple sclerosis. While she heard the diagnosis, she refused to accept it as part of her life. In doing so, she did not go around announcing this medical finding, nor does she use it as an excuse when the illness flares up from time to time. When it does, it makes walking for her a bit more challenging, and the cold weather is no welcoming thing for her either, as it makes it more difficult and uncomfortable to just function.

I am one of the few people who is aware of this lady's condition.

She is pretty well-known around the city, a vibrant wife and mother, and a friend and inspiration to all who know her. Yet she keeps this secret to herself as her appearance and level of functioning gives little indication of any challenges, physical or otherwise. Rather, she engages in this battle alone.

How brave, I thought. Though while she feels that acknowledging this illness is like embracing its presence, it leaves her open to insensitive comments from those who are unaware of her condition.

This is a prime example of why we should never be quick to judge another, as to why they appear or function as they do, because we are not always aware of their circumstances. The person who appears different than we do could be so for a reason to which we are not privy. We do not always know the story behind the person or their performance, and we are not entitled to.

It is like sitting back and seeing the young and active laugh at the elderly and slow, while taking their own youth for granted. And with a little luck, those youngsters will have the opportunity to make it to a point of old age. So don't laugh. You could very well be looking at your future.

The next time a person is moving a little more slowly or more awkwardly than usual, or when they appear less than what you imagine, take a moment to consider that there may be hidden circumstances that are painting a different and perhaps less appealing picture of their life before you. Think, be kind and keep your judgments to yourself.

Ethics And Morals

Our society has a value system that places family as the building unit. Just by living with their children and sharing everyday activities, parents are the first to teach children language, values, mores and manners. Since they literally shape our tomorrow, it is expected that these front-line teachers will be models of moral integrity. However, it is a commentary on changing times that the conduct that formerly set parents apart has pretty much disappeared from the inner cities of America.

Values learned at an early age essentially set into motion those choices we make later in life. The instruments used to examine and set the parameters about how people behave towards themselves and interact with other individuals or social groups are called ethics or morals. They determine whether we will be cordial or hostile, tell the truth or lie, be charitable or greedy, will study or cheat to pass an exam. It comes down to fundamental judgments of what is morally right or wrong, good or bad.

All of us are confronted with choices and questions: "What good am I seeking?" and "What is my obligation in this situation?" Ultimately, we must decide what's in our personal interest, what we owe to other people or what is good for society as a whole. It is usually through the balance of values such as freedom, tolerance and dialogue that communities define what is bearable and acceptable. Unfortunately, too much of what is socially unacceptable dominates our way of life.

Seldom do we consciously do what is bad for ourselves, although we may do what is bad for others if it appears that something personally good will come of it. Should we base our decisions on personal pleasure? Is knowledge, virtue or service to one's fellow human being paramount? At the same time, we are reminded that atrocities have been heaped on people of all races, ethnicities and religions under the guise of some greater "good."

In America, we have a system of law that helps us determine and enforce established rights and duties. Through this structure, we should be able to inhibit and punish those who would deviate from ethical standards. Most of us try to live by a personal sense of ethics and integrity that is reflected in respect of the laws, rules, and the rights of others. So why do we have so much gratuitous turmoil?

It may be that too many families have too few signposts. Everything is laden with ambiguity. But only when parents are armed with a predictable moral compass – and use it to raise children – will communities be capable of rebuilding the connective tissue and playing a deserved role as guardians of decency and respect. It is imperative that we discourage the culture of selfish corruption.

I do not apologize for my desire for ethics and for good. I'm convinced that there must be a moral underpinning, a moral gravity to what we do. No viable social or economic order survives without the moral support of personal responsibility and honesty in its dealings.

Further cultural and moral decline can be the only result from yielding to the worship of self. And while no single institution has the power or obligation to protect all of its citizens from all the unsavory outcomes of human nature, it is imperative that we have well-ordered communities where people can be "reasonably" free of contention and chaos.

I exercise my duty to positively guide children on their way to becoming adults in communities where morality has almost become a dirty word. Meanwhile, I persist in seeking answers to the question: What are the qualities of truth, goodness, and beauty?

Ministers Miss Chance To Promote Electoral System

A few days ago the Reverend Jesse Jackson and Reverend Al Sharpton held a press conference to denounce the alleged tactics of Ed Rollins, consultant and campaign organizer for New Jersey Governor-elect Christine Todd Whitman. Mr. Rollins has been accused of spending half-a-million dollars paying black ministers to urge their congregations not to vote in the New Jersey gubernatorial race.

Apparently, the thinking was if blacks went to the polls they would almost automatically vote for the Democratic candidate. Unfortunately, Mr. Jackson and Mr. Sharpton missed a great opportunity. It didn't make much sense to criticize Ed Rollins, it certainly wasn't his job to mobilize those who would likely vote against his candidate. He was only doing what was politically expedient. I'm not aware of anyone being physically accosted while on the way to the polling place. His actions may have been unethical, but not unlawful ... notwithstanding how some would interpret the 1965 Voting Rights Act.

Perhaps we all would have been better served by the press conference if Reverend Jackson had made the point that each and every one of us has a responsibility to evaluate a political candidate and vote accordingly. Should we go to a church only to be told what political candidate to support? Furthermore, is the black church the force it once was in the political lives of black Americans? According to C. Eric Lincoln, Professor of Religion at Fisk University, "no longer is the black church the dependent bastion of black prudence."

For too long it has been assumed that black people would vote automatically for a Democratic candidate regardless of his or her position on the issues. This attitude had made it relatively easy for black ministers to be targeted and pursued by the so called "walking around money" made available to precinct captains on Election Day.

If African Americans are going to make the political system work, they must make a conscious political effort to get involved, become informed and vote. The political process is simply not working for blacks in general because of indifference in the black community. Today there are roughly 17 million blacks of voting age, but only about 10 million are registered to vote.

Rutgers University public policy professor Henry Coleman was absolutely correct when he stated that "if the Ed Rollins allegations are true, they were aided by an uninspired electorate." He went on to say that "interest in the election was low in black communities because there wasn't a significant effort to embrace or pay attention to the African-Americans by either candidate."

The Ed Rollinses of the world are not going away. There will always be those seeking to exploit and demean certain groups of people. However, tactics like the one Mr. Rollins allegedly employed can succeed only when people are indifferent and uninformed. If we vote and vote intelligently, we have the ability by our sheer numbers to elect and defeat candidates. We should start by giving our support to individuals, not political parties.

If the Ed Rollins allegations proved to be true, African Americans should be angrier with black ministers who participated in this conspiracy than with Mr. Rollins. And ultimately, those African Americans who choose not to vote should bear the greatest burden of all.

Was Stevie Ever Really "Cute?"

Early on most people in and outside of the family were amused, if not comforted in knowing that the DNA matched. Little Stevie was a chip off the old block. Even at the tender age of two his temper tantrums were pronounced when he didn't get his way – this wasn't your usual case of the "terrible twos."

This pattern of behavior was manifested in almost every aspect of Stevie's behavior. Nonetheless, he was cute and cuddly, and his ability to get away with anything and everything was a direct of result of those two overwhelming attributes.

As years passed, little Stevie grew into big Stevie, and his outbursts grew along right with him. Who in the family saw this behavior as a growing dysfunction?

Little Stevie's shenanigans are an example of why families must teach appropriate social and functional skills to their children. Life requires us to understand, appreciate and work with people. Human relationships are not an abstraction of sociologists – they are required in organized life and we learn to shape them, dysfunctionally or functionally, in our families.

Families are where we learn to relate to each other with manners and respect. But for Stevie and many others like him, such primal instruction was lacking, and as a result his growing bad attitude took its toll in many ways. The cute tantrums Stevie had as a child evolved into uglier, more violent and dispirited behavior, simply because he was never told that "this behavior is unacceptable."

At what point did the family bother to make sure Stevie was taught the essentials of handling anger or resolving conflict? When was time taken to teach empathy or impulse control?

Stevie's lack of civility became the norm, taking root in his psyche, unable to be shorn. His incivility infected every nook and cranny of his life like a raging virus immune to an antibiotic. Rude, crude and violent behavior became par for the course in his everyday actions, making civility toward others impossible. As a result, Stevie began to get into trouble by lying, cheating and stealing, being mean to people, demanding attention, destroying property, disobeying at school and home...yes, the tantrums were still very much alive and well.

By acting in such an aggressive and destructive manner, Stevie was saying, "I don't like you and I don't like myself." Somewhere, during his formative years, Stevie didn't learn that to act out so foolishly shows a disdain for authority and a lack of discipline.

What happened to Stevie is a cautionary warning that small actions eventually turn into big actions if the offender goes unchecked. That's what happened to Stevie. For years, he got away with brash, reactionary behavior, which evolved from being "cute" and "amusing" to brusque and brutal.

There are many Stevies in the world and the numbers are steadily increasing. Many of them now call jail home. They have taken up this new residence because they never learned effective conflict resolution, anger management or understood the importance of civility in our society, which all starts and ends with the quick and early intervention of the family. They did not develop a love or respect for themselves and consequently didn't develop a healthy respect for others. It is virtually impossible to form healthy relationships with others if you have not developed your own positive sense of self-worth.

It appears that civility is becoming an outdated form of behavior because many adults aren't willing or able to teach children right from wrong. Time has become a precious commodity now, and adults are so consumed with other matters such as providing shelter, food, and other necessities for their children that character development falls by the wayside.

A colleague of mine, who worked in the criminal justice field, shared stories with me on several occasions regarding the Stevies of the world. He described individuals who had developed conflict resolution, problem solving and anger management skills that could best be described as sociopathic. These Stevies didn't grasp what was wrong with their behavior; they truly believed that their way of life was normal. They had been taught that problems and conflicts are resolved with violence, not discussion. For them, anger was released by striking out instead of working through stressful emotions with a long jog or a game of basketball.

As her son awaits his fate for allegedly murdering someone because, in Stevie's words, "he disrespected me," Stevie's mother can only wonder every day, "Where did I go wrong?" Perhaps, though, a better question for her to ask herself would be, "Was Stevie ever really 'cute?' "

The Prospect-Killing Aspects Of Rudeness

Once upon a time in America, decorum and good manners were celebrated and admired. Bad manners were a sign of vulgarity and uncouthness. Over time, though, rudeness became the rage. Where did we go wrong?

It seems that those of us who live in the urban core have lost our polish. We've tried but haven't been overly successful in legislating against hooligans, abusive nosy neighbors, public drunkenness, graffiti artists and other bad behavior. Discarded trash, dumped tires, and abandoned cars blot our neighborhoods. Aggressive begging is the norm in downtown areas. Coarse conduct in our communities has become commonplace and may be completely out of control.

Rude and careless employees – along with those who could care less – are found everywhere. Numbskulls who play home stereos loud enough to cause walls to vibrate; who drive through city streets with windows down and boom boxes blaring; parents who allow children to run wild in grocery and other stores are among them. Go to a movie and you'll likely find hordes of inconsiderate or outlandish people in the theater talking loudly, using cell phones, screaming at the screen, rustling fast food wrappers or kicking the back of your seat. Clearly this type of conduct falls between disrespectful and discourteous.

The etiquette of a lot of cell phone users is particularly crude. Some sales people inappropriately answer cell phones in the middle of transactions and never stop to even say "thank you." Ear piercing tones that emanate from cell phones drive me crazy. I've come to the conclusion that the tackier the ring, the tackier the owners. Simply put, they're jerks. Nobody cares what he or she is talking about or how loudly he or she speaks.

Or take the urban American tendency toward casual dress or over dress. In some cases employees need rules and regulations to prevent them from getting too competitive about their appearance and clothing. In other cases, some of our young women need to be told that "after five" attire usually means after work.

One would think that being courteous to customers is the way to go for anyone who wants to stay in business. Yet we're constantly exposed to people with bad attitudes even though their job is to serve the public.

Throughout the service industry are ill-mannered supermarket cashiers, sales people and fast food workers exhibiting abusive mannerisms. I've seen instances, for example, where customers walk up to a cash register to ask a question or pay for merchandise and the salesperson gets in a huff, acting as though the patron is disrupting their leisure. Heaven forbid if the clerk is having a conversation with two other clerks about what they did the night before.

This discourteous treatment of customers is a perilous pit that businesses should not want to put their foot in. An unfriendly reputation sends the message that the business doesn't care about customer service. Because jobs have left our inner cities in droves, we must learn to successfully combine business performance and efficiency with etiquette. After all, offended customers tell their friends about being treated boorishly by unnervingly rude service personnel. And most will refuse to do business with the company again.

The irony is that many of the successful challenges to urban American business have come from suburban communities that champion etiquette in the world of commerce. The lack of hospitality hurts the bottom line of companies trying to survive in the city, not to mention the local economies.

The basic principal behind etiquette is thinking from the other person's point of view. To be expert at it requires early training. To that end, we can almost pinpoint the decline of manners, etiquette and civility in our culture.

Children's first classes in manners should be in the home where parents model good behavior, reinforce good behavior and then reward good behavior. Prior to the 1960s, families ate together at the dinner table. Protocol-- including listening skills, basic human relationships, as well as the notion that you didn't take telephone calls during dinner-- was reinforced at every turn.

Low marriage and high divorce rates have since splintered the traditional family. Many single mothers must work and are not at home to raise children and instruct them in appropriate behavior. Fathers, once authority figures, live outside the home and often aren't able to provide needed discipline. And because the two-parent family is no longer in vogue, the family no longer eats together as frequently, the basics are no longer taught to children and time-honored community conventions and values aren't instilled as part of upbringing.

About the same time, a growing underclass began to exhibit what sociologists describe as "underclass behavior." In too many of our communities it is manifested as an utter lack of respect for property and people. Not only do they lack manners, too many have difficulty following most social norms. To make matters worse, ill-mannered people may actually think their actions are normal.

Codes of behavior are essential in a civil society. Good manners need a moral base. So we need to find a way to again tell our young they can and will do better in the world if they know how to behave. They must also understand that rude behavior is ugly and not knowing how to properly present themselves to polite society can put them at an extreme disadvantage for success and acceptance. Most importantly, we must drive home the point that seldom does this crazy world give them a second chance to make a first impression.

Part IV
The Family and Children

"Call it a clan, call it a network, call it a tribe, call it a family. Whatever you call it, whoever you are, you need one."

Jane Howard - 'Families'

When I was growing up, I believed and felt that it really did take the whole village to raise me. In that era, I was watched and scolded by any mother in my neighborhood. If my friends and I were unusually rowdy, any parent could come and straighten us out. If I was disciplined at school, I was disciplined again when I got home. We had good adult role models, and we accepted adults as authority figures even if at times we may have rebelled.

Of course, sometimes father did not know best. Even so, we knew that, by and large, the adults in our lives had our best interests at heart. I feel very blessed that I was able to give some of these supportive underpinnings to my own children. In many neighborhoods and communities today, however, this idyllic situation does not exist. Especially in large cities, families are often fragmented, they struggle with limited resources, they live under the threat of crime and violence. Drug dealers prey on their children and they lack adequate support structures. As a society, we are divided by class as well as by race. And yet we learn of success stories where the parents themselves take over the streets, clean up the neighborhoods, demand improved policing and other municipal services and provide a safe environment for their children. In some cases, local, state and national leaders come together to address the crises that face our large cities and urban centers.

Yes, it does in fact take a village to raise our children. However, has the village become too fractured to properly nurture and guide? In the movie; The Shawshank Redemption *the lead character, Andy, states, "Hope is a good thing, maybe the best thing. And a good thing never dies."* So we have hope for a better future, but we must also act.

In the following stories or passages, I share what I learned from my parents and my "village" as a child. I also share my experiences in providing leadership to address the crisis situations and circumstances that many families are experiencing in these times.

The Heart And Soul
Of Family Values

I met a young couple last summer in their latter years of an extended college education, both levelheaded, good students. They seemed happy together and so it was a surprise when I recently learned that they had parted ways.

Her main complaint was the amount of time he spent working at two and sometimes three jobs. He was too ambitious, giving too much time to work and not enough to her, or to other human relations.

He is young, energetic, and smart, with opportunities ahead of him to achieve whatever he decides to do. He has a strong work ethic, and is taking advantage of opportunities that he has sought and won. His ambition is helping him become the success he wants to be. His ambition has also cost him the girl he loved.

Her idea of life with him was not to sit at home alone every night while he worked overtime at the office. She didn't want a slave to the office and the dollar. She saw it coming, determined she couldn't change it, and so, for better or worse, got out. He now works harder and longer than before, in part to make up for his loss.

Another couple, twice the age of the first, is in trouble. They have been together eight years, and now she has told him that he must decide between her and the extra and excessive work he does which keeps him occupied – in body and spirit – throughout the day and many evenings each week. Her idea of a life with him is not to sit at home alone every night. She has told him that he must decide soon, or she will. The last time I heard from them, there had not been a let-up in his work schedule.

He is very good at what he does. He is an expert, in fact, very talented and highly educated, in demand from his colleagues as a leader.

Because he is associated with education, his financial rewards have been limited, but his achievements have not gone unrecognized. He has succeeded in what he set out to do with his life and career. It has brought him recognition and the respect of his peers and his students. It has brought him satisfaction and a modest sense of security and self-esteem.

But his expertise and the strongly felt necessity to involve himself in his work may cost him a loving relationship.

A simple answer would be for the men to lighten up, lower the ambitions that push them on, rediscover life, have fun, and save their relationships. But not everything is quite that simple.

As we know, for many men rewards come from success in a career. It is often the case that our achievements or our position at work bring us more recognition and opportunities than what we do at home. I am invited to many functions in this area because of my job; not because I am a father or a husband, or a son, or, black male, or that I am 5' 11" tall, or that I like the Detroit Pistons.

I thoroughly enjoy my work. I can easily get caught up in what I am doing and could spend most of my waking hours in some capacity doing my work – I love it! When I am working, I'm often happy. I'm meeting challenges; I'm reducing the "to do" stack on my desk. Sometimes I feel like I really am accomplishing things.

But, in addition to the personal satisfaction and opportunities my job offers me, it – and this is important – also offers me the means of providing for my family a more abundant and secure life than I knew. Like other husbands and fathers, I want my family to be safe and secure, and my work helps me provide that security.

But I nearly always also feel terrible inside about being at work in the evening, or on Saturday, instead of being with my family. I feel torn when I am not available to do the things that many families do together in the evenings and on their weekends. Whether it's going and doing, or sitting and watching, being together is the heart and soul of family values.

Providing for our families is also a major part of family values. We need to re-examine a social ethic, which, for economic success and self-esteem, requires the neglect of family and abandonment of life outside the corporation or institution.

This would take a major change in how society views the roles and rewards of fatherhood and motherhood vs. the rewards it now offers for success in the workplace. Though the company output may suffer a bit if men really did decide to give more energy and time to their families, if they began to find more internal rewards there, if they could really feel that being a good father and husband were as important as being a successful employee and provider, people and society would surely benefit.

Father Doesn't Always Know Best

At this writing I am 45 years old, which means by my calculation I have been around almost one half century. I have had more than a few extremely responsible jobs; I have met and worked with a lot of accomplished people; and I have traveled extensively; and I have had more than my share of failures and successes.

With all this being considered, why is it that suddenly my teenage children, barely out of diapers, seem to know more about everything than I do?

Or at least they tell me they do.

According to my 13-year-old son, all of my clothes are antiquated. He reminds me more than occasionally that I dress as he says, "Like people did the 1950s" As if somehow he was there (and he wasn't).

I'm even beginning to feel a little insecure about the way I wear my hair, well, that is the little I have left. My son thinks I would look sharp with one or two of these funny designs carved in some strategic location on my head.

However, my debate with my son over my sartorial splendor (or lack thereof), pales in comparison with my frequently spirited discussions with my 16-year old daughter. Suddenly it's a case of "father doesn't know best" because my daughter now believes she is much smarter than I am. There are times in fact, that I feel I am only appreciated for my car keys and my wallet.

When the music pounds too loudly through her bedroom walls

and I insist that music isn't supposed to be played that loud, she reminds me that in these "modern times" music is meant to be loud.

Also, it's all right if she cleans her bedroom only on her birthday – after all, she contends, "It's my room and how it looks shouldn't annoy anyone else."

Another interesting issue is that of homework. I can't recall the last time either of my kids welcomed any of my input about studying techniques. For to do so would mean more time studying than they feel necessary.

Oh yes, let me not forget, there is that technological wonder of the telephone, which my daughter mistakenly uses as a headset to share the sound of newly purchased CDs with her friends. As a matter of fact, my daughter has applications for the telephone Southwestern Bell has yet to consider.

A dear friend of mine also shares my sense of lost credibility. He said to me, "I'm a professor at a well-known college and an accomplished author and my teenage children won't take my advice about much of anything."

He also commented that he recalled finding an error in her algebra book and couldn't convince her that the book was wrong.

He continued by saying, "I took her to my study to show her a book that I had written. She was startled and only then did she consider that I was right and her book was wrong."

Honestly, there are times when I'm not sure who is raising whom. As teenagers, children also want to be the teachers, and possibly even the parents. This is requiring us, as parents, to engage in serious self examination.

Sometimes fatherhood is a 24-hour test, one that we don't always pass.

Strict Discipline Policy May Not Be Such A Bad Idea

A few weeks ago when the DeSoto School District announced its new discipline policy, I was incensed and prepared to do everything within reason to oppose what I thought was an unusually harsh and rigid discipline policy.

I was bubbling with idealism. Surely the administration could be more creative and a bit more sensitive. For you see, I momentarily drifted back to the Utopian values that under-girded how I thought I would discipline my yet unborn children. I would never spank, raise my voice, discipline when angry, and never discipline my children for what some authority thought was unacceptable behavior. After all, my kids would be a part of the new generation, and the writings of Dr. Benjamin Spock had prepared me well. Seventeen years and two children later helped serve to crush my romanticism with Dr. Spock.

The language of the policy was disturbing. "Students may be taken into custody," etc. I thought I pondered all the right questions. What guarantee of fairness is there in deciding who will or won't be arrested in any incident? Who will make that decision? How? Will it be objectively made, applied equally?

The answer to these questions began to unfold in a most dramatic and gut-wrenching manner at 1:45 p.m. on Tuesday, September 2nd in the death of 15-year-old Demarkous McLemore, who was shot at Roosevelt High School. This served as a wake-up call and once again reminded us of how violent our schools have become.

Our teachers and administrators are not perfect and I, like most, can be quick to criticize. It is time to come to grips with what our schools are being asked to do. Clearly, a problem as serious as violence in schools needs more than casual analysis and some suggestions for change. I think we are all becoming weary of simple remedies that do not resolve complex problems. It's easy to point fingers and look for someone to blame. However, it's time to go beyond the blame game. We can all own up to some of the problem and begin to be part of the solution.

Schools are no longer the safe havens that so many from my generation remember. Today the threat of violence and disruption is a very real issue and one that detracts from the goals of teaching and learning.

Somehow, we as parents must find ways to support our schools in their search for new models and policies to help deal constructively with the inevitable conflicts between school rules and the behavior of our children. We won't have a proper educational environment unless parents support teachers and teachers support parents. There will be disagreements, tensions and honest differences of opinions, but ultimately we all want the same thing.

We, as parents, should not expect more from our schools than we are willing to contribute of ourselves. If we won't discipline our children, the school can't succeed alone. We must instill in our kids the faith that if you live by the law, you will be a whole person. If you break the law, it will break you.

I don't want to come across as being unconditionally supportive of our schools and suggest that there is not room for improvement. I'm simply suggesting that we have got to start somewhere. We must let our children know that teachers and parents are on the same team.

Let's keep in mind that the issue of discipline in our schools is just the tip of the iceberg. Take a moment to consider the frequently occurring incidents involving some of our children that sadden us. Cursing like drunken sailors, committing thefts, having no respect for law enforcement, not valuing other's property, and worse, not valuing life – and the list goes on.

I stated earlier that some questions needed answering. Unfortunately, I did not ask the one really important question. Can we help students behave as civilized, reasonably well-mannered, decent human beings? That, I believe, is the overriding question. How we answer it will determine whether we attain the quality of life we all seek to enjoy.

Role Models Should Consider Their Responsibility To The Children

As an impressionable teenager growing up in the Texas Panhandle, more often than not, I had the impression that the successful people in my community drove Cadillac Eldorados, wore colorful wide-brimmed hats, and enjoyed the company of a variety of beautiful women. Of course, that was not reality, but it was certainly my perception and the perception of many other young black boys I grew up with. Is not my perception my "reality?" How many times have you heard that pop psychology tossed around?

I wonder if Charles Barkley, this year's MVP of the National Basketball Association, who proudly proclaims that he's no role model, has ever given much thought to the perception versus reality notion.

Surely he has not embraced the ideas as having much validity, for if he had, I doubt whether he would dare allow himself to shy away from the opportunity to be a role model to millions of kids.

By the way, Sir Charles, you are a role model whether you choose to be or not – just not a good one. The thought depresses me. Equally depressing is when some of our talk show hosts and guests proceed to butcher the English language – although, I guess that's acceptable, since some of them are raking in as much as $4 million a year.

Should they not at least say to their young audiences, "Listen, young boys and girls, it's all right for me to speak as though I never progressed beyond the third grade. After all, I carry a football for a living. Communication skills aren't a prerequisite for scoring a touchdown."

And what about those expensive gold earrings a lot of those "superstars" wear in each ear, complimented by the darkest pair of sunglasses to be found. Would you let the kids know that that "suave look" is suitable only if they are a multi-millionaire jock, or if they are interviewing for the bouncer's job in one of the local night clubs?

It is my contention that by virtue of the professional athlete's high profile and visibility he has a unique role to play, especially in the lives of young black boys. You see, when one considers the breakdown of the family within the black community, I can assure you that few of us who qualify as Afro-American adults can afford the luxury of saying "we are not a role model."

Only a few days ago, *Newsweek* reported, "For blacks, the institution of marriage has been devastated in the last generation; two out of three first births to black women under 35 are now out of wedlock. In 1960, the number was two out of five. A black child born today has only a one-in-five chance of growing up with two parents until the age of 16." According to University of Wisconsin demographer Larry L. Bumpass, "The impact, of course, is not only on black families, but on all of society. Fatherless homes boost crime rates, lower educational attainment, and add dramatically to the welfare rolls."

It is not my attempt to exempt parents from their responsibility as teachers of their children, but it is important that we understand that we all have a role to play.

We as parents have a responsibility to work with our young people. Every parent should make room on their agenda for their children. No parent is too impoverished, and no wealthy parent is too busy to do this.

As adults, we have an obligation to look after all young people, regardless of where we find them. Many of us have a mind to say that if a young person is not a member of our family, he is not our responsibility. But we cannot ignore the problems of our young people because they have not been designated as our primary charge. The children of this community are at our table and it is the responsibility of each of us to serve them.

And finally, for those athletes who say that they are not role models, I can't tell you how much I wish that were true. There's a tremendous waste of human potential, which could be halted, with the application of just a little genuine concern for our responsibility to the children.

Cuban Boy, All Youth Need Our Help

Elian Gonzalez, the handsome little boy on the cover of many magazines, has become an international celebrity in only a few months. Before that, his life wasn't easy, but it didn't differ much from that of the other boys his own age in his community. Now, as a result of family differences, he is featured in newspaper headlines and on the nightly news. Elian's relatives in Cuba want him to come back to live with them, and his relatives in America want him to stay here. Because relatives from two countries are involved, this has become an international situation with lawyers and negotiators and interviews with the press. Elian went from obscurity to international fame overnight.

This kind of experience is hard to imagine for most of us, and it must have both positive and negative effects on all the people involved, especially Elian. For example, Elian must know that both sides of his family love him deeply and want to take care of him. Probably, a boy his age would be excited about seeing himself on TV and in the papers. There might also be some new clothes to wear for publicity pictures, and lunches with officials at fancy restaurants, although most 5-year-old boys don't enjoy those kinds of things very much.

There are negative effects of being in the news, most of which we outsiders can't see. For example, just the pressure on both families to win the case and the fear of losing Elian must be stressful, and constant interviews can be annoying and exhausting. There is no question that Elian and his family have a problem, and solving it will require a lot of time and energy. But since both sides of the family want him and vow to take good care of him, in a way Elian has two positive choices.

Unfortunately, there are a lot of children around the world who do not have any positive choices. They couldn't name anyone in the world who wants them or would help to feed and clothe them. They don't have a home to go back to. The problems these children suffer seldom make the newspaper headlines, and there are probably a lot of reasons for this, too.

We can identify with Elian: one child with a serious, but not life-threatening problem, and his family and how they are trying to solve the problem. However, for many people the problem of hundreds of homeless children seems too overwhelming to solve. We have seen images of long lines of sad, hollow faces, waiting for a cup of milk at a food distribution center, or gangs of teenagers, mugging people for drug money.

It is easy for us to think that short of adopting one or two street children, or donating a lot of money, there is very little any individual can do to remedy such a difficult situation. And considering the problems of homeless children in America where it's possible for parents to get welfare, when churches and shelters distribute food, and where basic school education is free, it's hard to imagine the plight of homeless children in third world countries with none of these support systems.

In addition to feeding children, we have the problem of helping them avoid having their own babies they can't support and sometimes don't want. However overwhelming these problems seem, ignoring them and hoping they will disappear doesn't work either.

If we are really concerned with solving problems of homeless children, we must first look at what they are facing. Children growing up by themselves will have an impact on our society when they become adults, but unfortunately, their lifestyle may teach them the kind of behavior that is harmful to themselves and others. If we could pay positive attention to them while they are young, maybe we could avoid paying them the negative attention of a trial or jail sentence later in life.

Many children who do have homes face serious, even physical, danger every day. These children need help and unless we give it to them, their problems will only get worse. So any articles that focus on children like Elian, and especially those which focus on serious problems that affect many children, will help us understand what is needed and will attract attention so those children will get the help they should have to live happy and productive lives.

Children Should Remain Top Factor In Welfare Equation

Numbers don't always tell the truth. Let's take a look. It's virtually impossible today to discuss any level of welfare reform without invoking the name of Charles Murray, the famed sociologist, who advocates ending benefits to anyone now getting them. Not reducing, not phasing out – but ending.

Faced with a welfare system that enslaves more recipients than it liberates – the welfare rolls have grown by 1.3 million just since 1988 – many states are inching toward watered-down Murrayism.

One idea is to cap welfare payments to unmarried mothers regardless of how many extra children they have.

The big question is, to speak bluntly, "Will not getting an additional $50 or so tucked into each month's benefit check prompt welfare mothers to curb their sexual behavior?" Charles Murray certainly thinks so, and the unfortunate truth is a lot of policy makers are listening.

Well, it's pretty clear that the reverse is true. Public policies can induce people to have more children. Consider the East German example. Since the Berlin Wall came tumbling down in 1989, the birth rate in the former East Germany has plummeted 65 percent. Currently, according to the *Wall Street Journal*, "babies are being born in the East at the annual rate of five per 1,000 men, a third of the U.S. rate."

What has caused this remarkable decline? Evidently a large factor is the cutoff of state incentives to those who bear children.

In the defunct German Democratic Republic, families with newborns got first choice on scarce apartments, while the terms of state loans were eased according to how many kids a family raised.

These carrots produced the desired effect. Until the GDR crashed, the births in Eastern Germany exceeded those in the western sector.

Since 1992, when New Jersey began denying extra cash to mothers who have babies while on welfare, officials claim the birth rate among these mothers has dropped eight or nine percent. Charles Murray would say the trend in New Jersey is heading in the right direction.

What makes even many conservatives flinch when considering what Charles Murray is proposing, is the certainty that innocent babies, who have no control over their circumstances, will suffer when welfare checks are cut or stopped.

For those of us who may be quick to judge the sexual practices of women on welfare, let's remember that our multi-billion dollar welfare system is a mélange of uncoordinated programs. These programs have been created by a variety of federal, state and local agencies.

While the numbers, as Murray sees them, may point in one direction, we should understand that there is more to this welfare equation than he seems willing or capable of pointing out.

Numbers don't lie, or do they? Remember, it's image that drives the politics of welfare. For anyone with both heart and brain, welfare reform is an issue almost too difficult to take a position on. In our deliberations, we should never forget the children who in the end will pay the greatest price.

Teen Pregnancy: Yesterday's Disgrace Now The Norm

Take a look at how things have changed. It wasn't too many years ago that having a child out of wedlock was deemed a disgrace.

Young women mysteriously disappeared for no reason; or for contrived reasons, such as "She's gone to live with Grandma. She's gone to live with Aunt Marie who recently lost her husband."

They would suddenly disappear rather than endure the embarrassment of pregnancy in their hometown.

Today it's a different story. Gone forever are the days when young pregnant mothers are embarrassed by having a child out of wedlock. So many young mothers have never been married that neighbors think nothing of it.

At last report, two-thirds of black children, more than 38 percent of Hispanic children and nearly 22 percent of white children are born to unmarried mothers.

In three generations we've gone from attaching a stigma to illegitimate children to fostering a generation of children who have babies so that they can have somebody to love.

One out of every four women who had a child in 1990 was not married. Overall, the nation's out-of-wedlock birthrate jumped from five percent of all births in 1960 to 27 percent in 1990.

Some estimates indicate that as many as 10,000 extremely young women, age 12 or even younger, become pregnant every year.

The younger these children are when they have their first child the more likely they are to have at least one more child before their teen years end.

These children who have children are particularly at risk of dropping out of school and becoming social throwaways that face a bleak future, destined to a life on the streets. Later, unable to get and hold jobs, they will drop out of the labor market as well, creating or perpetuating cycles of deep, depressing and unrelenting poverty.

A new Census Bureau survey shows that children are almost as likely to be living with a never-married parent as with a divorced parent.

It's not that marriage is going out of style. The number of married persons increased from 95 million to 114.5 million between 1970 and 1993.

It's just that unwed motherhood has become so common that in some communities it's considered the conventional lifestyle. Unwed motherhood has public policy implications because many of these women are poor, unemployed and supported by the taxpayers under the Federal Aid to Families with Dependent Children Program.

New Jersey has been refusing to pay the additional benefit to children conceived while the mother is on welfare and several other states are planning similar experiments.

Times are changing. There is a new breed of intolerance of social programs. Some time back, this nation decided as a matter of policy that certain activities properly belonged in the public sector – thus the welfare system was born.

This was a decent and compassionate thing to do, and says a great deal about the kind of society we are and wish to be.

Along the way, however, and especially in the last 20 years, a curious thing happened: a damaging and persistent inflation and a national debt well over one trillion dollars came into the equation.

A couple of harsh lessons have been learned from recent elections. First, taxpayers are truly weary of paying for a number of lavish social programs that don't work very well, and second, the cost of income redistribution through various entitlement programs has grown out of proportion to our country's ability to pay.

We would all be well advised to listen to what the new leadership in Washington is now saying, particularly as they talk about their contract with America. Welfare reform is at the top of the list.

Finally, it is my hope that every young woman in America is aware of the times in which we live. Who's going to pay for those babies?

Children Suffer From Inadequate Parenting

When I was in college, I have to admit, I was a bit selfish – I thought the world would be my oyster. I would be able to do what I want when I wanted with no questions asked. However, I was not alone in that viewpoint. There were quite a few of us who fully embraced being a part of the "me generation."

Moral consensus had given way to moral relativism – a doctrine which makes an individual the sole judge of his own action and which is designed to give full leeway to the pursuit of individual appetites.

We had it all together, or so we thought. We would follow the American Dream by getting married and raising perfect kids.

However, when pop-philosophy individualists from the "me generation" got married and didn't get expectations met, we were, for lack of a better word, mystified.

And we also found out rather quickly that we were in fact, like everybody else, with lives filled with anger and family strife. All this strife, it turns out, harms children, according to a new study. The 25th annual Survey High Achievement conducted by Who's Who Among American High School Students reports that young people, even those who make good grades and take leadership roles, are more prone to high-risk behaviors.

For example, teens were almost five times more likely to smoke if they came from tumultuous homes, and twice as likely to drink to the point of drunkenness.

While 20 percent of students from happy homes were sexually active, the figure was 46 percent among those from unhappy homes. Saddest of all, 18 percent of the unhappy home group reported trying to take their own lives; among children from peaceful families, only two percent.

Another implicit finding of the study was that home environments that are emotional war zones stunt children academically and socially. Only six percent of the "Who's Who" high achievers said they came from unhappy homes, suggesting that such domiciles are a steep obstacle to success.

Unfortunately, the parents of many of these children were infatuated with the notion of doing their own thing unhindered by family obligations. We were surrounded by activities aimed at helping the individual to maximize his personal happiness and do his own things.

Remember, we got married and had children. No one tells our story better than the author of these words: "Parents today are caught in a crunch of conflicting values. They value children, but they value other things as well, such as time for themselves, material goods, status and their careers. Given these conflicts, in a number of instances they neglect children, or don't give them a fair shake."

We did it our way, but not necessary the right way.

Reforming Families Only Way To Improve Welfare System

All the empty rhetoric surrounding welfare reform continues to miss the mark. The larger issue – when we take a deep and objective look – is the breakdown of the family unit.

No amount of money or social miracle will fix welfare if family responsibility is left out of the equation. Welfare reform won't mend broken families. At the center of the welfare tragedy are children having children.

More specifically, we have got to do a better job of understanding the environment that fosters dependency. Too often our children are in trouble from the very beginning – from the day they take their first breath.

They are all too often born into dysfunctional settings with no way to escape, and they are hurting. Let me share with you comments from two children who have known trouble. "I was born to a woman I never knew, and raised by another who took in orphans. I do not know my background, my lineage, my biological or cultural heritage."

Second, a teenage girl who confided to her teacher: "Ma'am, my older brothers and sisters have hit the streets. I don't know where they sleep at night and I don't know what they might be getting into. My mama's had a lot of different boyfriends, but lately she's been sick and they don't come around any more. My brothers and sisters say 'Why don't you leave, why don't you get out of there?' Ma'am, I don't want the kind of life for myself that Mama has had, but I don't want to move out. I feel she needs me. How can I help her?"

These confessions represent the issues we must find a way to address. The big question is, how do we stop the trend of children having children, and thus perpetuating the vicious cycle of welfare, as we know it?

New statistics from the Census Bureau confirm what many have long suspected – that "children having children" is the essential cause of poverty and family disintegration in the United States.

The census report, based on a survey of welfare mothers, shows that women who receive Aid to Families with Dependent Children (AFDC), often had their first child as a teenager. Many never had been married and nearly half did not have a high school diploma.

Women on welfare tend to be younger and more likely to have additional children than other mothers. Among the findings in the report are these:

More than 68 percent of the first children of welfare mothers were born out of wedlock, and nearly 28 percent of their mothers had their first child when they were less than 18.

About 48 percent of the nation's welfare mothers have never been married and only 13 percent were living with a husband.

About one in four black mothers and one in five Hispanic mothers between the ages of 15 and 44 were on welfare. Eighty-seven percent of welfare mothers didn't have a job.

Children having children is a recipe for social chaos which is why we must look beyond the politics of demagoguery and the blame game.

To understand the real issues surrounding those receiving AFDC, one has to isolate assumptions about those who are on welfare, why they are poor, and what can be done to alter human behavior.

I don't think I know anyone who wants children to suffer. The tough issue is finding some viable approach to allowing the family unit to reclaim its proper place in American society.

It Truly Takes A Village To Raise A Child

At the dawn of the new millennium, we have been bombarded with how it takes a whole village to rear a child. Many of us reminisce about how this African proverb worked for us, as we tell stories of how so many individuals from our childhood communities were involved in our upbringing.

If we strayed on the way home from school, it was not at all unusual to be chastised by a neighbor and have parents ready to send us to the backyard to get a tree branch for our own switching when we got home. Also, if the teacher had occasion to get the paddle out at school, you knew there was going to be something waiting for you at home. We were not abused, as most would interpret it today, but we definitely had many layers of correction and expectation.

Today we smile as we remember the stories of our life experiences, and we are proud of all the people of "our village" who took the time to nurture us. We recall the village in terms of people: the neighbors, the Sunday school teacher and the principal, without realizing that many of those people were, themselves, members of solid, functional families. Today we acknowledge the fact that the missing concept of "village" has jeopardized effective child rearing.

Part of what sustained us during our childhood was the resilient nuclear family that nurtured us on many levels. But our "village" is disappearing fast into the complexity of today's society. Gone are the days when we would sit quietly in church or Sunday school to listen to the pastor or our Sunday school teacher. Today we consider it lucky if we can get children to sit quietly for 30 minutes in school or church. Their minds are fractured by the many influences of their community, including video games, music, movies, and, above all, television.

Most people are quick to blame the parents for failing their children.

Perhaps some of the reasons the village is not as effective today as it once was are that it has been undermined by an assault from society on our families and the many forces influencing our family value system. We know that poverty, teenage pregnancy, divorce, incarceration and addiction have taken their toll on family life. We see the consequences in school performance, behavioral problems, over-extended mothers who juggle jobs and family life, and in absent fathers who see their children wrongfully used to express their mother's anger.

Our village is no longer comprised of stable families and is less able to take care of at-risk youth because it has been undermined and rendered impotent by society. How quickly we forget that the African-American community has a history of survival that was made possible by strong and extended family ties. Even the assault during our years of captivity and slavery could not destroy our family life because it was needed and it was valued.

At this point in the African-American journey and history, we need to revisit the family support system that encompasses the village concept in order to create cultural survival and the restoration of the village. We are in great danger because for the first time in our history, technology and media influences have made it possible for us to have the illusion that family is no longer necessary. Many of us carry this alien, toxic value within us.

If we as a people are to survive in this new millennium, then we need to restructure our family value systems. We must strive to reduce juvenile detention, high school dropout rates, gang activity, violence in our schools and sexual promiscuity.

Many of us have assumed anti-family values without realizing it. We have internalized an alien value system that causes us to put ourselves in danger of non-survival. In order for us to rebuild the kind of family and community that are so unique to our existence, and the village concept that once worked for us, we must stop perpetuating dangerous values and outcomes.

We romanticize family life but often make choices that are inconsistent with that family life. We place emphasis on "self" and have become like children as seen in our ownership and possession without sharing. We teach our children to be self-sufficient to the point that it is difficult for them to establish the compromise needed for excellence, cooperation, or marriage.

We are quick to defend our children when they do not get along with other children, or meet high standards by declaring that they are exceptional. This is a lot easier to accept than to see their qualities as selfish or weak. We encourage our friends who have marital conflicts not to take it anymore, rather than encouraging them to try to work their marriage out so that the relationship can be restored.

Many of us are so tolerant of mothers who choose to have children and care for them with the aid of child support, instead of the support from the presence of their husbands, because child support is so prevalent and because it takes the pressure off of us. We do not have to hold ourselves accountable for our choices and our failure to heal. It is hard for us to remember that our children really perform well when they have the security of their parents.

While this may be true, it denies the fact that society sometimes has greater influence on our children than both parents do. For example, you can bring up your children in the most respectable family setting, but they are still vulnerable to influences of the community in which they live. They must interact with other children from whom they may learn bad and dangerous habits.

Another sad example of how our village has been destroyed is the fact that some adults who live alone are so wounded by their childhood demons, or their nightmare relationships, that they seek comfort in their own solitude. Fear of future family trauma is more powerful than hope for future family blessings. For many people, marriage is regarded as a trap instead of a sacrament of love. It seems as if we have an anti-family orientation. We love our mothers and we love our parents, and we love our children. Yet the work that we must do within the context of love and relationships cannot occur when our individual interests take priority.

As adults, we have responsibilities and we cannot run away from those responsibilities. But oftentimes we support those who run away from their responsibilities. We sometimes support those adults who do what they feel like doing, be it creating debt, being promiscuous, or quitting their jobs without thinking about the consequences. We support those who rear children that do what they feel like doing – be it talking back to their parents, disrespecting their teachers, or engaging in violent behavior.

Discipline as it used to be in our "village" may mean subordinating feelings to principles. The value of the strong family is not easy to establish, but it is worth it. It may be easier to take care of your unwed daughter's infant, but it may also reflect a value that undermines the fabric of our village concept. We are so tolerant of undesired outcomes that we find it hard to recapture the values that are necessary for our culture to survive. If our family life goes, eventually the individual desires that are held so highly will become unattainable. Doing what we feel like doing indiscriminately weakens character and ability and eventually destroys our once cherished village.

We as a people lack the tools to rebuild love, family and community commitment. The experience of being in family relationships where we place the needs of others before our own is absent. It becomes increasingly difficult for us to cultivate the values of family and community and we default to accepting futile efforts for individual personal success.

But there is hope. There is still time for us to look in the mirror and see whether we have inadvertently shifted the focus away from family. If we have, we know what works and must accept our responsibility to reclaim the values that work. We must teach others that love, discipline and even the "village" concept continue to support the healthy family value system as they did in the past.

Even when we have been deprived of such love, the opportunities to heal and recover still abound. We can and must have healthy lives within our healthy families. There can be no nation building without the solidarity of the African-American family, or revisiting the concept that it truly takes an entire village to raise a child.

Together we will win.

Love Lets Kids Be Kids, Grow Safely Into Adults

People have always accused kids of getting away with murder. Now that is all too literally true. Across the United States, a pattern of crime has emerged that is both perplexing and appalling.

Homicide is now the leading cause of death among children in most American cities, and about half the assailants are other youths.

From 1983 to 1990 the number of minors arrested for murder increased by a startling 31 percent, even though the number of people age 12 to 17 actually decreased by eight percent during this period of time.

Several days ago, as I sat with my son watching a television documentary showing young people discussing crime, it occurred to me that we were watching a room full of victims.

Some were young men mostly under 20 years of age. Some were victims because they had witnessed a tragedy; some were victims because of a loss or destruction of a loved one. All were victims because their lives had been altered or touched by a senseless act of violence.

As we sat watching the program I thought a lot about a good friend and colleague who had dedicated her life to working with young people. She left the convent many years ago in an effort to go into the inner city of Dallas and open her home and heart to our youth.

She is small in stature with a heart that belies her tiny frame. She had been teaching college chemistry for 17 years and no one questioned her unconditional devotion to her students.

I thought of her as I watched the program on youth and crime and remembered her admonition to me: "Whose fault is it that there has been no way to control this epidemic of senseless violence, waste and pain? How do the guns get into our children's hands?"

Almost anybody in Dallas can tell you the story of how Roosevelt High School's 15-year-old Demarkous McLemore's young life ended. How many times have we witnessed similar scenarios in the city of Detroit? The hard part is to determine "why?"

Why have those who claim to speak on behalf of children not made an outcry for tougher laws, no-nonsense sentencing, more police officers, safer schools, and fewer drugs?

Why have they initiated no campaign for putting the full weight of public protection on the side of babies and school children instead of on the side of mothers who poison their offspring with crack cocaine and thugs who bring guns into the classroom?

We have a responsibility to provide our children with a sense of right and wrong. I strongly believe that it is also my responsibility (and that of others as well) to provide my children with a sense of morality, honor, integrity, and ethics.

It is part of their birthright that my children be given life, love and the pursuit of happiness. But above all, it is my love that should nurture, protect and provide my child with an opportunity to be a child and a chance to be an adult. No one said the job would be easy.

The most influential source of violence, by and among children, is "family breakdown." More than 64 percent of all children born today will spend at least some time in a single-parent household before reaching the age of 18.

Drugs are one root of this curse on our young. Our children, in some instances, are going to schools that are armed camps.

Deadly weapons are found every day in lockers across the country. Our children are killing each other with no hint of remorse.

I still get this crazy sensation in my stomach when a 15-year-old boy explains why he shot another teen: "Wasn't nothing. I didn't think about it. If I had to kill him...I just had to kill him. That's the way I look at it, 'cause I was young. The most I could have got then is 18 months."

Ask your child if he knows how to obtain a gun or whether he has been approached with an offer to buy one. You may not like the answer.

Maybe if we talk with our children a little bit more, we can move toward curing the curses. Maybe if we listen a little more, we can help a child reach adulthood. And maybe, just maybe, if we love a little harder, we can help a parent have another day with her child.

Responsibility for Teenage Pregnancy Needs To Be Shared

I wrote a column a few weeks ago that was myopic in opinion. I was soundly chastised by one of my colleagues for not considering the issue from at least one other angle. She was right to do so.

I talked about teenage pregnancy and young mothers having babies out of wedlock as if they made the babies all by themselves.

In many ways what I had to say may have supported what we know to be true on the part of many young fathers; they engender and run. After all, too many of us have subscribed to the view that "boys will be boys."

Few would argue that we keep a sharp eye on the behavior of moms; they are the subject of endless scrutiny, demagoguery, and sermonizing. We ask young women to be young mothers as well as fathers, and, at the same time, to be economically independent.

But as my colleague correctly asked, "What about the father?" It was as if women brought all these kids into the world alone.

It was recently noted in *Newsweek* that fathers in 66 percent of all out-of-wedlock child support cases are never forced to be responsible for their acts. Only 18 percent pay child support.

The current system of child support is a disgrace. Often the problem is not that the father can't pay. By most estimates, an aggressive child support system could collect an additional 20 to 30 billion dollars from fathers.

The current system essentially lets the fathers off the hook. We have done more than enough to send the signal that absent fathers have taken no responsibilities.

There is no more widespread and profoundly consequential example of lawlessness in our society today than fathers' refusals to care for their children.

Listen only casually to the discussions around us when unwed mothers are the topic of conversation; it's not likely that much of the talk will center on the absent father.

We should never allow ourselves to forget that more than half the men in America who have been told by a judge to pay child support disobey the order, forcing millions of mothers and children to live in poverty.

To make matters even worse, some mothers seeking child support are afraid to contact the fathers, fearing retaliation in the most violent way. It should be easy to understand how some women are afraid to pursue child support when one considers that the men who are not paying child support are obviously not model fathers. If these fathers paid, they would get more involved with the children and that would mean more responsibility.

According to this view, the so-called inadequacies of the current child support system represent a desirable accommodation to the unpleasant realities of life and should not be tampered with.

Clearly, there are some fathers who are dangerous to their children and the mothers of their children. Forgoing child support in order to make a clean break with such fathers may be in the mother's and the child's best interest. However, there are countless cases where the support would be forthcoming without the threat of violence or the need for the father to negatively influence the child.

President Clinton is making noise about remedying this country's child support problem. He proposes making comprehensive reforms – the toughest child support measure in the history of this country.

Fathers who don't pay child support would lose any professional or occupational licenses they hold, as well as their driver's licenses.

Six hundred mothers who don't cooperate in tracking down the father of their child would be denied benefits. Every state would have to create a central registry of child support orders to help find delinquent, deserting fathers.

I'm glad my friend and colleague reminded me of how tunnel visioned a lot of us are on a number of important social problems. On the issue of out-of-wedlock children, it seems that we have factored fathers right out of the equation.

There was a time in our country when a father's responsibility for children was moral, not legal. What a wonderful concept.

I know what you are thinking – we can't legislate morality. Well, maybe not; however, we can present deadbeat fathers with undesirable consequences.

To Stop Violence, Focus On Children, Not Guns

The school shooting in Colorado was becoming old news when a brokenhearted boy in a Conyers, Georgia high school decided to open fire on his classmates. Then, two men on Detroit's Belle Isle shot and killed a man for soaking another woman with a water gun.

The world is moving too fast to dwell on one particular tragic event. Unfortunately, the impetus to change things – to try something new that might lower the chances of another tragedy – is also swept aside as we focus on a new problem. The factors in our culture that influence the motivation behind the plotting and carrying out of violent attacks remain. Therefore, as we have experienced in the past few years, the violent acts become more horrible and more frequent.

One solution to the problem of guns in schools is to install metal detectors and ban all backpacks. Another is to insist on uniforms. Uniforms might help minimize children's tendency to base their self-esteem on their parents' income and what it can buy for them. However, installing metal detectors and banning backpacks promotes the unspoken assumption that school violence is here to stay, so we might as well avoid as much of it as possible. In fact, many people have accepted the notion that our society is crumbling and it's too late to do anything about it. At the same time, many of our leaders don't hesitate to assume we can and should change the outcome of a civil war in a foreign country thousands of miles away. If we can do that, they say, we can reduce violence in our schools.

To focus on reducing violence in schools, we must focus on schools and the children in them. Our children's welfare must be important enough to be put first.

Some parents put their children first so often that they don't have a life of their own. But the biggest problem is neglect.

Many parents rarely talk with their children. And, many young people don't even want to have children. For some, raising children means having less time and money for their own enjoyment. Children require a lot of time, energy and attention. They can get involved with things that are dangerous, especially when the parents are just too busy or worn out to notice. Children like to have secrets but it's not good for them to think they can get away with anything.

One way parents protect children is by keeping them away from dangerous things – matches, knives, poisons, alcohol and drugs, etc. Many parents believe that violent movies and electronic games can be dangerous influences, encouraging children to feel comfortable with violence and to become experts in killing cartoon characters to win the game. It isn't obvious that watching violence makes children violent since most are able to maintain good relationships with adults and peers. On the other hand, aren't there other activities more beneficial to children's growth and welfare than watching or "practicing" killing?

If parents really think violent games lead to violent real life acts, they should make an attempt to limit their child's exposure to them. It might be too late to ban violent games but it's never too late to explain your position to the child. It would be useful for the child to learn to think about what he or she does and the results from those actions. Maybe if the child could explain what is attractive about the violence, it might become easier to choose a more positive alternative. A lack of involvement and no restrictions from parents can seem like a signal of parental approval to the child.

In addition to giving children more time and attention, if we really want to make our children's welfare number one, we will have to cut back our involvement with guns. Many deaths from gunshot wounds would never have occurred if there were no guns available. It's much easier to shoot someone from a safe distance than to engage in hand-to-hand fighting. The distaste and fear of physical injury would deter most angry people from a fight, but a gun makes killing the opponent and winning the argument easy.

Our current lifestyle is hectic and stressful even for children. There is little or no encouragement to take it easy as we work harder to make and spend more. This generates frustration and exhaustion, which can easily lead to anger and sometimes violence. If we agree with people who say "it's people who commit the crimes, not the guns," then we must be responsible for keeping guns away from anyone who could hurt himself or another. Some may feel they need a gun for self-defense, but no one needs a semi-automatic. And no one should be allowed to carry a hidden gun anywhere. Strengthening gun control laws may seem like an invasion of our right to bear arms but it may be the most effective way to slow down school violence.

If we really want to provide safe schools for our children, we must take whatever steps are necessary to accomplish that goal. It's not easy to put our children first, but we will have to face the tragic consequences if we don't.

Children Need To Know About Death

I read an article in a national news magazine last week that tugged at my heartstrings. I strained to hold back tears as an 8-year-old girl struggled to deal with the untimely death of her mother who had recently died of AIDS.

According to a recent report issued by the National Academy of Sciences, "The children most deeply affected by a death in their immediate family are usually young children who have lost their mothers."

It occurred to me while reading the article that millions of young children suffer the same tragic experience. When this happens, we as a society of adults are often caught off guard in terms of our ability to help children face the issue of death.

I guess the thing that struck me most profoundly about the 8-year-old girl was how she fantasized about being with her mother again in an imaginary world. She would spend hours drawing pictures of her mother fitted with wings and a halo soaring high in the heavens. Several of the pictures included the entire family with the mother as the center focus offering the kind of security that perhaps only a mother could provide.

From time to time every parent will give some thought to how to communicate to his or her young children the inevitability of death. This is in no way an easy topic to discuss. Few people are comfortable talking to a child about death.

Anytime I've attempted to discuss death and dying with my 13-year-old son, it has been quite clear that it's a subject he would rather avoid. I might also add that I don't attend to the subject much better.

David Perety, M.D., describes why so many of our children today deal with death as an abstraction. He says that "children today are not exposed to life and death like many who were raised in rural areas in previous generations." He further commented that "it is unfortunate that we can't go back in time and provide every child the learning experience of a simple life on a farm with its closeness to nature, with the experience of birth and death in the natural surrounding of the child." For the most part, children today don't know what it means for life to vanish forever. Only gradually do they recognize that there is a thing called death and everyone must die. However, according to Elizabeth Kubler-Ross in her book, *On Death and Dying*, "This gradual realization of the inevitability of death can take up to the ninth or tenth year."

My newfound curiosity with this subject caused me to query other adults about their feelings when they have had the unfortunate experience of watching a child struggle with the loss of a parent. A common thread ran throughout the stories they shared when observing such an event. Children would construct fantasies to cope with their loss and to explain the mystery of death. We, as adults, would lend support to this means of coping by saying things like "mama will be gone for a little while," or "your mother has taken a brief trip, but if you are good you will see her again."

Children need to be told the truth. The expectation should not be created that death is anything but final and irrevocable. The question is how to communicate harsh realities in a loving and sympathetic manner.

One of the greatest difficulties for a child is the death of a parent. The thought of losing a mother or father is the one thing that a child simply refuses to accept as a possibility.

I don't offer the answers here, but it's my hope that we will all be inspired to reconsider how our children are struck by the notion of death.

Why Do the Opinions of Others Matter?

I couldn't help but listen more closely as the mother explained to her daughter that what the other kids were saying about her didn't matter. The child was saying that the kids made comments about her being spoiled and saying that she didn't like to do things that her friends wanted her to do. She only wanted to do what she wanted. I would characterize that as being selfish, only the children were obviously too young to know that this behavior had such a big name.

Nevertheless, the mother asked if the child was being the friend to others that she wanted the others to be to her, which sometimes meant sharing and compromising. But, as my ears continued to follow the details of this pretty good advice that the mother was sharing, my thoughts returned to one of her earlier comments, that what others think about us doesn't matter.

I seriously had to give deeper thought to the validity of this statement.

It almost seems as if much of our existence is very dependent on the opinions that others have of us. Consider first the evidence that proves that attractive people get better jobs, are helped first at a sales counter and are considered to be more intelligent. Isn't this an immediate result of another's opinion of the most apparent of our characteristics – our looks?

Think about school, a place where we begin at an age sometimes as early as two or three, and remain until we are clearly on the threshold of adulthood. A friend of mine once commented that a grade was simply the teacher's interpretation of how well the student understood what the teacher was trying to communicate. The friend asked whether a less than ideal grade meant that the student didn't understand, or that the teacher failed to explain adequately. Either way, this was an additional example where another's opinion made a difference. Getting a bad grade, or a good grade for that matter, helps to further set the stage for future educational endeavors for the recipient.

Let's talk sports. From the time that kids begin Little League play, they are encouraged to perform for the purpose of garnering the approval of the coach and the applause of the fans. The opinions of others.

What about musicians and movie stars? Their careers are based on, and steered by, the opinions of their agents, talent scouts, producers, and ultimately the fans.

Perhaps it is better to say that only the consensus of many people really matters. While I understood that the mother was simply trying to teach her daughter the importance of not allowing the words or opinions of others to dictate her view of herself or her actions, I couldn't help but take this subject through a mental journey. Even in the arenas of life where the opinions of others do matter, the mother's advice was good. After all, opinions are like the weather. They change from time to time, and often without any obvious provocation. So, it is best not to be swayed by the opinions – whether negative or approving – of others. It sets one up for dependency and possible letdown.

It is, however, good to have a balance. It is said that sometimes others can see you as you fail to see yourself, so a good dose of reality, if given graciously, can help make for a better person.

On the other hand, one must always be armed with a comfort with oneself and a confidence that can withstand the negative opposition that we all surely encounter throughout life.

Self-confidence with a healthy dose of humility will surely prove more potent and effective in helping us improve ourselves than anyone else's opinion alone.

Gun Law Creates Environment Of Fear

It should have been a normal send-off for my 19-year-old son the other morning as he left to start his day. Yet, as a result of a weapons law upheld by the Supreme Court, it was not.

My wife and I have worked hard over the years, as so many parents do, to instill basic values from which we hope a mature, well-balanced and overall good person will emerge. And by all indications, our investments have paid off. Our daughter is a recent university graduate and our son currently is a university student, both very successful in their studies.

More than that, they are good children. They are honest, respectful, kind and moral. This summer my son is home doing an internship. He leaves home each day with qualities that make him a better person, but which will not protect him from the social ills that have just been unleashed by the Michigan Supreme Court's ruling.

Those ills allow more average Americans who say they want to protect their family and property to carry a gun. The law also allows those who harbor fears of those who are different to carry and use a concealed gun.

We move so fast and recklessly today that it is already difficult to recall those things that we know make life better for everyone. Tolerance, consideration, and thoughtfulness create a better person and society. Now, however, guns make those attempts at reconciliation and social harmony less necessary. The trust and understanding that we should have or should be working toward are no longer necessary. You do not need to trust, listen to or attempt to understand someone else because you have a gun.

When confronted with an uncomfortable situation, will one who has a gun take the time to consider or remember that this momentary "opponent" is also another living human being, someone's family member, friend or neighbor? Or will he attempt to resolve any conflict or calm his fears with a gun?

The usual send-off for my son now includes a big hug, and "Have a good day and be careful." I have to give him a brief rundown of situations that he may encounter that could jeopardize his life. Our society expresses many fears, especially of those who look or appear different. We frequently see or hear about the victims of those fears.

When we look into the eyes of a stranger, we cannot always see the fear and hate that may live in their heart and soul. Our young people, especially, already saddled with the baggage of negative perception, may be worse off as they are sometimes automatically looked upon as troublemakers, radicals, and rogues.

Why is it that in America more than in any other country, our modern mode of solving problems, of getting our way, of proving our point, has become guns rather than common decency and civility, traits necessary for a successful social order?

Civility is not easy, just as democracy is not easy. Civility means that sometimes you do not get your way. It is the slow, thoughtful, consideration of others.

Guns so easily give opportunity to momentary anger or revenge, allowing situations to happen that were not intended and that are regretted later. Guns do not require thought, just a quick trigger finger. Guns get you what you want for a moment or two, but they also get you a lot more than you bargained for later. There are consequences to our irrational actions.

America has opened its doors to many people and remains a true melting pot. Yet, hate and resentment still run deep through the veins of this country. They are now about to surface in ways that many could not possibly comprehend.

It is my duty as a father to now teach my son one more aspect of being a good person – survival. Not by suggesting he carry a weapon, but by preparing him and cautioning him not to unintentionally incite one who may be carrying a weapon and unjustifiably decide to use it.

Children And Violence

Another school shooting – a six-year-old little girl this time. It was closer to home this time. More than usual we felt the pain and outrage as the newspapers and radio and television commentaries broadcast the details and scenes of the families grieving. Again, as usual, we looked for someone to blame – someone we could punish to insure justice was done and set our minds at rest. In this case, we couldn't blame either the criminal or the victim, assuming that six and seven year olds should not be held responsible for their actions.

But looking beyond the scene of the crime, we could blame the errant uncle, a man who had his own trouble with the law, and owned the gun used to kill. Once the blame is placed and legal action begins, it is easier for us to focus our concern on the criminal proceedings and our desire for justice and closure; the less emotional concept of prevention takes a back seat. There is less talk about a stricter gun regulation, so gun owners, gun salesmen and the NRA breathe a little easier.

This time it was easy to see the connection between a dysfunctional family and a child's violent crime as the *Detroit Free Press* reports: "Mother evicted. Father in jail. Living with an uncle wanted by the law. And a teen who keeps a gun by his bed."

We expect children deprived of care, attention and love to grow up with serious problems. However, giving children a good home doesn't always keep them away from guns and crime.

Unfortunately, the focus of blame appears to be spreading, from indicting one irresponsible parent to passing laws which hold all parents legally responsible for their children's criminal acts. This seems reasonable for immature parents who don't pay attention to their children or monitor their negative behavior. On the other hand, statistics show that even children from "good" homes with loving, attentive parents sometimes defy all expectations and lash out in violence against innocent victims. We can't always place the blame for these crimes on the parents.

Children are just as capable as adults of getting angry and wanting to hurt someone, but just like adults, they usually avoid face-to-face violence. So, like many adults, they think of using a gun as a "safe" way to get back at someone, from a distance. And, like many adults, their experience with violence – in the nightly news, movies and interactive games – has made shooting someone a more common, familiar way to express anger. In addition, some states have concealed weapon laws that allow people to carry guns almost everywhere, every day. Now, instead of being considered the ultimate household weapon of defense, guns have become something to collect and display with pride, and target practice has become a hobby – a live interactive "game."

Even young children can tell the difference between pointing a finger, a water pistol or a cap gun, and using a real gun. But no one in our culture can escape the message that guns mean power, the ultimate power of life and death. Although we glorify gun ownership, we haven't emphasized the result of gun use. Those feelings of power can cause severe injury or death when used against another person.

In fact, gun clubs are encouraging children and adults to take gun safety courses and to practice target shooting. They are sure that the more familiar people are with guns, the safer they will be. And schools have new rules too: no trench coats, no backpacks, no purses, and no clothes with big pockets that could hide guns. Many schools have installed metal detectors to deter kids from bringing guns to class. Unfortunately, protective rules and devices are no match for the child who is determined to bring a gun to school. In fact, some children, as well as adults, enjoy the challenge of outwitting the opposition, and would love to sneak a gun into school, just to prove they could do it.

In addition, we live at a time when the image of a gun has changed from the old shotgun dad used to keep the coyotes from killing the chickens or the six gun used by the western sheriff to maintain law and order. Now, although most of us don't need a gun to do our everyday jobs, thanks to our current concealed carry laws, lots of people carry one anyway. No matter how many new rules are proposed or safety programs are initiated, people will still get angry, and with more guns in circulation, the greater the chances are that the anger will be expressed with a gun.

Gun enthusiasts are very concerned that restricting or outlawing guns would violate their second amendment rights to bear arms. However, parents of the victims of gun violence are concerned about their children's rights to attend school, to play sports, to visit the mall or McDonald's without being injured or killed. They also wonder how many more children will have to die before something meaningful is done.

Key To Healthy Living Is Taking Time For Healthy Activities

I talked with an old colleague of mine the other day and he told me that seven teachers at his campus had recently seen a doctor for stress and anxiety. They all went home with a prescription for Prozac. A few years ago, this might have seemed a bit unusual. Today, taking medication for depression is an everyday event. Unfortunately, too many students in our public schools who are supposed to be enjoying their carefree youth are, in fact, suffering from stress and depression.

In spite of all the labor saving devices we have invented, and the fitness centers we have to help keep us in good physical shape, we experience more stress and depression than we ever have before. And although we have poured money into drug education programs and increased jail time and fines for drug use and abuse, young people are still making an effort to solve their issues by escaping with illegal recreational drugs. Many of our youths are so frustrated that they actually bring guns to school with the intention of killing their classmates and teachers. Why do we have so much stress and depression in our lives today?

One over-used phrase – "the good old days" – seems to define a period of happiness for many people. It brings up images of extended families, closer relationships and love and support for the family members. It inspires us with the images of the whole family sitting down for dinner and talking over the events of the day, solving problems and enjoying each other's company before the arguments started about whose turn it was to wash the dishes.

Our modern lifestyles don't allow very much time to sit around watching the kids play. There are very few, if any, extended families anymore. The fast-paced schedule of every member in the family makes a family meal a thing of the past. Between the children's after-school activities, church and community activities, housework, homework and the regular trips to the store, at the end of the day all we want to do is fall into bed – without enough energy to pay attention to each other's needs.

These problems have no easy solutions. On the one hand we are constantly encouraged by "the experts" to manage our time more productively, which translates into doing more in less time. On the other hand, we are encouraged to relax and enjoy our lives. This assumes that we will not accomplish everything we set out to. Most of us feel the need to be "good" at what we do. This may mean being a good housekeeper, employee, parent, friend, wife or husband. Giving up something we need to do for time to relax leaves us feeling guilty. We know that to fulfill the many roles we play and meet all our expectations requires more than the 24 hours a day that we have.

How can we apply what the experts say we need to do and what we know we must do in reality? Enjoying life and quality of life are the same thing – and for most people this means money. Any time away from work means having fewer resources to participate in those leisure activities like traveling, eating out, or going to the movies or a play. We work such long hours that there is very little, if any, time to enjoy the benefits of our labor. This is a common problem among women, who constantly manage multiple roles, working 40 hours a week and returning home at the end of the day to the other jobs of being a parent, tutor, cook, housekeeper, caregiver – and the list goes on.

Medical experts say, "In today's high stress lifestyles, it is important to relax," but few of us believe that there is any health risk if we don't. Some of the stress-related illnesses are high blood pressure and heart attacks. Many of us would rather take the gamble that this won't happen to us than to carve out just 30 minutes a day to do something to improve our quality of life through exercise.

One of the advantages of the so-called "good old days" was that everybody, even "city folk," got more exercise. There were fewer cars (many of us did not have access to those that were available) and this resulted in a lot more walking. People walked to church, to school, or to the corner grocery store. On those cold, snowy, icy, windy days, walking home from the store with three bags of groceries was probably no more fun than getting in the car and driving some place to exercise. Although walking with bags of groceries was exhausting, it was still good exercise.

For some of us, taking 30 minutes every day is virtually impossible, but most of us can find minutes sometime during the week to walk or involve ourselves in some other form of exercise: basketball, dancing or golf. Whatever your thing is, you need to do it regularly. Deciding to take the time to participate in these activities will make it easier for you to take the time for other relaxing pastimes. The usual chores, the dirty dishes, the laundry, homework, or taking care of the yard will always be there, but staying free from stress and depression requires an active choice of what is best for us, and taking the time to do it.

Domestic Violence: Family Terrorism

Domestic violence is shocking our human consciousness into horrified silence. Women and men are victims and victimizers of America's fastest growing violent crime. But the worst effect of this pervasive social ill is found among children who witness acts of family violence. These kids repeat what they see as they go through adolescence and grow into adulthood.

Terror is what happens within families beset with domestic violence. Also known as intimate partner abuse, the term simply describes a situation when someone physically harms the person he or she loves, with whom he or she has, or used to have, a relationship. It is the number one reason for injury to women, at the hands of their husband, boyfriend, partner, or ex-husband. Many of the assaults involve severe aggression, such as punching, kicking, choking, beating, gunshots or knife wounds. Women are more likely to be battered by a known assailant than by all other types of attackers combined. In fact, a husband or boyfriend killed one of every three women murdered in the United States in 2000.

The frequency of this behavior numbs the senses. In many urban areas, domestic violence calls to police are second only to false alarms. And during the weekend, domestic violence may top all emergency calls to the police.

It doesn't just happen in two-parent families; it occurs in any relationship and across all socioeconomic lines. Other incidents involving family violence – child abuse and neglect, child sexual abuse – are extensive and increasing as well. But it doesn't end there. Each year, millions of elderly people are victims of various forms of maltreatment by relatives.

Until recently, the issue of violence against one's mate was cloaked in silence or denial. That's no longer true. Today, more women are willing to report such crimes. These statistics, though disquieting, tell only part of the story. These insidious categories of family violence are still severely underreported.

For the record, not all domestic violence victims are women. As a general rule, men engage in more hostile acts, more severe acts, and multiple aggressive actions against their female partners. With men's greater physical strength, it should not be surprising that these acts usually, but not always, result in quite different outcomes for women than for men. Even the imitators aren't always clearly defined. Surveys show that a nearly equal number of men and women have committed at least one act of aggression against their partner. Yet there is no measurement of actions when they are undertaken by either party in an act of self-defense.

It's easy to imagine that this type of violence has lasting side effects. Female victims have many of the same reactions as casualties from other types of trauma. While under attack, their primary focus is on self-protection and survival. Later, we find that the common responses are shock, denial, withdrawal, confusion and fear. Nearly half of domestic violence-related homicides end with the assailant taking his or her own life.

Those who study the phenomena have discovered that it is not easy for a victim to just walk away. Women worry that calling the police will result in the family being broken up or the man being removed from the home. Many refuse to testify against the alleged abusers because they fear further attacks, or they will be financially unable to live on their own. What makes it all the more complex, is that most domestic violence homicides occur once the victim has already left, or is in the process of leaving.

The root causes run the gamut. Therapists say domestic violence is about power and control. Abusers exert their power over family members to compensate for insecurities or powerlessness elsewhere in their lives. It's called scapegoating. But there is another, more painful, reality. Legal and medical experts have come to identify those accused of family violence as victims of abuse themselves.

What this says is that children born into dysfunctional homes where domestic terrorism reigns are more apt to be abused, neglected, and more socially unstable than those who are not. Statistics reveal that almost two million child abuse reports are filed annually. And more than half of the men who abuse their female partners also abuse their children. Substance abuse – drugs and alcohol – and domestic violence have been identified as prevalent factors in child neglect and abuse cases.

It gets worse. Recurring violence produces violent children. Parent-on-parent hostility and physical and emotional abuse of children have an undeniable role in shaping the future delinquent. A child who witnesses one parent beating the other may do the same thing to his or her mate as an adult. It makes sense then that violent families can produce violent youth, violent communities, and generations of future parents that are equally brutal. Is there any wonder why we have so much chaos in our neighborhoods? The data paint a grotesque picture of a society steeped in violence that is so common and widespread as to be seemingly accepted as the norm. We call ourselves a civilized society, while wallowing in gratuitous assaults on family members. Should we merely label intimate violent behavior as a social abnormality and treat it like we would any other incurable disease?

Why Are Babies Dying?

Across the nation the case is firmly established that urban communities are notorious for their social ills. Not the least of what can be described as "scandalous" behavior is a distinction involving the needless loss of life. Our core cities have become the infant mortality capitals of America. They are graveyards where countless babies are prematurely laid to rest in their first year of life.

We've never seen a more extreme measure of excess death. Statistics from national health agencies tell the story. On a national scale our infant mortality rate of 6.8 deaths per 1,000 live births is more than twice that of other developed countries. Our dismal ranking of 21st among industrialized nations in premature infant deaths has not improved measurably since the 1970s.

It is among the black population that infant mortality leaves its most wretched mark. For black infants, the rate is a staggering 20 per 1,000 births, almost three times the rate for white babies and the national average. To make matters worse, whereas infant mortality in the rest of America has stabilized or, in some cases, modestly declined over time, the death rate for babies born in inner cities has actually risen in the past two decades.

No health predicament is more misunderstood, misinterpreted and lies without immediate solution. What is it that ails black babies? Politicians and public health officials have either been unwilling to give a straight answer, or have been stymied in trying to pinpoint the origins of the problem. What I can't help but wonder though, is whether the fact that most of the mothers and victims are black is a root cause for the reluctance of policymakers to weigh in on the matter?

What we do know is that the dire statistics threaten to unravel the very fabric of life in our cities. To some extent, the burgeoning rate of infant deaths among blacks is associated with inadequate prenatal care and poor nutrition. Black infants are many times more likely to die as a result of maternal pregnancy complications. But for that matter, blacks lead other groups in death rates from 14 of 16 life-threatening ailments. So rather than being a single cause, the origins of high mortality levels are likely complex and deeply rooted in the black culture.

One indisputable contributor is the trend towards black out-of-wedlock births, particularly among teenage mothers, who, because they are single, are most at-risk. For teens, pregnancy poses greater hazards and complications than for women in their 20s. Teenagers' babies, in turn, are in danger of being stillborn or born prematurely. They are also more likely to have low birth weight and physical and mental handicaps.

These teen mothers' youth makes them ill-equipped mentally to understand the biology of reproduction. So they are apt to develop serious nutritionally related medical problems. By some estimates, more than half of all black babies today are born to young, single mothers who also tend to be socially, economically, and psychologically immature. By any reasonable definition, these are kids having kids. To them, motherhood is a lethal flight from reality.

Sadly many of these incompetent mothers inordinately account for and suffer from disproportionate drug abuse, higher incidents of smoking, alcohol use and the use of other chemical substances during pregnancy. They are primary contributors to the phenomena of "crack babies" – crack being a cheap, highly addictive cocaine derivative that is foolishly used in epidemic numbers by young expectant moms – only adding to an already dismal situation.

There's also a relationship to access – or lack thereof – to existing prenatal services. Health officials often have no way to reach young mothers who may never seek treatment, or go to a doctor before delivery. Either through ignorance or neglect, many babies are born with long-term, and often fatal, disabilities that result from their fragile condition.

Poverty may, indeed, play a role in mortality rates, but probably not to the extent social scientists would have us believe. Even among college-educated, middle-class mothers, black infants perish at disparate rates. But even that doesn't explain why one of the very richest black populations of the world suffers from one of the worst infant mortality rates.

I shudder to think that the prevailing hypersensitivity about race would account for the lack of a vigorous investigation of why black babies are dying at genocidal rates.

But let's be real! There's really no mystery to why we have the highest infant mortality of any group. This crisis is easily understood and explainable if we would just look inwardly and would be willing to face what we see. And what we can see is that this perverse state of affairs is best described as dysfunctional or even pathological behavior by young mothers, including those who are neither poor nor poorly educated. It boils down to the choices we make.

What's saddest of all is that most of this dying, mourning and hand-wringing is unnecessary. We are not powerless to deal with this self-inflicted death sentence. Diabolical behavior can change. Saving defenseless babies from preventable death is a test of black America's resolve not to become extinct. Are we up to the challenge?

Communication Breakdown

I was fortunate to grow up in Amarillo, Texas, with a mother, a father, and six other siblings. In retrospect, my parents were powerful transmitters of the values that laid the educational foundation that became the cornerstone of my life. From this union flowed indelible wisdom about fostering a love of learning.

My mom, a homemaker, was a caring and nurturing matriarch. Dad was a strong, authority figure who in the early years toiled as a construction worker. Later he worked for the Atomic Energy Commission. An uncompromising work ethic was bedrock in our home.

My parents constantly stressed that good citizenship and scholastic achievement were a necessity, not an option. I was encouraged to be a professional from the time I entered kindergarten. It was there that the basic lessons of life and learning took root.

Mom and Dad epitomized the idea that parental guidance is essential to helping children act more deliberately and choose more wisely. This mindset enabled me to better cope with issues beyond the home.

It's this mindset, that has been instilled in me for decades, that has me thinking about a recent survey conducted by the Michigan Education Association, the results of which were printed in a recent newspaper article. It appears that while parents and teachers want to see children receive the best education possible, there is a great lack of communication between the two parties as to how that should happen.

In this survey, two-thirds of the teachers polled say they desire parental input; however, a great majority of teachers (84 percent) say they are sometimes frustrated by defensive parents. It's not that the teachers think the parents aren't concerned about their children, in fact, quite the opposite. But these two groups of people who are so key to the educational, spiritual and emotional development of children are sometimes not on the same page when it comes to determining how best to nurture a child's intellectual capabilities.

The disconnect that exists between parental involvement and learning means that not all the failures of education can be heaped on large, metropolitan school systems. Families with wealth and talent have long left the city for the suburbs and a better way of life. Those left behind are overwhelmingly single parents, unemployed or marginally employed and living below the poverty line. Adults in these families typically have less formal education and often find it difficult or impossible to help their children navigate the learning process.

Somehow my parents instinctively knew that arming children with the knowledge and habits needed to enter a demanding world of work was fundamental. An appreciation for knowledge, in their eyes, was the key to self-empowerment. Parents from contemporary families are less likely to teach children at an early age that academic excellence is to be prized. It's no mystery that their offspring tend to enter school lacking home instruction about even the basics of reading or writing.

To this end, parental involvement is key to allowing for the transfer of authority from homes to schools through a partnership in which educators have more freedom to better counsel, guide and motivate students to grow successfully and intellectually. When teachers and parents jointly expect that children will strive toward excellence, students are more likely to do so.

For these and other reasons, a formal education is correctly termed an investment in human capital. True, it requires an outlay of money and time, but I know firsthand that the degree to which a community progresses or atrophies has much to do with the education of its citizens.

Flipping Channels

In recent weeks, Detroit has had much to be proud of. The Pistons defied the odds by winning the NBA championship, and even better, residents defied national media speculation and gathered peacefully to celebrate in Hart Plaza during the parade that drew nearly one million people.

However, Detroit's good news was marred during the 4th of July fireworks celebration when several people were shot by a single gunman as residents flocked downtown to participate in the fun. As crisis hit, a well-prepared emergency response team handled the situation expediently, caringly and competently. Leading this effort was the Chief of Police of the city, Ella Bully-Cummings, who put into perspective correctly that the perpetrator of this crime does not represent the citizenry of Detroit. Her capable professionalism and leadership enlisted the efforts of our community resulting in a suspect being arrested within 24 hours of the incident.

As responsible citizens, we all have a broader issue to examine and attempt to resolve. Why is it that some people are predisposed to violence? What is causing young people to take matters into their own hands and settle a dispute or a grudge by using a gun? Is the onslaught of violence we see everyday on our televisions playing a more insidious role than we realized?

The often contentious debate over whether television violence causes violence in real life among kids may not be far fetched. The evidence is pretty much overwhelming that boys and girls who grow up watching a lot of television violence are more likely to engage in aggressive and violent behavior as they become young adults. Studies confirm that young people who watch more than one hour a day are four times more likely to be violent as young adults than those who watch less.

Based on recent findings, responsible parents should not let their children watch more than one hour of television a day during their formative years. Boys in particular, who are exposed to violent programming, show an increase in the number of assaults, robberies and other hostile acts in later years. For these and other reasons, parents must limit the amount of time their kids spend in front of the tube.

Most children spend many hours a day transfixed on television, video games, computers and other media which offer a range of violent content. In the typical home, the television is on for almost eight hours a day. Youngsters spend more time watching the tube than they do studying for school. And by age 18, the average child has seen 16,000 people get murdered on television. On average, children spend less than one hour a week in meaningful conversations with their parents, but almost 20 hours in front of the television screen. Even children's shows have 20 to 25 violent acts per hour, compared to three to five violent acts an hour in other shows.

Too much of anything is a bad thing. Television is no different. Overdosing on television is an unhealthy outlet for young minds. After seeing their favorite video game or television superhero performing a karate chop, kids are inclined to try it on their friends during playtime.

Why? Children become desensitized to violence. They come to see it as normal, acceptable behavior. Numbed by its intoxicating effect, kids lose the ability to identify with the real hurt, reality and cruelty of pain. Subconsciously many young boys even glorify such violent behavior, which probably explains why they are more affected by it than girls. That's why many kids today seemingly act out without a conscience.

This pipeline that feeds our young with negative behavior needs to be minimized. We need to launch a collective effort to begin a transformational process for children already reeling under the trance of violent programming. Anger management, psychological counseling, and other productive outlets should be accessible options for young minds searching for energy outlets.

Mothers, fathers and caregivers must be more engaging and monitor their children. However, the amount of time children spend alone in front of the tube may not be as important as the act of parents watching television with children and discussing what they see. The harmful effects of watching battering, bloodletting acts, even terrorism, may be reduced if parents are present to explain the difference between fiction and reality.

Better yet, parents should provide developing minds with extracurricular activities like indoor games, outdoor sports and reading. If not glued to the tube, our children can get involved in constructive things that lead to a more promising, richer and fuller life.

Protecting Our Children

It was both sad and painful to read recently that foster care in America is plagued by a shortage of funding, reduced staffing, high case loads and too few high-quality foster homes. This disturbing reminder of a chronic crisis affords all of us a fresh opportunity to commit to the betterment of poorly reared, often maltreated and lowly regarded children who are deprived of permanent homes. The problem is not new.

Thousands of hard-to-place youngsters are known to be shuttled between foster families – sometimes for years or until they "age" out of the system. Most are children of color. Many cry out for loving and nurturing families and there are loving and nurturing families that want to take them in. Yet they are not allowed to. In many instances the decision of where to place these children is often based on outmoded standards of evaluation regarding the qualifications of potential adoptive families.

Race should not be a factor in determining the fitness of foster or adoptive parents. There have been concerns over whether children of one race should be placed with parents of another ethnic background, but what should be of more concern is that because of this debate over interracial adoption, thousands of children are trapped in the maze between foster and permanent homes.

So it defies logic to suggest that for all the problems a black child will face growing up under these conditions, they will be significantly worse off if raised by white parents. Do we continue to allow a disproportionate number of children of color to be represented in the foster care system in the United States? Of all ethnic and racial groups, African-American children are at the highest risk of remaining in foster care for longer periods of time without a plan for permanent placement. It is tragic that too many infants and children are allowed to stay too long with biological parents who can't or won't provide love or care. More often than not, the result is abuse and neglect that is sometimes irreparable, (despite the care and concern of foster parents), leaving the children without a place to call home. It is equally tragic that once these children are removed and parental rights are terminated, we compound their condition with philosophical arguments that fail to resolve the right to a safe home.

Years ago as Commissioner of Human Services for the state where I then lived, I saw firsthand the challenge of helping children cope with the trauma of separation from their home and their biological families. Often, children would get lost in the "system" and never return to the type of caring, stable home that was the American ideal.

As I write this, I am reminded of a painful and ultimately tragic experience that symbolizes exactly what I am talking about. As Commissioner it was often I who had the final say over whether a child should be removed from their biological parents, and one decision I made years ago illustrates the need for adoption reforms.

A local hospital had reported the possible abuse of a three-month-old infant. The report stated that the mother may not have known how to care for the child, who suffered from sleep apnea. Additionally, three other children who suffered from the ailment had died under her care. The child had a state approved foster parent, with whom he could have been placed – yet he wasn't. Since then I have often wondered what alternatives could have been chosen, because having options is the fundamental cornerstone upon which a child's future is based.

Children should be our highest priority. There are a lot of things that we treasure, and among these should be young people. Our collective philosophy must be that the care of these children is a communal function; there should be a family for every child. We should put aside long held perceptions of what the perfect family should look like and think about the long term ramifications for needy children who continue to lack the one thing they truly desire – and what many of us take for granted: a loving home.

Rethink And Restructure

A few days ago I read an excellent article that appeared in a major metropolitan newspaper which outlines some of the problems blighting higher education in our country. It didn't paint a pretty picture.

As we enter into the 21st century, all of our great American institutions, it seems, are under siege. Little seems to work properly anymore. We appear bedeviled by one appalling and apparently irreversible problem after another.

Over the past few months, there has been a dramatic resurgence of interest in education in our country. We have been virtually inundated by a wave of studies and reports placing education at the top of the nation's agenda.

Let's take a sampling of just a few of the problems in higher education outlined in the news article: too many professors teaching leisurely schedules; scant emphasis on quality; classes needed for graduation not being offered; disproportionate use of part-time teachers; tuition cost beyond the purses of many; and business leaders complaining about the lack of basic skills of college graduates. Are any of these on the mend?

We can be sure that the public won't stand for much of what is now being reported. Some citizens are already suggesting that the federal government should get more involved in protecting its investment in higher education, chiefly the money it provides for student loan programs.

According to Joan Stark, professor of education at Syracuse University, "We should expect detailed examination of institutions, refunds to students for inadequate services, warranty periods on purchased education, and even malpractice insurance for faculty."

If we find all this a little disconcerting, then maybe those who serve in higher education leadership roles will be challenged to act. They must first admit that regulation and review have come about largely because of their own short-sighted vision.

Arguably, to some extent, administrators have abdicated responsibility for improving undergraduate education to state legislators and state regulatory agencies, thus issuing a serious, troublesome new set of consequences that permeate education.

The movement toward greater accountability and the assessment of educational outcomes is being discussed by public officials at all levels, often in specific terms, considering such issues as academic governance, curriculum, student retention and satisfaction, and a variety of other matters regarding institutional policy.

As state government boards become substantially more involved, we should remember the adage: "He who has the gold makes the rules."

Higher education's reliance on state governments has ballooned dramatically over the past 20 years with a proportionate level of influence and control.

Hold a casual conversation with any state school board official and the first word that is likely to come out of his mouth is "accountability." Your educational outcomes must be "measurable" he will say.

For all educational institutions, accountability is the new watchword. The state agencies are demanding that those in charge be responsive and responsible in the use of resources being provided.

As I found myself pondering about the state of higher education in this country, I was struck by the notion expressed by a respected author: "Just maybe the prime function of education is not measurable."

Perhaps there's something to this line of thinking. It sounds good, and if nothing else, should we all buy into it, a lot of well-meaning bureaucrats would be searching for another line of work.

In spite of the way I tend to see things, whatever the present shortcomings of our colleges and universities, the recurrent response to setting things right is responsibility, better management systems and doing more with less. It is time to retrench, restructure and soberly rethink in regards to the excesses of the recent past.

Returning America
To Prominence

As we evaluate what it is we want from our schools, we should continue to remember that there's no shortage to excellence. It seems, of late, that there are many discussions on the national level concerning the value of homework.

I can vividly remember being shocked in 1983 by the "rising tide of mediocrity" mention in the report, "A Nation at Risk." Many who read the report were left to feel that students and teachers were in effect, saying to each other, "If you don't bother me, I won't bother you!"

The *Washington Post* finds that much homework in suburban D.C. goes ungraded by teachers and undone by students. Now, I'm not advocating homework for the sake of homework, but what better way to teach independence and individual responsibility? Was Laura Ingalls wasting time doing her "sums" all those nights by an oil lamp, or is something bad happening here? At present our education system in some places is long on theory and short on tradition.

Surely, it's the latter. Hard, purposeful work usually pays dividends in any human experience. When students assume responsibility for acquiring a formal education, they also assume responsibility for activities that create classroom excellence. Yet today, an activity that has been proven over centuries is getting hammered all around.

Unfortunately, some school systems, determined to move students along almost regardless of their performance, won't discipline kids who refuse to do their homework. Will it take another report like the Nation at Risk or Sputnik I before we suddenly decide we needed to be smarter than the Russians to get our attention once again? Russia's sudden sprint ahead in the 1950s in the space race left many Americans concerned about whether we were losing our edge.

For American children, homework is especially important because they go to school fewer days per year than most of their overseas counterparts. A rigorous homework schedule could do much to close that gap while also fostering the good habit of independent study. Show me a kid who understands the significance of homework and then does it, and I will show you a good student.

A thought to keep in mind: students in Great Britain, Ireland, Spain and South Korea, among other nations, do more homework than American students. Further rubbing salt in the wound, education critic Chester Finn estimated, "The average eighth-grader in 1988 spent 211 hours a week on television and five and a half hours on homework."

Watching all that television has familiarized American students with the athletic shoe slogan, "Just Do It." That philosophy, so unwise in many applications, should become the rallying cry of concerned adults regarding homework. Most children are in school about six hours a day and out for 18. Also, a child is in school approximately 175 days of the year and out for 190. Children spend more hours from the time they enter kindergarten until they graduate from high school watching TV than they spend in the classroom.

Finally, while homework is important and should be a part of a child's curricular activities, schools cannot control it alone. Parents must determine a child's schedule once the 3 p.m. school bell rings. There is no substitute for the values nurtured at home.

Welfare System Needs To Find Reform, Lose Misconceptions

Here we go again: Welfare reform has again become a national priority. Almost every president since the passage of the Social Security Act in 1935, which established Aid to Families with Dependent Children (AFDC), has promised some sort of reform of the welfare system.

There is an abundance of books about welfare reform and almost anyone able to mumble a syllable can offer suggestions on the topic.

President Johnson made the war on poverty his major domestic thrust. President Nixon, developed a "Family Assistance Plan" as his domestic policy centerpiece. George McGovern tried to get his campaign moving in 1972 by promising $1,000 a year for everyone. President Ford tried to develop a plan in 1977, and quickly made welfare reform one of his first domestic priorities.

All attempts to reform the welfare system have failed and the problem of welfare reform is still with us. Before I go much further, I speak on this subject with a fair degree of knowledge, experience, and heartfelt concern.

I have dealt with every conceivable issue related to managing a multi-million dollar welfare agency. I have witnessed first hand the day-to-day realities of those living in social isolation struggling to endure the impossible when forced to decide between food, clothing, health care and shelter.

On the other hand, I have seen up close the flagrant and open fraud perpetuated by a sizable percentage of welfare recipients. There is no question that a huge percentage of our tax dollars is lost to those who receive welfare benefits that they have no right to collect. However, it's important to add here that most major welfare and food stamp fraud is accomplished by welfare aid workers, not recipients.

I would be remiss if I did not say I agree with the widely held perception that a sizable number of welfare recipients cheat. I think it would also be fair to say that many rules and regulations encourage people to cheat. Under the current rules there are no incentives for working.

While the great majority of us would agree that welfare reform is in order, I hope that we can also agree that there are some notions about reform that are without foundation. These ill-conceived notions ought to be addressed and corrected.

It's essential that welfare reform not become the politics of provocation and have debate pursue that wrong direction. If our problems with our welfare system -- including decades of half truths, myth making, and downright lies, usually for political end -- go unchallenged, we will surely not achieve our objective.

We can perhaps start with the ridiculous notion that women on welfare keep having babies to get more money. I can't think of anything further from the truth. In fact, when all is said and done, there are no economic rewards for having additional babies on welfare.

"The average per capita amount of a welfare grant decreases as the number of persons in the household increases. Having more babies, in essence, makes a family poorer" according to the *Green Book*, published in 1991 by the U.S. House of Representatives, Committee on Ways and Means. Furthermore, can we imagine any woman seeking to go through the experience of childbirth and taking on the incomparable responsibility of raising a child to increase welfare benefits? Even conservative intellectual Charles Murray supports this point when he states, "It assumes that poor women get out a calculator before getting pregnant."

We should also correct the myth concerning those who receive welfare. While a disproportionate percentage of African-American and other people of color fill our welfare rolls, whites are also part of these rolls at a rapidly increasing rate. In fact, according to an article in *U.S. News and World Report*, April, 1992, "Slightly more than half of all AFDC recipients are white."

The National Urban League asserted the following in its 1988 report: "Among the poorest of the poor-single mothers, living below the poverty line with minor children to support, 39.7 percent of AFDC clients are black, single mothers and 38.1 percent are white women with children. Food stamps recipients are 37.2 percent black and 46.2 percent white. Medicaid benefits are paid to 27.5 percent black recipients compared to 48.5 percent white clients." Again, I share these numbers to demonstrate the importance of not having the welfare reform debate underscored by half truths.

Based on everything I have read or heard, the Clinton administration's welfare reform proposal will likely evolve around the concept of "two years and out" with job training as a key piece. Essentially it will impose a two-year limit on welfare benefits after which recipients would have to enroll in a work program or face financial penalties. The aim here would be to prevent parents from becoming chronic recipients.

In an article in the *Dallas Morning News*, David T. Ellwood, one of three who co-chairs President Clinton's reform task force, acknowledged that many questions remain. "The whole question of how exactly the jobs will work is still very much under discussion," he said.

Many are concerned about what would happen to those suddenly cut off without any kind of cash assistance; however, given that an appalling one in seven children now receives AFDC, it's highly unlikely that President Clinton would approve any type of reform package that would cut people off "cold turkey."

During almost 20 years in public service, the president has clearly demonstrated his unwavering commitment to children. I'm betting the "farm" that the new reform package will include a significant commitment to programs for children.

Our welfare system has helped a lot of people and should continue to do so. However it's time to talk once more about individual responsibility: The social contract between the individual and society. The dependency on some type of welfare assistance has now reached epidemic proportion.

Is it unreasonable to say we should stop handing out checks without expecting anything in return?

Perhaps it is here I should repeat a line from Walter Lippman, who wrote, "There is nothing for nothing anymore."

Can Mr. Clinton deliver to us a welfare system based on integrity and the necessity of work, the need to maintain family stability, and the avoidance of any incentive toward welfare dependency? I think he can.

Giving Is The Greatest Gift Of All

If the man's right, the world just has to be right.

She was a little girl, hardly more than five or six years of age, and her mother was busy at the sewing machine trying to finish a dress. As it sometimes happens, little girls don't take naps and can be something of an annoyance when their mothers need to get some important task finished. The mother had tried almost everything she could think of – games, toys, TV, radio, records. As always, quickly the little girl tired and returned to tug at her mother's dress and fret for something else to do.

Finally the mother had a brilliant idea. She got a magazine and in it found a map – a map of the world.

With her sewing scissors, she quickly cut the map into pieces, jig-saw like, and gave the pieces to her little girl, saying, "Honey, you go in the other room and put the pieces of the map back together again."

The mother congratulated herself for her ingenuity, thinking, "Now, surely, it will take enough time for me to finish the dress."

But to her chagrin, in only a few minutes the little girl called her mother to look – the map of the world was precisely put back together.

Exasperated, the mother said, "Honey, how did you do it so quickly?"

"It was easy, mother," she said. "There was a man on the back of the map. I put him together first. I knew if the man was right – the world would just have to be right!"

Out of the mouths of babes…sometimes…priceless gems of wisdom!

And so, on this Thanksgiving Day let us all remember that we should focus on life. On this special day the virtues of people and human relationships should be hallowed and exalted, made special by generous deeds and innocent enjoyment.

There is nothing more gainful than the glory of giving. We are all challenged to understand the beauty of giving. We receive by giving.

Years ago, as the story goes, told by one of my dearest friends, a minister was preaching in the city of Pittsburgh one Sunday on "the glory of giving." At the end of the service, a businessman friend in the congregation came to him and said, "Minister, I know first-hand what you were talking about tonight." He then recounted the story:

"I was leaving my office and catching a bus to go home. As I was standing there by the corner drug store, I saw a little boy crying as if his heart would break. I went to him and asked what was the matter. And he said, 'Mister, my dad gave me a dollar (and you have to realize how long ago this was) to buy some medicine. When I got here I reached in my pocket and the dollar was gone. And now I'm afraid to go home.' " The businessman tried to comfort the boy. He said, "Just go hone and tell your dad what happened. He'll understand." And the boy cried even louder. "No, you don't know my dad. My dad's been drinking and he will whip me."

Finally, the businessman did what I imagine any of us might have done in a similar situation. He reached into his pocket and pulled out a dollar and said to the little boy, "Sonny, go into the drug store, buy the medicine and go home just like nothing happened."

The little boy took the dollar and ran into the store, purchased the medicine and started to go home. But then, in a moment of magic, he turned to run back to the businessman and caught the man by the coat. Looking up into the rich man's eyes, he said, "Gee mister, I wish you were my dad." And the rich businessman told the minister, "Sir, I didn't go home that night. Not then, at least. I walked, and walked, all over the streets of Pittsburgh, looking for other boys who had lost a dollar and needed a dad."

I am thankful that I understand that one must give love in order to get love.

This Thanksgiving will be of special importance to me because of the opportunity to share it with you.

Together, we will harvest the fruits of our vineyards and our lives; we will ensure that our relationships are well-meaning and never-ending.

As a community of humankind, a community of warmth, we encourage one another to do our utmost to share. Is there a better way to celebrate the harvest of Thanksgiving?

Don't Blame The Children

Every parent hopes that their child will be productive when they grow into adulthood. But success must be ingrained in children at an early age. It's during the first nine or so years of their lives that the majority of their most ardent beliefs on how they should live their lives are formed. The influence a parent can exert during these years is substantial and crucial.

A child who steals and tries to lie his way out of it doesn't necessarily make him or her eternally dishonest or a criminal. It's fair to say that at one time or other during their growing-up years, many children will display behavioral problems. Most outgrow them with the proper stewardship. And if we were honest, most of us would have to admit that as youngsters we were no exceptions to the rule. But when children throw tantrums, fight, kick and are noncompliant beyond the early years, it is indicative of serious problems to come, and parents have a special role to play in taking corrective action to prevent poor behavior from becoming an indelible part of the child's personality.

There's a pretty good bed of research showing that the single most important factor in the development of antisocial behavior in children is the conflicts that occur among their parents. Outside the home, undesirable behavior also becomes a problem for other children, teachers and other authority figures. The result is learning problems, poor academics, isolation, and low self-esteem for the child, and ultimately, communities in crisis.

We tend to define the mission of public education as providing an environment where students will acquire the knowledge, the skills, and personal confidence they need to succeed. Yet our schools teem with a myriad of severe kinds of misbehavior, not the least of which are disobedience, fighting, damaging property, classroom disruption, bullying and harassment. Boys and girls, or a combination of both, routinely intimidate others through foul language, carrying weapons to school, spitting, pushing, shoving, or kicking others.

From the earliest age, many students don't learn at home that to be crude or discourteous is socially unacceptable. So at school they show an attitude of disrespect by yapping when teachers are talking. They broadcast that they are not interested in listening or learning. But such actions also say that they believe their own interests take priority over the concerns of those around them. In other words, our schools contain many selfish, self-centered, undisciplined children who show no respect for those who might want to learn something.

I am reluctant to blame the child. More than anything, family characteristics put children at risk for developing aggressive behavior patterns. Those with parents who are inconsistent with their discipline, physically abusive, highly critical and hostile are more likely to act out both in school and at home.

So it's important not to forget the adage that actions speak louder than words. It still rings true. Parental role modeling helps teach children to be caring and kind. In other words, parents have the power to nurture, guide and instill – to teach kindness, responsibility, and gentleness in an often rude and angry world.

This isn't always easy in a culture where kids are exposed to a barrage of media images – many promoting uncivil or discourteous behavior.

Even though many of us are under constant pressure stemming from our own responsibilities and concerns, we must be vigilant and be on our best behavior around children, and make good manners a part of the daily routine. Teaching children manners gives them character, and character produces lifelong survival skills.

At the end of the day, children who are honored, valued and respected learn to honor, value and respect others. Teaching them about respect is the most important and enduring job we as parents will ever have.

America Was Built On Immigration

I'm going to dare to share with you my thoughts on a very controversial topic – immigration. Why are you here? How did you get here?

I would be less than honest if I did not admit that I have always had a rather jaundiced view of immigration in any form. This is an emotion sprinkled with irony, particularly given the fact that the greatness of this country was, in part, founded on immigration.

The United States has historically welcomed immigrants to a much greater extent than any other modern society. So why do I, at times, tend to feel this way? I'm at a loss to explain. I wonder if it has a little to do with my circumstances growing up as a kid. There were times when relatives would just drop by unannounced just around supper time causing my share from the dinner table to be painfully diminished. However, as our beloved governor has been known to comment, "That dog won't hunt." If there's one thing my parents instilled in me, it was the value of giving and sharing.

Why am I, like so many other Americans in this country, so possessive, so unwilling to share? Only Native Americans can claim true roots in this land -- everyone else has come here from somewhere else. The fact that I'm African American further complicates my feelings on the topic of immigration. My descendants were neither immigrants, refugees, nor exiles. We know that the mass of blacks originally arrived shackled in chains on overcrowded slave ships. But practically nothing is known of the great transfer of Africans in the century after 1660.

But with all of America's social upheavals, it is still the land of opportunity. Listen to the elderly black gentleman who served with distinction in World War II in a segregated unit (a unit proclaimed by General Patton as one of the greatest fighting units in the world).

Recently, while being recognized for outstanding service during WWII, he had this to say when asked if he was embittered by the way black Americans were treated in this country at the time he fought on foreign soil: "I can't worry about all of that now. All I know is that America is the greatest country in the world, and I would do the same thing all over again if I was asked."

I know, like so many black Americans, the passion we have for the only country we have ever known. We are protective, possessive and just a little bit insecure. We are insecure about the thought of losing blue-collar jobs that, for the most part, have been traditionally set aside for blacks.

If there is indeed competition between immigrants, legal or illegal, black Americans are likely to be more affected than any other group — at least that's the perception, real or imagined. Many blacks will tell you that they resent being constantly compared to Asians and other recent arrivals to this country. It's said that Asians in particular have outpaced blacks in terms of academic achievement and economic development. If other minority groups can assimilate and achieve, why can't blacks? This may be the most revealing question of all, and somewhere deeply hidden beneath the rhetoric is the painful truth.

There is one other piece to this immigration thing that is still a little bit puzzling. We seem to be more than biased regarding whom we welcome to this country, which has not done much for my psyche as an African-American. Asylum preferences have a solid justification, given all the regimes in the world, but they have been seriously compromised by our foreign policy biases. When both Nicaragua and El Salvador were in turmoil in the 1980's, Nicaraguans fleeing a communist dictatorship were accepted as refugees. Likewise, Cubans were admitted as refugees from the time Castro took power. Yet no dictator has been bloody enough for Haitian refugees to be welcomed in this country.

My views on immigration are just that – mine. They are views that have been founded on baseless information. When all the facts are understood, America is not being inundated with immigrants. While the volume has risen steadily since the national origins quota system was scrapped in 1965, the rate of immigration relative to the nation's base population is far below historic levels.

The immigration scare does not reflect a genuine problem, it reflects a genuine panic. In fact, recent studies show that the unemployment rate among blacks living in or near immigrant enclaves actually fell.

Let's continue to invite people from around the world to seek refuge in our great country – even people from Haiti.

Mandatory School Attendance Not Always Beneficial

I'm a little concerned that the Michigan Legislature is considering a bill to amend the law that currently mandates school attendance for children between six and 16. The proposal to extend the time students must remain in school to the age of 18 may not be the best solution to quell high dropout rates.

Without question, the high numbers of school dropouts are a national problem. In many urban school districts, close to 50 percent of students who enter high school leave before graduation. Many are permanently disadvantaged in finding jobs and resisting drugs, crime, prison and premature death. Simply put, where you find a high number of dropouts you'll find communities with less than a viable labor force and crime-prone environments. Changing this dynamic is a legitimate concern of policy makers.

Put into perspective, the first compulsory school attendance law was enacted in Massachusetts in 1852. By 1918 every state in the Union had a law requiring children to attend school until they earned a high school diploma or until they reached a certain age – typically 16 or 18. Michigan's law has been on the books since 1871. But I question whether forcing young people to stay in school until they are 18 is good for them, whether they are fully committed to pursuing their education or not. Close examination of the subject exposes the potential for all sorts of unintended consequences.

Educators already know that the problems inherent in hiking the compulsory age to 18 may be worse than the solution. Fourteen states have already done so. But there's nothing to show that an increase in the "school leave" age increases educational outcomes. For the most part, the primary effect of amending current law may be to merely increase the amount of time children who aren't learning spend in school. I'm sure teachers would agree that there should be a place for academically deficient students, but it is not in the traditional classroom.

Nor does such legislation address the root causes of academic failure. When students aren't taught to read in the third and fourth grades, they fall behind and are incapable of catching up. Requiring them to remain in school can only contribute to accelerated mayhem in the classroom. Those who don't want to be there will have two additional years to make trouble, intimidate teachers and students and disrupt the already fragile learning process. Thus the undereducated troublemaker will deprive willing and attentive students of the education they desire and need.

I'm open to counter arguments, but I'm afraid that while a hike in compulsory school attendance to age 18 might seem like a good idea, it may prove to be a disadvantage for students attending schools with fewer resources.

Parental Involvement Is Mandatory

A half-century after the U.S. Supreme Court's landmark Brown v. Board of Education ruling, there remains a widening achievement gap between black and white students. Educators at the state and federal levels tirelessly pursue reforms designed to address this problem. However by making schools their exclusive focus, policymakers are ignoring an area that is vital to priming the learning curve: parental involvement.

What we know to date is that for a variety of reasons, the deck is stacked in favor of students versus others when it comes to educational attainment. Social class, differences in nutrition, socio-economical status, childrearing experiences, housing quality and parental background all play pivotal roles in how well children learn and ultimately succeed. None, though, is likely to supplement a child's advancement more than a supportive family.

The need for parents to be engaged in the life of a school-age youngster is overwhelming. It is, after all, within the family that advantages or disadvantages are conveyed. There's no question that the family is the primary source of "social capital."

Religious training, by example, stresses the importance of living in unison with moral virtues such as honesty, responsibility, and respect for authority. It follows that youngsters grounded in this belief system would be more likely than those who aren't to show respect for parents and teachers and to regard stealing, skipping school and rowdiness as morally unacceptable. This kind of foundation serves as a deterrent to bad behavior since young people in this network are inclined to attract those with common values and interests.

Positive "social capital" in families also lays the foundation for strong relations between children and school. In this framework can be found the seeds for essential social, cultural and economic resources. Parents who benefited from higher education tend to pass on the importance of learning to their children. An abundance of evidence shows that children have better educational outcomes if they come from families where both biological parents are present and work. Thus, it can be argued that the absence of either adult is a "social capital" deficiency in the development of children.

Studies of Asian-American families can help us understand a parenting style that may be conducive for educational achievement. Mothers and fathers within this group seem to have exceptional parent-child communication. They insist on lots of homework and severely restrict television watching. Close and nurturing connections, combined with firm direction appear to make up a workable blueprint across most cultural and ethnic lines. At the same time, we know that growing up in a single parent family is not necessarily detrimental to a child's chances of success.

Unfortunately, too few of our schools have a dedicated group of super-parents who make it their job to show up at parent/teacher conferences, chaperone extra-curricular activities, supervise homework or run off flyers on the copy machine. Most parents in the city's core are working, single parents. Some hold down two jobs just to break even. School officials have vainly tried to increase their involvement. But for too many parents, just getting their children dressed and to school on time is about as far as they can go to be involved.

The sum of these and other factors make it difficult to make the case that parental involvement should be mandatory. How would we ever force parents to participate? But while it is difficult to exact some sort of punishment for parents who opt not to get involved, we need to be relentless in searching for carrot-and-stick approaches in response to a growing sense of urgency about some parents' disconnection to school, children and learning.

The Curse of The Elderly

When we don't understand something, we seldom want to talk or even think about it. It remains an abstraction, an idea with meaning to others but not for us or at least not now. We can get worked up over abstractions, they can motivate us to action or ideology without us ever clearly seeing what it is that we're excited about. Or we can dismiss those things that are not at the moment relevant to us and not bother with understanding or action.

It is harder to do so, though, once the abstraction is made real by a specific example. It is harder to remain a racist when you have friends of another race who are as kind and as decent as you are. It is harder to ignore burglary after your house has been burglarized. It is harder to ignore the needs of children when you are rearing some of your own. You are more aware of the special needs of children and adults when you have a family member or close friend who is handicapped or has special needs that many others don't.

And you are more aware of the almost unfathomable fear of growing old in America when you see the confusion and distress on the face of an old man or old woman about to leave home and familiar life behind, heading for a nursing home. When they lose control of their lives, when they lose their home, and often their spouse and best friend – what is left for them? If their retirement finances are uncertain or inadequate, they look forward to the last years of their lives in poverty.

Until we're there ourselves, aging is for others, for those ahead of us, and we hear about it sometimes but it's easy to ignore. Only when we are forced (as kids) to go visit someone in a nursing home or an old relative in the back room of and old house somewhere do we get a glimpse of what life might be like for us later. Much later we hope so that we can shake off the aura and resume our active life.

But we ignore aging at our own peril. If we hope to live long, we'll be there sooner or later. Preparing for it early can only help. If we're lucky to have steady and gainful employment over our working years, with an adequate and dependable pension for our retirement, and if we have a full Social Security check to anticipate as well, we can look forward to at least a comfortable life if we are healthy. We can likely afford to stay in our home with its familiar and secure surroundings longer with all the benefits the comfort of home may bring.

But if our retirement income is inadequate, or if our pension has gone bankrupt or was heavily invested in Enron stock, or if we have no pension other than Social Security – our life will be very different. I think a definition of fear is having no money when you're old, or having an inadequate amount to live on – those two abstractions that will have a different meaning to each of us someday when we are longing for them.

Very quickly, low-income elderly Americans dependent only on Social Security can expend their meager checks, and soon find themselves having to sell their homes and move into nursing homes after depleting whatever resources they have managed to accumulate. They lose their home, their belongings – the place and things most familiar and meaningful to them at a time when they are again alone. They go to an unfamiliar place we all dread all our lives.

Instead of finding assistance, they often find bureaucracy. There is no friendly society to embrace and lend a helping hand. They are easy victims to scam artists, easy prey to the unscrupulous or the mean. They feel powerless and afraid. Is that what it finally comes to for so many aging Americans? An age group that in some cultures is honored and revered, whose wisdom is still valued, and whose experience is ironically so different in America, the wealthiest nation on earth.

In effect the elderly become dependent wards of the state. They are also sometimes entirely dependent on Social Security. That is why it is vital that its integrity be ensured, and that it not be surrounded by a veil of demagoguery where the beneficiaries are the wealthy and the lucky. A reliable Social Security system is both fiscally and symbolically necessary – the one return even poor people have faith in their lifetime of investment in their government. It represents some semblance that their government cares a little about them at this time need.

This need was never more apparent when I visited a nursing home to see a woman who played such an influential role in the lives of the neighborhood children where I grew up. She was a woman who was not blessed with children, but made it her duty to watch out for the children who surrounded her. She was a woman full of pride and dignity, who unfortunately, had that taken away from her when she was eventually confined to a nursing home.

We must take a more proactive, respectful turn toward the elderly, ensuring them that their golden years are not tarnished by doubt, fear and instability.

Part V
Wit, Words and Wisdom

"Things do not change; we change"

Henry David Thoreau

In the movie Chariots of Fire *an Olympic distance runner asks the question, "From where does the power come to run the race to the end?" His answer: "From within." From where does the strength come for a lifetime journey of meaningful significance? The answer: "from within." The nurturing of these spiritual and transcendent dimensions of life gives us the strength we need for a lifetime journey of successes and failures, of ups and downs. I speak here of the inner impulses of our heart and soul, of the love, hope, faith and joy that make us a leader or a follower, a dreamer or a doer. All of these qualities are crucial when it comes to imparting valuable life lessons.*

Since a major portion of my professional life has been devoted to leadership roles, I want to explore how this inner journey toward meaning and personal fulfillment relates to the development of leaders. Warren Bennis stated, "Leadership is first being, then doing." The leader must make this personal inner journey to build self-awareness of his or her ethical or spiritual center. That is, the core values that will guide daily actions. Through this inner journey, the leader becomes his or her authentic self. With this foundation of being, the leader is better equipped to proceed to the act of doing, to take the outer journey of engagement in organizational and in community life.

In this set of stories or passages, I share what I have learned from my personal journey of being and doing, experiences in providing value-based leadership and observations of others who are making this same journey.

Keeping The Brass Polished

During my professional career as a teacher, counselor, public servant, college chief academic officer, and now as college system chief executive officer, I addressed the staff so many times on the subjects of service, attitudes and responsibilities that I became concerned that I had said everything that needed to be said. I presume preachers share the same experience of feeling they are constantly repeating themselves.

However, there are certain verities of both life, in general, and of public service and higher education, specifically, which require perpetual reiteration. I have always been concerned with the untapped capacities of human beings who only occasionally live up to their own potential. It has always bothered me knowing people with tremendous capabilities that are wasted because they fail to use them.

One of the most popular of my lectures on this subject deals with a comparison of human beings to brass. I cited a visit to the bridge of a naval vessel where the brass fittings gleamed like gold. I asked the captain how often they had to shine the brass. He replied, "Every day. From the minute you stop polishing it, it starts to tarnish, and as beautiful as brass looks when it is glowing, conversely it looks dirty and repulsive when it is dull."

I correlated this description to human beings saying, "None of us is made of gold, we are made of brass." But we can look like gold if we work as hard polishing ourselves as a sailor does polishing the brass of a ship. It is not something we can do only once a week; it is a consistent, daily effort that makes both the brass and our own performances shine. We can all rise to greater heights if we are willing to make the extra effort.

Looking good, as good as we are capable of looking, contributes to success. Employers naturally gravitate to bright looking women and men; those with whom we work daily enjoy associating with those who look bright, just as the ship with shining brass is happier than another whose metal is dull and tarnished.

Scores of times I have been impressed by all levels of people in management, and in the workforce, simply because they appear to be bright and shining. Those who are engaged in shining invariably have shining eyes, a sense of alertness and a quality of responsiveness, working with them is more fun than working within those with dull and negative qualities.

That advice may sound very trite, but it must have made an impression on many hundreds of people, for almost every week, even today, some former associate comes up to me and says, "I am still polishing my brass."

Changes In Health Care Must Be Carefully Charted

Now that President Clinton's proposal for health care reform has been released and the great national conversation is in full throttle, it's time for all of us to seriously consider the kind of health care system we want for our country.

Today's U.S. health care system is in economic trouble because it may be too good. Will people give up their cherished one-on-one, patient/physician relationship? How will we feel about the inconvenience of disrupting established relationships with our local doctor and neighborhood hospital?

We must think carefully as we consider overhauling our health care delivery system. After all, it does deliver the world's best medical care for the vast majority of the people.

As Commissioner of Human Services in another state, with oversight responsibility for Medicaid and Medicare, I had a unique opportunity to observe our health care system up close. I have long been convinced that there are some things about our system that we need to change; however, we should not "throw the baby out with the bath water." We should tackle the problems of healthcare without destroying the very strengths we have worked so hard to build. Let's fix the things that are not working – an example being the abuse of hospital emergency rooms. I have had more than my share of visits to hospital emergency rooms seeking treatment for a family member, but mostly as an observer associated with a job assignment. As a result, I have concluded that the emergency room is often the most misunderstood unit in hospitals.

Just speak to someone who has visited the emergency room as a recipient of services recently and they will surely tell you that they had to wait too long to see a doctor. They are also likely to say that the medical care they received was somehow substandard. Further, if you really want to see a bunch of unhappy campers, take time to drop by a hospital emergency room.

Why are all these people so agitated? Well, for the most part the overwhelming majority of people being treated in emergency rooms don't belong there. Recent surveys have shown that more than half of the patients seen in emergency room departments are not emergency room cases. Patients frequently misuse infections and general aches and pains. Not only is this type of misuse of the emergency room costly for everyone, it may not be the best place for treatment of chronic conditions.

Physicians and emergency staff agree that the emergency room is not the best place for chronic problems. For example, asthma patients and others with chronic illnesses are frequently placed on medications that must be closely monitored and adjusted by a primary physician.

We are told that 37 million Americans are uninsured with no access to health care. What we see in the emergency room is the result of 37 million people without health insurance. So often the working poor represent the largest percentage of those we see in the emergency room. Because they work they don't qualify for Medicaid and they don't have the kinds of jobs that come with health care benefits. Therefore, their access to medical care is often through the emergency room.

It seems to me that a good first step would be to consider increasing the number of publicly funded clinics and insist that non-emergency patients be treated in these clinics. Let the emergency rooms do what they do best – treat emergency room cases only. Most practitioners agree that the problem of emergency room use will not be solved until people have easy access to other doctors and get out of the habit of using the emergency room as a substitute clinic.

We must get a handle on the high cost of health care and strive to assure that every American has access to proper and affordable health care. There is no quick fix and it's essential that we do it right. Finally, it is my belief that the health care system that will work is one that is driven by market forces – and not by government control.

Why Me?

Traveling through our home state of Texas was always a fun experience for me as a youngster. It was "quality family time" before I knew that is what it was called. If nothing else, it was fun. But, it was also a game of social lessons and strategy that I learned, although I didn't realize that I was being taught.

Thinking back, I can recall one day in particular when we stopped at a roadside restaurant. The day was a typical summer day. The sun was hot, the air dry and the day seemed endless. My dad stopped the car just short of the restaurant entrance. He got out of the car, and told me to do the same. Upon exiting the vehicle, he began to instruct me on how to get food for us.

His directions seemed normal and not out of place. Except for one thing: I had to go to the back door. I wasn't quite sure why. I associated the back door with the source of discarding trash, or for criminals looking for an easy out, or the hideaway for lazy workers. Why, for any of those reasons, would I have to go to the back door, I thought.

As always, I listened to my father, and it worked. I didn't realize that there was a method and reason for why it worked. I thought it would have worked regardless of where I asked, or even how.

Yet, it wasn't until years later that I learned of the inability for us as a black family not only to walk to, but least of all, to walk through the front door. That was true of any establishment, especially here in the South. It wasn't until years later that I also learned that father sent me – a child – because he felt as though there might be some sympathy and compassion toward a child, regardless of color.

It wasn't until years later that I learned why it was me that he chose to do for my family what we were otherwise unable to do for ourselves.

One Step At A Time

Millions of us have just begun 2004 together. After all the parties, or at least a long night waiting for the ball to drop, a lot of people think about trying to make themselves better, or happier, by making a few New Year's resolutions. Most people can find several things they would like to change about themselves. A lot of us would like to lose weight, stop smoking, start exercising, eliminate clutter in our homes and offices, become more productive, and this is only the beginning of a long list.

Unfortunately, it's much easier to think of things to improve than to begin the labor of improving them. As a result, most New Year's resolutions are accompanied by nagging feelings of anger at ourselves because we've failed to reach the goals we aspired to. These goals are very difficult to achieve. If achievement was easy, we would have made our changes for the better a long time ago.

However, most people aren't quitters. They continue to think about their goals even if reaching them seems impossible. Most of the people who stop to formulate New Year's resolutions are already doing almost everything they can to make their lives productive and successful, seven days a week. Often the best thing they do for themselves is to drop one or more of the activities they're involved in, or take a vacation, rather than taking on a few more projects.

Those who are caring for small children or aging parents, in addition to a full time job and household chores, rarely enjoy a free hour of time for themselves, much less a real vacation from their responsibilities. A vacation away from home costs money, and many aren't fortunate enough to have a job with a paid vacation. Often, they barely make enough to pay bills when they are working, so taking time off from work seems financially impossible.

Even those who own their own business usually anticipate their income going down when they are not at work. So their vacations have to be very short – an extra hour for an extended lunch, an hour in the library or the gym, a half-hour walk in the park, or even 15 minutes to look through a favorite magazine, listen to a CD, watch a DVD, or finish a game of Free Cell. Fifteen minutes can't possibly compensate for all the stress accumulated in 24 hours, but it's a little break from responsibilities, and hopefully, it will be worth extending to half an hour on the weekend.

Ironically, those who are the busiest are the least likely to feel able to take an hour off, but they are also the most in need of free time. Sometimes their self-esteem depends on their productivity, so cutting back on what they're doing makes them feel inadequate. It's especially hard for them to say "no" to a new project and "yes" to a little free time. And, it's impossible for them to think of a long-range project, for example, taking a class, losing 25 pounds, learning Spanish, or organizing all their files. Such thoughts would cause them to dwell on what they have to give up in terms of time and energy in order to complete just one of those activities.

Instead of looking for an enormous long-range goal, maybe we could learn to break down the steps required to achieve that goal into small goals we could succeed at every day. For example, 30 to 40 minutes of exercise, three times a week, is often recommended as a bare minimum for better fitness. If adding that to a weekly schedule is too much, what about five minutes, three times a week. That's certainly not enough exercise to lose weight or protect the heart, but 20 sit-ups or jumping jacks, or leg stretches will definitely make a difference over a period of time.

If organizing files is the goal, maybe it's a good idea to start with organizing one file a day. Taking a Spanish class requires a lot of time and effort, but learning one new Spanish word a day doesn't take much time at all. Some people like the method of labeling household objects with their Spanish names, so that walking around the kitchen for five minutes is actually a mini-Spanish lesson.

If learning to dance or play the piano or guitar is the goal, start with practicing five minutes a day. If raking the whole yard or planting flowers is the goal, start with one bag of leaves a day, or one or two flowers at a time. If the goal is spending more time with children, or communicating better with teenagers, take one to lunch on Saturday, or just take 30 seconds to give the child a compliment or ask the child's opinion about a movie, sport, current fashion, and the like.

The first step in a New Year's resolution is the hardest and also the most important. The first five minutes of exercising, planting a few flowers, practicing the guitar, learning a new Spanish word, organizing the garage and your files, talking to a child about a movie, or just saying "no" to the extra calories of a soft drink, or candy bar, may seem insignificant, but they represent the beginning of completing a goal. So if we compliment ourselves for starting, and try to focus on the five minutes, or half hour, we've accomplished, maybe it will become pleasant enough to keep going and eventually achieve our New Year's resolutions.

College Leader Finds Brave, Old World

For the first time in my life I felt like a real celebrity, though it took about four days in Beijing for me to realize it. As I walked around people stared at me intently; they would point and gesture with their hands about my size and height. A few came up to have their picture taken with me. One old gentleman walked up and said "I love you" to me in English.

They were fascinated with my white beard and black skin. In some rural areas they had never seen a black person. This attention made me very uncomfortable for the first few days, until I learned their gestures were a compliment. When I finally asked our guide why I commanded such huge attention almost everywhere I went, he said, "Because you're so big."

In China to be big is to be rich. I may have looked big to the Chinese people on the streets, but Beijing looked overwhelmingly huge to me. Located in the northeastern corner of China, it's a city the size of Chicago, but with 12 million people moving about everywhere. The old city is giving way to new buildings in almost any direction you look. Established more than 3,000 years ago, Beijing burned to the ground in 1215, but it has arisen time and again after being overrun by enemies, to become a mixture of the very modern alongside the ancient.

For more than 500 years, the Forbidden City was in fact off limits to nearly everyone. Today, it has the best preserved ancient buildings in China, and they are awe inspiring.

I had the opportunity to visit Beijing University. I looked at books and materials for their courses and talked with groups of students. I learned that the average Chinese family saves 35 percent of its income a year and much of the remainder goes to education. In China, education is taken very seriously. Only about four percent of the population will have access to higher education, and as in many other countries, they have to pass rigorous exams in order to gain entrance to the university. The students are especially good in math and science. Perhaps because of the long influence of Confucius, they think of education and learning as important and they take their studies very seriously. Despite their seriousness, the Beijing University students I met were friendly and curious.

Their educational system is similar to ours with grades K through 12. Not all students finish 12 years of school, however, and the goal is to have everyone finish at least the eighth grade, even though some students have to leave school to work at home on farms. Parents and the extended family support education. I saw grandparents meeting their grandchildren after school and walking them home, and getting involved in their schools and school homework.

At Beijing University I had an English translator, which helped significantly. As might be expected, the language was a barrier at all points. I did manage to learn a couple of phrases and eventually was able to at least say "thank you" and "hello." Being in another county without knowing the language is an effective reminder of the usefulness of learning other languages.

I was surprised about many things that I saw in China, and my surprise is due in part to my ignorance. The country is much more developed than I'd expected. There was far more modern technology than I'd expected, and I was also surprised to learn that they are a society driven by e-mail. I was also surprised to see the ultra-modern airport. The streets and countryside are clean and free of litter. It's almost as if their personal discipline and cleanliness come from a sense of national pride.

Another surprise was the absence of children. To combat the

country's population growth, in 1980 China passed a law limiting families to one child each. As a result, today you rarely see children, or you see only one child at a time. I did see twins once, but it was a strange feeling being in a world where there are so many people, but with the eerie absence of children.

Ironically, for this nation with such a long history, the two-parent family is still the norm. With a very low divorce rate there is family stability, which, in turn, contributes to social and cultural stability.

I can't really describe the feeling of standing on top of the Great Wall of China. History books and pictures and even the Internet cannot prepare you for the feeling of exhilaration and awe of actually being there, of standing where millions of others have toiled, sacrificed their lives, or just stood and gazed in amazement. More than 6,000 kilometers in length, it zigzags its way north of Beijing into the mountains. Part of the wall was built as a defense in the seventh century B.C. It has been said that the wall is visible from the moon.

Something else I was not quite prepared for was some of the food we ate. There was no mistaking the pigeon, as it was cooked and served with its head still on. We were served what was called a "delicacy" which turned out to be an entire pig's head served whole. We had to be shown how to eat it, after we made the decision to do so. We were instructed to pick the meat off with chopsticks and then wrap it in a tortilla-like flexible wrapper, and it was delicious. The Chinese also eat cats and dogs, which are considered delicacies. In all of my travels there I saw only one dog, even though I was consciously looking for them. Vendors on the sidewalks served all kinds of food as in mall areas in America – except we didn't have any idea what the food was, thus requiring us to couple courage with our curiosity. We were advised not to drink the water, and bottled water was provided in hotels and elsewhere. Other drinks, such as Coke, were available.

My most dominant impression of Shanghai is how absolutely crowded it was with bicycles. They are everywhere; by the millions it seems, ridden by old men and women, young men and women, kids, teenagers, businesspersons and housewives. I was amazed at what I saw people carrying on bicycles, including refrigerators. From atop a skyscraper it looked like a stirred-up ant bed.

There are far more bikes than cars, though the number of cars has tripled in the last 10 years. Drivers were crazy – I can't imagine trying to drive there. It looked like mass hysteria in the streets. There are no apparent jaywalking laws or consideration – people walk everywhere, across jam-packed streets in the midst of bicycles and cars, which make their way through hordes of people moving everywhere.

It was crowded like New York City, but with 14 million people in the space of Chicago. I was surprised to discover that at night these millions of people disappeared somewhere; the streets were nearly deserted by evening.

The architecture and engineering required to move that many people is amazing. Shanghai is also an ideal port, sitting at the gateway of the Yangtze River. It is a city that thrived before the Communist takeover but which has suffered neglect ever since.

In Shanghai I was also able to visit Jiatong University. There was no translator there, and no one else spoke English, which seriously limited our communication. I did chat with a man who is chairman of the American Language School there. He provides the more than 400 American university educators there a means of communicating with each other. He also provides information for American teachers and college graduates interested in teaching in China.

As a black American, I was struck by the fact that people of color had their own country. It was theirs, they can point to it with pride, their history goes so far back – how can you not have a sense of pride for that achievement, for sustaining a viable culture and society since many centuries before Christ?

As black people we have not truly made America – or anywhere else – our home. Our legacy in this country is slavery. But this is where we live, where we were born and raised, and we need to make America our home and our history too. We need to integrate ourselves fully into its story, which is also our story.

Seeing so much modernization also reminded me of our great

danger in underestimating the development and progress of other countries, especially those we have labeled "Third World." We don't have a monopoly on modern successes, and traveling to another country and observing it is a useful reminder of discovery for us. After all, we are not much over 200 years old as a nation, while the Chinese have been a successful society for more than 2,000 years. We can learn something from that.

"Please Hold For Further Assistance"

"Thank you for calling the ABC Corp. Please listen carefully as our menu options have changed. If you would like to open a new account, please press 1. If you want to inquire about an existing account, please press 2. If you are in dire need of something, press 3."

The automated telephone system in use today by most large organizations is the most frustrating innovation of all. You must be armed with an unbelievable amount of determination and patience in order to navigate through the many directions, instructions and seemingly endless prompts offered by these mechanisms.

These messages create an initial barrier between the company and the caller, and seem as though they were intentionally designed to be frustrating, to further complicate matters and dissuade callers. If nothing else, they are obviously designed to drive even the most sane to their limits.

"Thank you. If you have had an account with us for less than one year, press 1. If you have been an account holder with us for more than one year press 2."

In anticipation of these automated telephone systems, I usually let my list of "calls to make" to companies or organizations build up so that I can sit down knowing that I will be at the phone, pressing options and on hold for some time. When they reach a certain point, I gather all the papers and information that I need, and arm myself with as much patience as I can muster and head to the phone. My most recent setting included a call to the bank, insurance company and the telephone company. And so it began.

"If you want to access your account, press 1. If you want information from that account, press 2. If you want other information not related to your account, press 3."

Depending on where you call, your may hear music, promotional information for the company, inspirational messages, sales pitches and excuses for being left on hold: "Your call is very important to us. Please remain on the line and our next available representative will be with you shortly." Shortly. Now, there's an exaggeration. Waiting five, then 10 and sometimes even 20 minutes or longer hardly qualifies as "shortly" in my book.

"If you want to check your account balance, please press one. If you want to inquire about a loan, please press two. If you want to add new service to your existing account, press three. To speak to a customer services representative, please press four."

I was beginning to think that speaking with a human was not an option. OK, so I press four. Then, "Thank you. All representatives are busy assisting other callers. Please remain on the line for the next available representative." If you're lucky, you get an estimate of your wait with "your estimated wait time is seven minutes." Try quadrupling that time.

In all, I made six calls and it took me 90 minutes. While companies may be saving money and time by not staffing the phones for immediate answering, they are creating an enormous level of frustration and animosity for the public that have to deal with their mechanical systems. When you make a call to resolve an issue or obtain answers, you want to speak to a person. You want someone who will hear your concerns, and resolve your problems. You want to know that the company that takes your money also has some concern for you otherwise. You spend far much more time waiting than you do actually completing the transaction, much like the wait at the doctor's office.

In all fairness, once I was successful in reaching someone who could deal with the matter at hand, I found them friendly, courteous, competent and helpful in resolving my concerns. It's just unfortunate that it took so much time and so many commercials and sales pitches to reach them."Thank you for calling the ABC Corp. Goodbye."

Detroit's Future: It's Up To Us

As we all know Detroit is suffering from tough times, which has led to much heated and inspired debate, but I implore everyone to just take a deep breath and look at things from a new perspective.

I choose to focus on the potential of Detroit and be optimistic about its future. For if the city is to regain its former luster, all of us must embrace a vision of how great it can be.

Today, I see a city in the midst of a fundamental transition from an economy dominated by and dependent on auto manufacturing to one even more robust and diverse. That evolution includes an economy where a relatively few large companies are the major employers to one with a wide and changing mix of smaller, diversified employers who play a leading role in science and technology. To that end, Detroit has the potential to emerge as one of the real surprises in modern urban America.

Fastest growing in the city of tomorrow would be the service sector where most of the new jobs would be in managerial, professional or technical positions. This environment will provide us the opportunity to become one of the largest research and development centers anywhere. Our colleges, universities and R&D centers are already capable of producing cutting edge research. For sure, the Wayne County Community College District expects to be at the heart of this activity. In partnership with the corporate community and local governments, we can find a role to play in shaping Detroit into a center for software engineering, robotics, artificial intelligence, advanced technology spin-off companies, including biomedicine.

In the medical arena, the city stands on the threshold of being internationally known as a health care, medical research and teaching center. For one, the Detroit Medical Center is one of the top integrated medical systems in America. University, hospital and biomedical research and development projects will have specializations in circulation ailments, respiratory diseases, AIDS, cancer, Alzheimer's, hypertension and cardiovascular disorders.

As we become recognized as an education leader, we will see innovations in Detroit's public schools that serve as prototypes for other districts. Strong community support, parental involvement and development of gifted and science academies will contribute to the district's excellent reputation. Measurable results will drive test scores, lower dropout rates and signal a return of students from charter and private schools.

Because of Detroit's geographic make-up and climate, the city can become known as a four-season recreational center. Spectator sports already thrive year-round. For families, we would offer such amenities as the Detroit Zoo with its natural habitat settings. A strong park system and enhanced riverfront areas with planned activities throughout the year will supply wholesome recreational opportunities. Highlighting the city's turnaround will be a partnership between the city's leadership and business investors that culminates in the virtual rebuilding of both the downtown area and the neighborhoods. The rebirth of communities will be a delight as affordable housing contributes extensively to Detroit's livability status. New housing construction will continue to give families more options and allow them to move into larger homes. A strong neighborhood system will result in lower crime rates.

I am not naive. Detroit's transformational renaissance will not occur overnight. If we pool our collective resources, though, we can become a benchmark for other cities reeling from population and economic decline. Then we can be proud of having lifted ourselves from the rubble higher than almost anyone could have foreseen, and enjoy a quality of life that is among the richest in the nation.

Detroit is a city filled with passion and pride, and the people who call it home wear their emotions on their sleeve. They are committed to the future of all of its citizens, most importantly the children whose future sits on their collective shoulders. At the end of the day, despite all the controversy that swirls around our city, I know that the people who call Detroit home are committed to economic, social, and educational prosperity for all.

Part VI
Cultural Competence and Understanding

"We win half the battle when we make up our minds to take the world as we find it, including the thorns."

Orison S. Marden

We have in our bloodstream the whole of our experiences and the experiences of those who have gone before us. For example, African Americans have the slavery experience deeply ingrained in their psyches. When we read Harriet Beecher Stowe's Uncle Tom's Cabin or Toni Morrison's Beloved, we experience again the terrors of separated families, slave masters and nightriders. On the other hand, when we read Martin Luther King, Jr.'s Letters from a Birmingham Jail, we feel again the courage, spirituality, beauty, and majesty exhibited by those who have led and now lead the long march to equal justice and equal opportunity. We recall the cherished customs, music, arts and rules of conduct that characterized those who came before us. These triumphs, suffering and remembrances are all a part of our heritage and of our culture.

How has culture defined us – and how have we defined culture? Is the discussion about culture a valuable one or is it a concept that has been discussed too much, or perhaps too little?

We can judge that African Americans do have a shared heritage and a shared culture. The same could be stated in varying degrees about all racial, ethnic and national groups.

However, the mobility of our society is fragmenting family units and separating generations. The rituals, celebrations, and customs that once gave family, racial, ethnic, neighborhood and community groups their sense of oneness, identity and collective spirit are at risk of *disappearing as families disperse around the country.*

Countering this trend is the renewed interest in maintaining these cultural connections. Today, America is less likely to be seen as a melting pot, and more likely to be seen as a diverse collection of ethnic, racial and national groups, each with their own identity, language and community. In any case, all of us hunger for a sense of community and connection, and we are innovative in creating new forms of community when the old familiar forms are not accessible any longer. Our experience of national oneness and patriotism in the aftermath of 9/11 also reminds us that there are cultural dimensions to the overall "American" experience.

In this set of stories or passages, I share what I have learned from practical experience about how culture shapes us and how our increasing diversity as a nation impacts our cultural identity. I share as well my reading and personal experiences regarding the past and current triumphs and struggles of African Americans.

Despite Tragedy, Americans Remain Resolute And United

The exact day and time, while now more than a month and a half ago, seems more significant with every passing day. September 11 is forever etched in the minds of every American, for all that it took away and all that it left remaining. For all those who survived, it has been quite a rude awakening. For the families of the thousands who perished, it marks the beginning of life-long grieving and a healing that may never come. The magnitude of this one day of massive destruction and death is unparalleled by Pearl Harbor or Genghis Khan, or even the Crusaders who ravaged and killed all in their path.

This was not just murder of African Americans, Asian Americans or European Americans, Jewish Americans, or Hispanic Americans. This was simply close to 3,000 Americans comprised of all that make this country unique in its composition. They were our neighbors, our family members and our friends. Citizens from more than 80 other countries in the world also perished in this attack.

As we moved from shock and disbelief to anger, we mourned for those lost, as well as for those who remained. We mourn for our loss of loved ones, of our innocence and of freedom as we knew it. We have a new enemy, one that harbors a hate so intense that it is intent on destruction of any and all in its path.

Things will be different now. They must be. We cannot forget, yet we cannot let our fear, anger and memories consume or ruin us. Our reactions are being watched by the world, and will set the stage for our international relationships. While we call for retaliation and the demise of Osama Bin Laden, what would that really mean? Would it yield even more violence by fanatics driven to frenzy by the humbling of their leader? Nothing is easy anymore and so much more stands to be lost.

We are in a real war now, and we are all in this together. What will this do to our nation? Can it unite us, pull us together and end our pettiness and divisive race wars? We are all Americans – black, white, rich, poor, gang members and congressional members – and our enemies have proven that they do not discriminate. Since they hate us all, we no longer enjoy the luxury of hating each other. Someone hates us more.

We can use tragedy to learn something, to grow up a little and to make adjustments regarding how we think, live and treat each other. When we find ourselves getting back to what was normal before September 11, all we need to do is recall the images of burning buildings, or people jumping to their deaths – that are etched in our minds. Suddenly, not much else seems very important anymore.

The whole thing seems unimaginable. Being trapped in a building, knowing that there was no way out, or having to phone family or friends to say, "I love you, and I am about to die."

We find it unimaginable that one, or many, could stoop so low as to celebrate the deaths of innocent victims. We remember those fallen in valiant efforts to save lives – the firemen, the police officers, and the heroic efforts of strangers. I was walking through the parking lot recently and noticed an airplane overhead. I stopped and watched as it disappeared into the clouds, as I stood there cautiously staring upward. Then I walked on in to the building. That is now how we must travel and live our lives – cautiously. We must stop, watch, and then move on. If not, our enemies have won. They have stolen what makes us truly American – our freedom.

We should take this opportunity to rethink our values and adjust our behavior and attitudes. We must rethink and reconsider how we treat each other. We must move forward as we began in the days following the tragedy – as one. For it has now been proven that we may possibly perish the way we should be living – together.

With crisis grows opportunity, say the Chinese. We certainly have a crisis. Let's seize the opportunity to make a difference.

Diversity: The Key To Understanding

On a recent Saturday morning, I was driving around admiring some of the city's historic landmarks when I drove past what appeared to be a miniature golf course. I noticed a man with a leaf blower out cleaning the leaves and overnight debris from the carpets of the miniature greens. No doubt that man starts every workday by air-blowing overnight debris.

I've never worked at a miniature golf course where I have had to blow leaves off the carpet. But I've done other, similar things, depending on the job I had at the time. And as I thought about this leaf blowing, I thought about how so many millions of Americans – men and women, rich and poor, young and old, Gentile and Jew, tall and short – go to work or school every day, to thousands of jobs doing a multitude of different activities.

It doesn't really matter whether we blow leaves or make sausage biscuits, or teach children or haul trash, or repair VCRs, or grow tomatoes, or deliver mail, or sell groceries, or bake donuts, or patrol the streets, or drive a train, or heal the sick, or aid the needy, or govern the land – we all contribute to the common good. Despite the many differences in what we do – the different products we make or services we perform – our common collective efforts make this country and the economy go.

An interview I read not long ago with a human relations manager at a food processing plant recently caught my interest. The plant employs people from 21 different countries. "Too often we think in terms of what America has given these immigrants," she said, "(But) we don't stop to think about what they give us."

She said that by working with people from so many different places, she has learned about their celebrations, mourning rituals, food preferences, and religions. Her last comment in the article expressed perhaps the most important awareness of the customs and experiences of people from diverse backgrounds. "I have learned that our way is not the only way to do things."

We all need to reflect on the idea that there are other legitimate and sometimes even better ways of doing or seeing things, that our way is neither the only, nor always the best, way. It is so easy to assume that the way we do things or the way we see the world, the way we grew up, the time we grew up, the way we think or believe, or feel about so many things or other people, are the right ways to do or think, or believe or feel.

The problem of knowing that we are right is that we see no need to learn anything else, or try something new, or step outside our own boundaries or limitations and look around. We are so afraid of change and of difference, yet both are facts of life. We are also afraid of each other, of those who look, dress, or think differently than we do. Race in this country has been the primary source of division, religion serves that function in other parts of the world, national pride in still others. How can we overcome the inherent loss caused by our singularity of vision, purpose and assembly?

Bottom line, it's our attitude. At some point we decide that we believe that all people are created equal or that they are not. It's really as simple and as complex as that. But that's where it starts.

It's as simple and as complex as overcoming our prejudices, our fears, and our tendency to flock together with others of like mind, or heritage, or attitude, or fears.

If we believe that all men and women are indeed created equal, then that ought to mean something. That belief ought to mean that we have an attitude toward things and people and beliefs and ideas and values that – while we do not necessarily accept, embrace, believe, or even understand other ways of doing things – we at least tolerate and reserve judgment about that which is different about things we don't understand.

Tolerance is our capacity for recognizing, allowing, and respecting the nature, beliefs, or behavior of others, whether agreeing with them or not. Tolerance reflects the attitude that what we know, think, or believe may not be all that can be known, thought, or believed. It does not automatically assume that there is only one way to view or do something.

There are so many ways that we can find to differ. We group ourselves based on our gender, our race or ethnic background, our educational level, our religious preferences, our occupations, our politics, our degree of wealth, our views toward the environment, or football, or government, or abortion, or gun control, or education of our children.

We tend so often to stay within a few small circles of like-thinking people where we are comfortable, where our views are shared by those around us, and where our views and prejudices are reinforced, not challenged. When we limit our world to those who are most like us, we are generally safe and comfortable.

But we also lose out on a great deal. We miss the benefits that can come by knowing and learning about the customs, cultures, beliefs, values, and views of those from different lands or religions, or ethnic backgrounds, or even gender. It is naïve for anyone to believe he or she has the only truth, knows the only way to think, or do, or be.

We have so much to learn from each other.

At What Point Are We Grown Up?

I looked down a row of magazines last week and saw the lead article of one that was about growing up. The idea, "when I grow up," seemed to precede a lot of my thoughts in the past. But I rarely say this anymore since I realize, usually just before the words come out of my mouth, that this idea must no longer apply. At this point in life, in theory, I have already grown up. I have done plenty of the things society would accept as grown up, but in many ways I feel a lot like I did years ago. Assuming I have grown up, I couldn't pinpoint the time when that happened.

As kids, a lot of us read the book or saw the movie *Peter Pan* and learned his message about "Never Never Land," a place where you didn't have to grow up. We spent hours jumping off beds pretending to fly to "Never Never Land," and leave behind our future of adult responsibilities.

Although the idea of freedom from responsibility was enticing, most of us accepted adult roles and grew up. But there seems to be a difference of as much as 15 years between how old we feel and how old we are. A 50-year-old might feel about 35 to 45 most of the time. To feel this way we must have learned some kinds of standards for grownup behavior, some ways we are expected to act in order to measure ourselves.

We agree grownups should take care of themselves and their children and their property, and work and pay their bills. Doing a good job of this takes a lot of time and energy. But in addition, the society we live in makes other demands. Grownups are supposed to be quiet and reserved in their behavior and dress, and maintain the high standards and values of their society. Grownups are supposed to enforce the rules that young people rebel against. Unfortunately grownups also are supposed to pick up the pieces when things go wrong. This attention to responsibility often makes grownups more tired, less tolerant, less likely to be creative or to try something in a new way, and thus less spontaneous.

In addition to feeling stress from their own responsibilities, many grownups are trying very hard to improve things they have little control over, and naturally, they are worried about what could happen if their efforts don't succeed. What happens if their teenage, unmarried daughter does get pregnant, or if their teenage son crashes into another car – and he has been drinking. Worrying is not likely to help the situation, and it can be physically and emotionally draining. It is easy to understand why being a grownup can seem unappealing to younger people. In addition to coping with responsibility and stress, there is the general, more conformist, social attitude toward being a grownup.

Then there is the media promotion of youth. We have much more motivation to be youthful than we have encouragement to grow up. We are supposed to look young and beautiful and sexy, and be young and confident and successful. Better eating and exercise habits have given us better figures and health, so it is easier to look younger and more fit than it was 50 years ago. It would be difficult to change our society's tendency to focus on younger heroes and their successes.

However, there are still some advantages to growing up. For example, grownups have more confidence in their own choices and less concern about peer group approval. The popularity gained in high school from wearing the right clothes or driving the right car is much less important in middle age.

Another advantage to growing up is having years of experience in living, and knowledge to draw upon when making decisions. Most people have endured difficult and unhappy experiences in the process of growing up, and have learned just by living through these situations.

People's personalities, their past experiences and whatever they encounter day-to-day combine to result in some level of growing up. So, a person can be quite grown up in some ways and an absolute child in others. Unfortunately, our society expects grownups to be perfectly mature and still youthful. No wonder we all think growing up is difficult.

It would be more useful if people concentrated on growing up in the ways that are most important, for example, acceptance of responsibility, kindness toward others and placing a high value on life. The outward appearances – hairstyle, clothing, house, car and income – are poor indicators of whether a person is grown up or not; they are just the result of a lifestyle of choice or a higher monthly paycheck.

Tolerance, an open mind to new ideas, and spontaneity are positive qualities we associate with youth. But if grownups could maintain their responsibilities while showing a willingness to try new things and learn about new ideas – even if it requires changing their old opinions – they could enjoy the feeling of youthful freedom many regret having lost over the years.

What Is Our Most Defining Characteristic?

There are some things that I can't know in this lifetime. For example, I can't know – in the sense of understanding gained from first-hand experience from living and feeling – what it's like to be a white person in America.

I can't know what it's like to be a female, either black or white, because I am male. I can't know what it's like to be Muslim, Jewish, or Buddhist because I am a Christian.

I can't even know what it's like to be a youth today, even though I have two teenage children. I remember what it was like for me, in my time and my place, but this is a different time and a different place, and I can only observe.

There are, of course, some things that I do know from personal experience and from living, and in these experiences I find much kinship with others. I know what it's like to be father, and so I feel I share the common experience of fatherhood with other fathers the world over: black or white, rich or poor, Muslim or Jew. We may approach child-rearing differently, through different customs or life experiences, but we have in common the joys and hopes and worries and fears for our children.

I know what it's like to be a husband, and from talking with my friends who are married, I know we share some common experiences of married life that probably cross racial, ethnic and religious lines.

I know what it's like to play sports, and so I share that

background with others who have also played football, basketball and baseball: black or white, Hispanic or Asian, short or tall, Catholic or Jew.

I know what it's like to have faith in God, and I share that joyful experience with many others, regardless of race, gender, denomination, occupation or economic status.

I know what it's like to be a teacher, and I share that experience with many others of all races and religions and both genders.

I know what it's like to be a college administrator.

I also know what it's like to be a black man in America. I share that experience with other black men. Yet not all of our experiences are the same: a boyhood in Amarillo, Texas was quite a different experience, in some ways, from a boyhood in Harlem or Watts, or Detroit.

What is the common, core experience with others that unites us? With whom does it unite us? From whom does it divide and exclude us? Which of the groups where we find ourselves – not by our own choosing (such as race, gender, or height) – are most significant to us, mean the most to us, or define us most?

If I had to choose one group of people based on one of these experiences, with whom would I choose to spend eternity?

Would I choose my race, including both genders, religious and non-religious, and all occupations as the most important criteria? Or my gender? Would I rather be with males, regardless of race or religion, or with Baptists, regardless of race, or college presidents, regardless of race or gender? How about fathers, regardless of race, or husbands, or football players? With whom would I have the most common interest?

We can't ignore the significance of race, gender, ethnic heritage, religious choices, etc. Nor should we. But we should also downplay the absolute and automatic importance attributed to race alone as our main defining characteristic. Doing so limits us all, keeps our circle of friends small and closed.

It may be that a Methodist and a Catholic can indeed enjoy each other's company and yet respect each other's differences. It may be sometimes that a black and white man in Detroit have more in common than two white men from Maine and Arizona, or two black men from Harlem and Amarillo.

So, let's face it. Race alone probably should not be the defining characteristic that determines how we exist throughout our lifetime. We need the enriching gifts of the broad spectrum of culture, religion and resultant thought that exist in this world to complement our very own wonderful contributions. This is needed in order to gain the greatest value from the experience on earth that we call life.

Take Time To Reflect On Triumphs, Struggles Of Black Americans

As the month of February is upon us once again, 30 million black Americans will take time out to reflect upon the history of black Americans throughout society.

During this month, every black American is challenged to peek at the rear view mirror and see and embrace a heritage the world should know about.

When we give appropriate attention to the African-American experience, we ultimately provide one of the cornerstones for a much needed reconstruction of black history.

Gary Nash, in his book *Red, Black and White*, suggests that these three racial groups are inseparably entertwined and together have created what is a uniquely American culture.

To try to define the term American apart from the sum of its cultural and ethnic diversity is to grossly distort history and to deprive all Americans of a rich and varied past.

C. Eric Lincoln put it this way, referring to our past: "Because we have provided our youth with an interpretation of our history which has been highly stylized and selective, we have muddled their perceptions and compromised their preparation for coping with the hard problems of contemporary life. Neither Black Americans nor White Americans have an adequate perception of themselves or of each other."

Black History Month is important to me because like so many other people, I have lived the history. I lived the "separate but equal" experience in the downtown theaters and eating establishments that were off limits to blacks.

I felt my father's pain when he was not allowed to purchase services from gasoline stations, or when we traveled via the back roads on our annual 40-mile pilgrimage to visit aunts, uncles, and cousins. Clearly, the history of blacks in America is essentially the story of the striving of nameless millions who have sought adjustment in a sometimes hostile world. But for me the good stories outweigh the bad.

When all is said and done I know that the black contribution in American history is so rich and varied that attempting to confine the discussion to a brief period during the course of each year defies all that is logical.

As we discuss the many accomplishments of black Americans, we should take care to remember that black history is not separate from American history.

The struggles of black people in America strike at the core of our country's past and present. If nothing else, we have learned that studying the past helps us understand how our common heritage paves the way to an enlightened future.

It is not very difficult to understand why the distant past is used as a way to give blacks a sense of cultural identity. We truly have a history that is captivating and dynamic. Out of the midst of time has come evidence that blacks were prevalent in all of the old world cultures.

Today, historic sites, landmarks, monuments and shrines are scattered throughout this nation to commemorate black men and women as they achieved great things, often against fierce adversity, and overwhelming odds. But they achieved, and we can be proud of them.

When we learn to know our black ancestors and forefathers and learn of their achievements, we will be inspired by their deeds and their acts of courage and dedication.

In recent days, social and political pundits have encouraged a salad bowl approach to American history. While certain parts of that theory have merit, the theory itself fails to acknowledge that there are ways in which we have melded together.

Maybe a more accurate definition of American culture is the great "stew pot." And in this pot there is not quite the distinctiveness of the salad bowl, or the loss of identity found in the melting pot.

Rather, the carrots, potatoes, onions, beans, tomatoes, and beef become something new. They take on the flavors of all the components to make an exciting and flavorful blend.

In a multicultural society, there is a need to celebrate our cultural differences as well as our commonalities as human beings. I'm proud to be American and to acknowledge my entire identity.

Loyalty Is A Motivating Force

I overheard a conversation a while ago between two men. One was about to retire from 20 years of successful military service and starting to think about a second career. He was wondering what he might do, and wanted some advice from the second man (an acquaintance), who is an executive in a large corporation and in a position to speak about corporate hiring practices.

The first man said with the firmest conviction, "When I go to an interview, the most important thing I have to offer is loyalty. I am loyal to my organization and I am dedicated to doing a quality job."

The executive hesitated a few moments before finally answering (I felt bad realizing the peculiar irony of what he was about to say). "Well, you know in this era of corporate restructuring (meaning downsizing), loyalty doesn't necessarily mean the same today as it did when you and I were starting out. There are a lot of loyal employees who have lost their jobs in the last few years. The current trend is to run lean."

There followed a discussion of how the man should position himself in his quest for a second career. I soon moved on without overhearing its conclusion. But the implication of the man's answer, that loyalty is no longer a valued criterion, core value, or expectation between an employer and employee, is troubling.

In my father's generation, by and large if a man or woman went to work regularly, on time, put forth an honest effort and did a good job, then that person could reasonably expect to be employed by the same company through retirement. My father spoke often of being "married to the job" he worked at his last 30 years. He saw improvements in working conditions, hours and wages over the years; the company took care of him, and he, in turn, gave the company his best. He felt secure in his job and he was loyal to his company.

Years ago in college I was sitting in a small diner one day when I heard two men who were standing in line introduce themselves to each other. As is customary when two men meet, inevitably certain phrases come up: "Where do you work?" or "What do you do?"

"I've been with company X for 12 years," the one man said. With the same kind of pride he might have shown if asked about his happy marriage of that long.

"You like it?" the second man asked. "Yeah," the first replied. "The company's been good to me and it's a good place to work. How about you, what do you do?"

"I'm with company Z," he answered, adding, "I'll be there 17 years next month."

I still remember that both men opened their statements by referring first to the company they were "with," and only later talked about what they did there. They made their relationship with their company sound more like a community where they felt they belonged and were valued.

How different the situation is today for so many people who are valued less as human resources and seen more as economic liabilities. A firm I noticed recently advertised that it was now lean and trim, having reduced its "overhead" by laying off several of its employees. The first thing that often happens when a new executive takes over a corporation is widespread layoffs.

When people are considered no more than "overhead" at the place where they work, when their work can be taken from them without warning or regard to their long term success, it frightens them. When they can no longer count on an honest effort and loyalty as providing them the security of a job, it affects how they work and how they relate to the company.

According to Maslow's theory of motivation, physical safety and financial security are next to the most important of all our needs, behind only food, air, water and shelter. When we're insecure about our future, we can't focus on the present, we can't do our best, and we're distracted.

Loyalty is one of those intangible factors, like morale, which is an important but subtle motivating force. When morale is high, the place runs better; people are happier and more productive. People need to like where they work, to feel secure there, to feel their human and economic needs are also recognized as important, to feel they will be treated fairly. In return they need, and are generally willing, to generously bring their labor and talents to their jobs.

In a new book, *The Fourth Turning*, historians Strauss and Howe discuss their idea about four cycles of American history. The fourth turning is a crisis period into which we will move in a decade from now, they say, a time of upheaval and great social change. To help prepare for the time, they suggest that neighbors and public officials will newly prize classic virtues like loyalty, integrity and civic honor.

These virtues are necessary for social civility, cooperation and harmony. If we could rediscover and re-emphasize those values of loyalty, integrity and civic honor now, it could lessen the troubling times that are predicted for later.

Workplace Equality Will Only Come With Change Of Attitude

The Grocery Store

"The letter of the law or the spirit of the law?" – this is the rumination that kept racing through my mind as I sat in a meeting with several of my colleagues discussing a touchy phenomenon called "affirmative action." As the meeting progressed, I was struck by the thought that affirmative action may never work. Attitudes cannot be legislated.

In March 1961, when President John F. Kennedy signed Executive Order 10925, which created the President's Committee on Equal Opportunity, and thereby, brought the phrase "affirmative action" into usage, he apparently had no clue that affirmative action would someday become one of the most controversial and complex issues of our time.

The arguments offered for and against affirmative action have grown almost too frayed. There are days when I fully embrace affirmative action as a remedy to overcome the effects of racial and gender discrimination, and this feeling intensifies when I look around and see the scarcity of minorities and women in key positions in the workforce. For example, at one local university in the area, the ratio of minority faculty has not appreciably changed in 10 years. With nearly a 1,000 faculty members, blacks and Hispanics account for less than five percent, as the number is less than 50.

No one can deny that there are some solid accomplishments that can be attributed to affirmative action. There are times, however, when I think that, maybe the concept of affirmative action is somehow inherently flawed and a recipe for resentment. I say this because of what affirmative action has come to mean in the eyes of many. To a growing number, as observed by columnist William Raspberry, affirmative action means "that efforts to recruit women and minorities lead to lowered standards, reverse discrimination and quotas."

Harvey Mansfield, in his article entitled, "The Underhandedness of Affirmative Action" makes the same point. He says, "As a policy, it cannot claim success because to announce an 'affirmative action' as such is to insult the recipient by implying that he would not have got it on merit." These kinds of arguments, in some ways, are counterproductive because they imply that the people hired under affirmative action programs do not merit their appointments. To suggest that such appointments only come about in order to give less capable individuals a chance is unfair in most circumstances. Many times the applicants are over-qualified, or just as qualified as their counterparts.

Some would suggest that affirmative action means setting qualifications aside. I would hope that it never comes to that. While qualifications have been used in the past as discriminatory devices, setting them aside under the guise of achieving equal opportunity goals is in itself discrimination.

But as a black professional I can see that the "perception" addressed by Raspberry and Mansfield underscores my ambivalence on the question of affirmative action. Nothing much in my experience tells me it works very well. Furthermore, I believe that programs based on racial preferences are fraught with peril and are basically unfair. It may be difficult to construct a precise formula for curing past discrimination without engendering a new kind of discrimination.

During my career, I have held five different positions of authority and, in three out of five, I was the first minority to hold the position. In almost every instance there was a significant number of people who believed that my assignment had more to do with affirmative action and tokenism than competence. Perhaps this sounds like a cliché, but I have talked to many who have had this experience, and the story needs to be told as many times as it has repeated itself.

Colin Powell, who until recently was the nation's highest ranking military officer, could cause some to wonder if his outstanding achievement could have happened without the notion of affirmative action. Clearly this supposition is without foundation for those of us who have seen Colin Powell in action, yet this specter of affirmative action persists.

My ambivalence cannot either confirm or rebut the merits of affirmative action. For those of my readership who ask why, consider this observation from the *New Republic:* "Certainly it is hard to explain why a pre-school educated child of two black professionals should get admission preference to Harvard over, say, the kids of an unemployed white coal miner from a rundown public school in Appalachia."

There was a time in our history when we had to construct tortuous rationalizations for blacks were being forced to take a seat at the back of the bus, and the rationalization for sending blacks to the head of the line is just as tortuous. Both kinds of rationalizations say that sometimes it is all right to treat people of different races in different ways.

No matter how aware I am of the past injustices some minorities – blacks in particular – have been subjected to in this country, I find it difficult to not acknowledge an inequity, even when its purpose is to correct a wrong. Affirmative action is a social issue we must study and learn more about. We must think about it from the other person's point of view; we must listen to those with opinions different from our own; and then we must learn to understand and communicate with one another in the most earnest way.

We should think more in terms of doing what is morally right. We should move beyond the idea of social legislation (Affirmative Action) and think more in terms of diversity and the kind of richness that comes with it.

It is no longer fashionable to talk of moral dilemmas, but affirmative action is not just a legal question and it is not just an employment question – it is a moral question.

The question facing each of us is whether it is time to follow the dictates of our conscience, or to escape personal and moral responsibility by failing to treat every human with equity.

Perhaps we would all be well served to remember that every law has a component that is known as the "letter of the law," and also one known as the "power of the law." Both are sacred. They are not repugnant to each other.

Vignettes On Racial Awareness

There are some images that we all can remember more vividly than others. When I see it in my mind's eye even now, one experience that I had is almost as devastating now as it was many years ago.

My father and I were downtown, going into a grocery store. As I opened the outer door (this was before the era of automation) I saw a person approaching the door from inside the store with an armful of groceries (I was taught to always be polite), so I stood back and held the door open for the lady to exit.

She did not just walk through the door and thank me, as I had expected. No! The lady (who was white) looked at me with such venom, as if I had done something wrong or was a poisonous snake, and began to curse at me. "You little nigger, what are you doing, you don't belong here, just what do you think you're doing? You niggers ought to go home…" and turned and huffed off toward her car.

At that very young and tender age I was terribly surprised and quite frankly, shocked by her reaction, and her attitude toward me. What had I done? I could not think of anything that I had done – I just held the door open for her. What was wrong with that?

Well, now I see that there was absolutely nothing wrong in my holding the door open for her. I would do so today, for any lady, black or white. However today I would be surprised to get the kind of reaction I received when I was a child.

As a child I dissected this scenario, I could not think of anything that I had done wrong to her. Then I turned my focus inward and began to wonder what was wrong with me. I felt awful, and this experience left me terribly confused.

My Mother's Friends

A number of my mother's friends were white. She knew most of them through our church and, as a natural consequence, many of our social interactions involved persons of another race and at the time that seemed quite natural and normal. In fact, one of my best friends at that time was white. We played together at church and at home. We got along like two boys who had found common interests and activities.

One afternoon he told me that he couldn't play with me any longer. I was surprised and asked why. "Because you are a nigger and my father said I couldn't play with niggers," he said.

I really didn't understand – it made no sense to me. I told my father what had happened, and this was one of the very few times that I had seen my father speechless. I think that he was as devastated as I was to have heard such a statement.

I began to develop an awareness of racial attitudes from these and similar incidents.

The Christmas Doll

I remember my sister getting a white doll for Christmas one year. This doll had hair that was blonde and stringy. The texture of the doll's hair was nothing like what I was familiar with. What was this? Was this an aberration of sorts? I looked at the doll and looked at my sister and my mother. This just did not make sense.

Thus began my patchwork entrance into an awareness of race and the destructive victimization that occurs. I was blaming myself for some phantom thing that was eventually labeled "racism." You can only imagine the devastation of such interactions on one's self esteem, be it racism, sexism, or any other "ism." You go through life at one level always aware of race, and in most situations always being in the minority, wondering if the situation is OK. Wondering if the person you are approaching will rebuff or accept you, or just tolerate you. This adds a chilling dimension to stepping out into public areas.

In certain areas, one wonders if he/she will get home safely, without neighborhood boys throwing rocks at the car as you pass. You wonder about the safety of your children, whether some sick individual is having fun at your expense, or worse.

You hope and pray that someday your children won't have to know that fear. I am glad to say that in spite of a nation that still sees the world in terms of race and ethnicity, things do appear to be better.

I don't know if there will ever come a time when I will be able to drive out of my driveway and not be aware that I am a black man, and therefore in one way or another, "different" from a number of people that I will interact with that day.

It was not that long ago that a black man in many parts of the country (not only in the South) could leave home in the morning for work and have a good reason to wonder whether he would get back home that evening without some unusual incident happening to him, or whether his home and family would be intact when he returned.

As we all know, through our experience with others, especially in school as a youngster, a teenager, and as a young adult, people are fragile commodities. It does not take many experiences of flunking a test or a paper to start one believing that he is dumb or incapable. A few dropped footballs in a key game and you begin to wonder if you really do have the potential for that professional football career. An angry or harsh word from a parent or loved one when we have done something that is not acceptable quickly washes over a history of kindness that you have received from that same individual.

No doubt there are many children, black and white, who have played together when they had the opportunity. That is, before an adult made them stop and end their association. The result makes them think that they were different and that there was something wrong with them playing together, and that they would not be able to get along anymore.

I hope that over time this number has decreased for the good of all.

The Scourge Of Hip-Hop

The First Amendment continues to get a workout with the new stain of obscene, offensive recordings by rap groups. It's beyond dispute that much of the genre pushes the limits not only of speech, but also human dignity. However, I'm particularly curious to know why, with the violent anti-woman theme in many of these dehumanizing messages, more women aren't speaking out more forcefully against rap's degrading lyrics.

These lyrics include crude, raw sex and vile and degrading renderings that are laced with brutality of all sorts. Women are sexually denigrated and insidiously depicted as mere sex objects in unrefined and unflattering subservient roles.

A lot of rap music not only glorifies life in America where guns, drugs and sex reign supreme, it may also be a contributor to the turmoil. Popular rap themes are murder, rape, robbery, and dismemberment. They are all easily identifiable with the social problems that disproportionately victimize blacks.

Why should we be concerned? For one, there's a credible body of research validating that excessive media violence is harmful to children, and is a factor in real-life murders, shootings, knifings and rapes. Misogynistic lyrics and the dark underpinnings of the underclass are hardly suitable for young ears. Indeed, there is evidence that young people are more violent as a result of becoming desensitized to what once were cultural taboos. These findings notwithstanding, blacks have been conspicuously silent, as black music, with the advent of "hardcore" rap, has plunged into an open sewer. In turning a deaf ear, we relinquish the responsibilities we have. The taboos being violated are neither cute nor harmless.

CD and video producers, hiding behind the First Amendment to exploit violence, have exhibited no sense of corporate responsibility. Unless ordered to do so by government, the recording industry isn't about to adopt standards in the best interest of the traditional culture's preservation and health. After all, they are motivated by profits.

But should we be outraged that for fun and profit the groups they have under contract offer young people the lowest form of street culture where the greatest tragedy in black America since slavery is played out? Is their work immoral or irresponsible? Should we label the genre's minstrels for what they are: nothing more and nothing less than traitors to black advancement; selling out black aspirations by peddling a caricature of black life unencumbered by values?

These questions are part of the debate about whether rappers set an example we want our children to emulate. Do they also go too far in trashing family and community life? Equally important is the question of whether blacks place too low a priority on obligations of citizenship. There is little argument that this form of music appeals to prurient interests, is patently offensive, and lacks any redeeming values – tests used by courts to determine obscenity. And if we accept this as fact, should our focus shift away from the rights of those who dump their effluent into the cultural mainstream toward those who are adversely affected by it?

The situation is by no means hopeless. If we believe a culture defines itself by the limits it sets for people, we can change the dynamics. I don't mean to suggest we should resurrect restrictive codes. Reasonable alternatives are within reach. Current obscenity laws for example, permit suppression of material if it offends community standards. To take advantage of them calls for raising community ethics so high that the garbage spewing from rap groups is muted by even louder voices affirming high moral standards.

That would be a 180-degree change from the status quo. For the moment, not a peep is heard from black commentators. Nobody is organizing a boycott or picketing radio stations, leveling threats of boycotts against the music industry, or forwarding letters to the editors of newspapers. In fact, there's been a conspicuous silence from rap's critics.

We can't wish back into existence the good old days of strong communities where such conduct wouldn't be allowed to fester. Banning what we think are unspeakable utterances will never make us aesthetically pure. Anyway, that kind of cure could be worse than the disease. But if we accept the lowest forms of human behavior as the price for free expression, we will have gone beyond redemption.

The search for answers must start from the premise that liberty requires freedom of speech. By that, I mean that we must tolerate individuals and groups with which we disagree – no matter how despicable they are – and allow them to freely speak their minds.

If not censorship, what will make a crusade against misogyny in hip hop effective? The answer is simple. If hip-hop is forced to change its messages, the impetus must come from young people themselves. Central to the solution must be young women who are both the subjects and potential targets of the bloodbath. It is in their self-interest that young women in particular revolt against the spread of the moral pollution and exploiting of sex that's headed their way.

If that occurs, expect to see the older set, who have long been unbelieving that young women were not offended by the hateful and demeaning name-calling and representation, join the fray. Maybe then, may older women finally be weary of being called whores, bitches, or worse by their children.

Visit To Cape Town

In Cape Town, South Africa, a chicken sells for $1, but only the rich can afford to buy a chicken. Children pose easily for the camera and ask you for money once you snap their picture. In June 2000, I took my wife, Ola, daughter, Angela, and son, Marcus, to visit South Africa, having heard so much about the effect of the apartheid policy under the white regime – and of the independence, with a coalition of a mixed race government, under the leadership of Nelson Mandela.

For me and my children, this was history in the making. The experience was more than what could be written in a textbook. We arrived in South Africa after what seems like forever in the airplane, a country where there is a distinction between the rich and the poor. It is heart wrenching to see children as young as six years old beg in the streets. They run after passing vehicles begging, "Please give me a dollar. I am hungry and I need money to buy food." These are familiar voices in the streets. They can even follow a vehicle for several hundred yards before giving up their pursuit.

Let me take you back to our arrival and journey into the city from the airport. We drove through some of the most dilapidated shanty towns I have ever seen. Maybe these shanty towns stood out more graphically because it was my first time seeing such a sight. Here in the shanty towns, one comes face-to-face with abject poverty. The houses are made of corrugated tin metal, wood and cloth, and they are clustered together. The bathing facilities are outside and I could not imagine how anyone could use them. The floor area inside the shanty is the bare ground. Angela asked our tour guide, "What happens when it rains?" He tried to hide his feelings and gave an answer that none of us could remember, or we did not quite grasp what he said.

But soon, the shanty towns disappeared as our vehicle sped up the road to downtown Cape Town. Downtown Cape Town is a completely different world. Here is the wealth of South Africa. The stores are filled with goods and the streets are paved and cleaned. It is mind boggling to see the contrasts between the shanty towns and the modern living in the same country within a few miles of each other.

The hotel we stayed in was not a five-star hotel, but it sure was different. The locals who lived in the shanty towns must obtain passes to work in the city. The pass must stipulate their name, job title, and length of time they will remain in the city. The locals cannot remain in the city beyond the time stated on their pass as they will be considered trespassing in their own country.

In Cape Town, which is the southernmost point of Africa, the two oceans, the Atlantic and the Indian, meet. But the blue waters of these two mighty oceans mingle without the disparity that exists between the rich and the poor in the city. "This is awesome," remarked my daughter Angela, as she surveyed the oceans and the slapping of the waves against the shores. My wife, Ola, quietly remarked, "Here we are at the tip of South Africa. It is their winter, but we are wearing light jackets because it is not as cold as the winter we are used to in Detroit."

My family and I fell in love with Africa as we walked on the beaches, but at the same time we could not lose focus of what the locals are going through. It was our first experience in Africa and our first trip to the homeland. We are proud of our ancestry, but there were no kings and queens to meet us. Instead, we came face to face with abject poverty. My children were not prepared for such an experience. They were devastated by the poverty and I could see the tears in their eyes. I guess we don't appreciate how much we have here in the United States until we travel to another country and see what they have.

In his book, *Long Walk to Freedom*, Nelson Mandela writes,

"traveling to Robben Island was like going to another country." History recalls how Nelson Mandela was forced from his home in the winter of 1964 and taken to Robben Island where he spent 18 of his 27 prison years. For me and my family, going to Cape Town and not seeing Robben Island would have amounted to visiting Egypt without seeing the pyramids, or going to London without seeing the Wax Museum.

It was very emotional for me and my family as we took the guided tour to Robben Island, an island which was used to incarcerate Africans for their belief in freedom. As we toured the island, we remembered the names of such activists as Walter Sishulu, Govan Mbeki, Ahmed Kathrada, Robert Sobukwe and Neville Alexander that are buried in the annals of history. Only the name of Nelson Mandela stands out, and his cell is quickly pointed out by tour guides. It was emotional for me and my family to walk the prison halls where Mandela once walked. Now that the place is a tourist site, it holds memories of history and of a people fighting for freedom in their own country.

"I can't believe that they would do this to Mandela," my daughter remarked as she stared as the now empty cell. My son, Marcus, tried to narrate our historic trip in the family video. We left South Africa filled with memories of Africa and how the rich and the poor must live side-by-side, in a country that once recognized "equal but separate development" under its apartheid regimes. The apartheid system no longer exists, but its impact is still being felt in the country.

Trying to elicit a reaction to our historic trip from Angela, Marcus asked, "What did you learn while in South Africa?" "It's late Marcus, ask me tomorrow." In his usual relentless manner, Marcus pursued the question. Fighting back tears, Angela said, "It is an experience that I will never forget." She then fell into a deep sleep. It was our last day in South Africa and we were all anticipating the long flight back home to Detroit.

Smiles Are Universal When Bridging Differences Between Cultures

During this time of difficult circumstances, when we look at each other with "wondering eyes," the simplest of gestures has taken a front-row seat. While I stood in line recently, patiently waiting for the sales trainee to figure out the next step in the sales transaction for the customer ahead of me, I casually turned to survey the customers waiting in line behind me.

I was really wondering if they were being as patient as I was pretending to be, or whether their expressions would give away their true feelings of impatience and irritation. I looked over the group of maybe four or five people, most of whom simply held a blank and rather nonchalant stare on their faces. I was not taking any serious inventory of the people themselves, what they were wearing or even what they were waiting to purchase. In short, I was just looking, if for no other reason, then to kill time.

It was during this visual scan that I caught the eye of a particular gentleman. He appeared to be in his mid to late 40s and of Middle Eastern descent. I looked him in the eye, as he did me. His skin was a dark olive, his hair black, dark and shiny. His eyebrows were full and eyes were bright. In a split second, thousands of thoughts ran through my mind. I wondered where he was from, what he did for a living, if he had a family, and how he lived his days. I wondered, too, about the impact that recent events have had on him and his loved ones, and how he felt about Americans.

But wait; maybe he was an American too. Maybe he was born here as were his children, if he had any. Perhaps he had a typical "American" job, voted in the last presidential election, and owned and proudly flies the American flag. I thought about how others may look at him and place unjust blame on him simply because of his appearance and perceived characteristics. As an African-American man I, too, know what it is like to be looked upon as the responsible party for an entire race, and either blamed or credited for the bad and the good of our people. So was I now guilty of doing what others have long done to me?

I should most certainly hope not. How dare I pigeonhole this man with whom I shared a line. We had some things in common – we were men, we were shopping, and in both seemed tired of the growing wait.

I thought of making a comment. Perhaps something funny that would pierce the silence between us, and help pass the time. Maybe I could comment on the wait but I didn't want to in any way attack the clerk who was so desperately trying to master the sales transaction process and procedures. What could I do to let this man know that I was not harboring mental criticisms of him, that I was not like the others whom I am sure he had encountered? What if he did not speak English, or snubbed me for being who I was or appeared to be? What if he thought my innocent and well-meaning acts were simple disguises for patronizing him?

Oh, this was becoming all too complicated. I simply wanted to make my purchases and leave. Yet my thoughts made me feel almost compelled to say something, do something. But I did not know what. I took a quick inventory of my possibilities – I could speak, say something that I thought was funny, turn around and mind my own business, or continue to look around as though I was in search of something. Instead of any of those things, I stared him straight in the eyes and I smiled. Not a silly smile, or an amusing smile. Just a simple, genuine and heartfelt smile. A smile that I hoped would sincerely communicate my genuine and heartfelt greetings. Nothing serious. just a kind of "hello, hope all is well" kind of smile. In less than an instant I did it. I smiled, and in less time than it took me to get to this point the gentleman smiled back.

Regardless of our differences – however real or perceived – we shared one mutual and universal language – a smile. Perhaps he, too, was thinking the same thing as I.

Slowly, The Times Are Changing

Black Americans can point to pride at the remarkable growth in the number of families that can be called middle class. Unfortunately, the earnings gap between high and low income blacks is also growing. Even worse is the unmistakable link between family breakdown and poverty levels.

Statistics tell the good and the bad news. Incomes of the most affluent black Americans rose significantly between 1967 and 1995, while the earnings of the poorest blacks remained stagnant. Black households experienced an increase in real median income during the mid-1990s. And the 2000 median income of $27,910 was the highest ever recorded for black households.

The primary beneficiaries are families headed by married couples. More than half of them have incomes of $50,000 or more. But it gets better: almost 30 percent of black married couples have incomes of at least $75,000. So, it shouldn't be surprising that most blacks in the labor force have surpassed menial labor and gained entrance to higher status and higher paying jobs. Those with sharply rising incomes tend to be business executives and professionals and come from homes where both spouses work and education levels are high.

Black enterprise is rapidly taking root. According to the latest figures available, there were 780,770 black-owned businesses accounting for 4.2 percent of all firms nationally. This represents a 25 percent increase in black owned firms since 1992 and complements a 32.5

percent increase in gross sales by those firms. A recent article in *Black Enterprise* supports those statistics, stating that African Americans with advanced degrees are nearly twice as likely to go into business for themselves as their white counterparts.

And with the rapid development taking place within Detroit, this only bodes well for the city, as it was founded on the entrepreneurial spirit of people who ran the gamut of social, ethnic and religious backgrounds.

But there's a flip side to every coin. On the downside, nearly 24 percent of black Americans still live below the poverty line, a number that is twice as high as the poverty rates for the total population. It's only a small consolation that this number is less than the 42 percent of blacks who found themselves trapped in poverty in the mid-1960s.

Those most likely to be poor eke out a living in single parent, female-headed households. More than a third of black families headed by unmarried black women are in poverty, compared to eight percent of black married couples with families. Close to 60 percent of single black women have incomes of less than $25,000 and are sentenced by the choices they make to a potential lifetime of disadvantaged circumstances. But it is the fractured family structure that bodes the most ill for the movement of more blacks into the economic mainstream.

As disheartening as these numbers may be for some, the overall picture is one of good news for more black Americans. It shows for the most part that our economic system pays off when families are intact and educational attainment is a priority. And it is a validation that the chance to rise to the limits of one's individual initiatives is still there for those who choose to apply themselves and take advantage of the available opportunities.

The Fog of War

It's been a rough week for America and Americans – soldiers and civilians, at home and abroad. We have been adjusting at home to the stunning revelations of horrible Iraqi prisoner abuse, flooding us like a tidal wave with news we do not want to hear or believe.

And then the latest: I can't find words strong enough to describe the outrage and utter revulsion that overcame me when I heard the news and saw the photo of the premeditated execution of the innocent American man in Iraq. It is still hard for me to speak or even think about it. The deliberate staging for obvious public viewing of such an atrocity in retaliation for other unthinkable travesties incites in me a deep sense of ire and frustration.

We are no longer isolated from war "over there." Between the mass media and proliferating websites, the carnage and destruction, the violence and killing, the growing hatred is in our living rooms instantly. We're all involved now, for better or for worse.

War has always been atrocious, made ever more so with the advent of quick, technologically advanced deadly weapons. However, what makes this war unique is the sense of revenge that has promulgated throughout every aspect of it on both sides of this bloody and tragic saga. This has been a test for us, one that has already been seriously failed by a select group of prison guards whose actions run contrary to the honorable beliefs put forth by the men and women who have served as members of the military.

I would like to think we could rise above it and not think about exacting revenge, but no doubt most of us would feel some kind of satisfaction at seeing those butchers in the video suffer the same fate. We wish they could be caught and brought to justice – as unlikely as that may be, it is our hope. But there's a revenge motive as well: It is unthinkable to let anyone get away with such an atrocity.

However, just as we feel hatred and outrage at the savagery against an innocent American worker, so the Iraqis must also feel a strong hatred and outrage at the hideous abuses of their prisoners by American soldiers. I'm not sure that even a court martial with guilty verdicts would placate them or repair the apparent damage to America's reputation, either real or perceived. At the moment, there seems to be no satisfactory short term solution, no easy and quick way out, no easy way to stop the madness. Both military and political realities make a quick exit unlikely.

For long term solutions, we need to do a couple of important and very difficult things. We must look inward and figure out what we do that creates ill will. Anti-American sentiment didn't start last week with the announcement of the prison abuses. It didn't start when we went to war with Iraq last year, or even the first time, though those wars, and this one in particular, have exacerbated it. What do other cultures see in us that we cannot see in ourselves? We need to find out and examine that closely. The terrorists make it harder for us to focus on our side of the problem, but we still must if we have any hope of repairing the damage.

The other thing we must do, and which we will find equally difficult, is reduce our dependency on oil as a way of lie. We must speed up development and implementation of effective alternative energy sources and not merely dig up the rest of Alaska so we can carry on as normal. As long as we are dependent on overseas sources to sustain our consumerist way of life by supplying us with oil, our economic lifeblood, we are not free.

We're not very good at sacrificing in this country without a crisis occurring – we're growing complacent and selfish. No one wants to voluntarily reduce the amount of energy we consume, the amount of gasoline we use driving here and there. Yet our unwillingness to make changes in how we do things will ensure that we remain dependent on foreign oil. Do we need higher and higher gas prices, or higher fuel taxes, to force us to make sacrifices? In addition to more economic stability as a result of reduced oil dependency comes the environmental benefit of cleaner air.

Must we wait for a major crisis to reflect? Well, a crisis is here. We should seize the moment of this tragedy as an opportunity for serious personal reflection and national soul searching. Is this how we really want to be? Can we do better? What are our national values? How would we like others to see us? How do we get there? How do we start?

None of this is easy but we have to do it, for as Ralph Waldo Emerson once wrote, "The real and lasting victories are those of peace, and not of war."

Vote, Or Else!

It is quite amazing that people will now so publicly – whether shopping, exercising at the gym or fraternizing with co-workers around the water cooler – talk incessantly about the most private details of their lives, and about things we really don't need to know about each other.

However, despite this rash of candid behavior, there is still one topic that seems to instill a sense of dread and fear among a gathering of people, whether they're at a PTA meeting, a Mary Kay party or a morning coffee klatch at the neighborhood diner – a subject that undoubtedly dredges up a variety of feelings such as fear, intimidation, shame or pride.

Voting.

There's nothing that can bring a fun-filled gathering to a standstill like when a person asks in mid-conversation, "So do you plan on voting?" People seem to be able to take in stride being asked which candidate they prefer, but being asked as to whether they will actually take advantage of this privilege is too much too handle.

My grandfather, who lived to a ripe old age, was a staunch Republican – his argument was that President Abraham Lincoln freed the slaves, emancipating them after years of cruel conditions. He taught us from very early on that if you disagreed about something, there was a way to make your voice heard in respectful manner. Now, I try to encourage my children that the ballot is the ultimate tool in deciding their futures.

But this essay isn't an article about choosing one party over the other; it's about how our communities teem with disinterested, disillusioned voters who give new meaning to apathy.

Reasons vary. Many residents are too young to remember the life threatening sacrifices made so we could vote under non-discriminatory circumstances for the candidate of our choice. Some of us take this hard-earned privilege for granted. What's not in dispute is that these votes lost to indifference are the equivalent of a self-imposed disenfranchisement that threatens our future in countless ways.

Today, 40 years after the Civil Rights Act eliminated discriminatory practices that kept minorities from elected office, and made their voices heard at the polls, blacks have made dramatic gains. There are now few, if any legal barriers between minorities and the voting booth. More blacks than ever are registered and our voting potential is potent. However, the size of the eligible voter population by no means guarantees a turnout. In fact, the rising numbers of those who don't vote represent a huge plurality of non-voters. Clearly, we haven't been very successful in getting registered voters to the polls in recent years.

Voter participation in Detroit is down 50 percent since the late 1960s. Sometimes, less than 25 percent of voters determine the structure and representation of the entire city. Many non-voters do not believe that upcoming elections in August and November will make the slightest difference in their lives. And that train of thought is not healthy for a city that has lost a huge chunk of its middle class and desperately needs increased citizen involvement to recover.

Beggars And Vagrants Pose Threat To Civic Security

Street begging can be a frightening experience for everyone who lives, visits and works in downtown Detroit. Pedestrians are constantly harassed, and frequently intimidated by confrontational freeloaders. It's time we tighten up and enforce laws that impose penalties on beggars who engage in offensive, disorderly conduct.

Anyone who spends a lot of time in the central business district can attest to the explosion of vagrants. Their pushy pressure tactics can be ugly, claustrophobic and menacing. Not only do they exhaust our patience, they are difficult to ignore since they tend to get an attitude when anyone has enough nerve to say no to their demands. They don't have a right to our money.

These seemingly destitute souls were once called derelicts or hobos. They were thought of as outcasts who live in virtual isolation in what was known as skid row. However, a more tolerant society has allowed them to drift back into the public domain with more respectability. Today they are referred to, sometimes euphemistically, as the homeless. This is not to say that most street people aren't without a permanent home, but homelessness is the least of their problems.

Their Achilles heel is usually alcohol and drug abuse. Many suffer from serious health problems from years of habitual self-destruction. Most, though, are able-bodied school dropouts and ex-cons that have worn out their welcome and have been rejected by whatever families they had. Some, of course, have a history of mental illness. But rather than work, the majority support addictions from what they can get from you and me.

We try to ignore beggars, to avoid eye contact, or walk around them. But we can't always escape their demands or feelings of guilt when we can't distinguish between those who are truly down and out and those who are the unscrupulous.

As a matter of conscience, we are driven to have sympathy for the less fortunate. But while they may be pathetic, most beggars don't deserve our empathy or our cash. Some have perfected the art of street hustling and take advantage of our sense of compassion. So we tend to overlook the fact that the money we give them is used for neither shelter, nor self improvement.

Other cities have adopted measures that put a damper on behavior that's threatening. In some cases, laws impose criminal penalties, fines and/or jail, for panhandlers that accost, force themselves upon someone or approach or speak in a manner that causes people to be concerned about their safety. New York City cops routinely sweep street people from parks, roust them from sleeping in vacant buildings, and prevent them from loitering in parking lots and other public places.

A better idea than giving beggars cash would be to distribute food coupons from designated restaurants, or direct them to homeless shelters. People would feel better about giving a homeless person a meal ticket if they knew that it is being put to a good purpose.

Getting tough with beggars will likely evoke choruses of both support and condemnation. Homeless advocates will declare that a crackdown is heartless and a retreat from public compassion. And it's fair to argue that police have more important criminals to pursue. But the public's sense of insecurity is not altogether groundless. Beggars cause people to avoid retail and entertainment venues or even the city itself. Our right to enjoy safe streets unmolested is basic. In the end, a downtown where social breakdown and disorder prevail is one where society has neglected to provide a public environment that is friendly and attractive.

Midnight Basketball No Panacea

Every once in a while something happens to remind me how out of touch some of our politicians are. The rationale offered by some for not supporting midnight basketball leagues, which are among the crime prevention programs that will be funded by the new comprehensive crime bill, is beyond my comprehension.

One Senator dismissed the merits of a midnight basketball league saying that kids ought to be home with their families rather than walking the streets looking for a basketball game. Others who oppose midnight basketball see it as just one more unadulterated social program for undeserving inner city kids.

In spite of the pop psychology offered by some of our policy makers, many on the law enforcement side praise "midnight basketball" games for helping keep idle kids off the streets.

Now, back to the senator who says that these kids should be at home with their families, I wonder what planet he's living on. I, too, believe that kids should be home with their families. The problem is, Senator, most of these kids don't have families to go home to. Surely you are aware of the disintegration of the traditional family and how it bears on the frequency of crime?

We all know that the family unit is the primary educative and stabilizing force in a community, and the first line of defense against crime. Thus, those kids that grow up in stable family units where love is tempered with dependable discipline are the kids who are likely to be at home long before the clock strikes midnight. Basketball is not for those kids.

Midnight basketball is for those kids who have either not been taught to be in bed by a reasonable time each night or who rebelled against their parents' orders.

Midnight basketball is for those kids who are fixated with the jungle atmosphere of the streets, where survival at any cost is the name of the game.

Midnight basketball is for those kids who have no father at home to provide guidance and nurturing. And the stories describing the plight of children living in one parent households are only too well known.

We would be myopic to pretend they don't exist. Some of us have been conditioned to believe that if we simply look the other way, they will eventually go away. It's ill-advised for us not to meet this problem head on.

Can we afford to wait to lock those kids up after they have committed serious crimes? I think not.

As recently reported in *Newsweek*, "Lessons in aggression sometimes start as the umbilical cord is cut. By the time they're four, many kids can recite the bloody lexicon of rap; by eight or nine, some psychologists say patterns of violence may be too entrenched to alter."

Let's pause here for reflection! Aren't we coming at this whole thing from the wrong direction? Isn't it a little too late to try to teach a kid to abide by the laws after he has robbed a bank?

We now know that incarceration does not reform; it serves only to harden the young criminal mind. Our juvenile justice system is antiquated, inadequate and no longer able to cope with the crime wrought by kids.

Therefore, I'm willing to support most anything in the name of prevention. I'm encouraged when I see people around the country involved in community-based crime prevention.

Also, we should keep in mind that basketball is just one effort to keep kids out of trouble. Ultimately, the important thing is to find those programs that will effectively deliver the most change the soonest. With a little help, some of these midnight basketball programs will manage to get kids started toward productive lives.

The money earmarked for midnight basketball in the crime bill is miniscule compared to what it will cost to imprison these kids later. Can we agree in this instance that "an ounce of prevention is worth a pound of cure?" Furthermore, I would rather have those kids shooting midnight hoops than committing midnight crime.

Midnight basketball is no panacea. But it certainly is a step in the right direction.

We are increasingly a society that is trying to solve fundamental social problems through stricter punitive controls.

I continue to support swift punishment for serious criminal activity; however, I think the record shows that it is high time to give more than lip service to the idea of prevention.

Banish The Language Of Our Culture?

Black English, also known as Ebonics, is a distinct grammar and structured language spontaneously spoken within some black American communities. Its use is highly controversial with fierce critics and strong proponents. But because of its reputation as the jargon of the ghetto, it needs to be permanently exiled from our vocabulary.

I'm willing to concede that the dialect has a special significance in the evolution of American blacks. The roots of the hybrid dialect date back to the first slaves to arrive on this soil. Black English probably flowered from necessity. Slaves merged the strange words they learned with their familiar West African speech patterns. This code may have been a means to shield their thoughts and actions from slave owners. Over time, the means by which black people adapted to the English language changed significantly.

Black English was thrust into prominence in the 1960s and 1970s, about the same time the black pride movement gained acceptance. Prior to this era, utterances such as "he hungry" and "he be hungry" were erased from the blackboard as intolerable corruptions of speech. In 1973 African American psychologist Robert L. Williams, studying the language development of black children, coined the term "Ebonics," which joined "ebony" and "phonics" and means "black sound." Speech therapists started to officially recognize Black English as a dialect.

Supporters were of the mind that official recognition of the "language of their culture" would allow black children to develop a more positive self-image. Kids shouldn't be made to feel ashamed of how they spoke lest they suffer major setbacks in the learning process. If allowed to read and speak without having their grammar constantly corrected, they might eventually master standard English, proponents said.

Standard English teachers also had to be sensitized to the fact that many youngsters speak a dialect perfectly acceptable in the home and peer environment. Making them feel that careless, lazy pronunciations, incomplete sentences and sloppy language phrases meant they were inferior to those who spoke "White English" was insufferable.

From this cultural symbolism came landmark concessions. In a famous 1979 lawsuit, Federal Judge Charles W. Joiner ordered the Ann Arbor school board to create a special plan to accommodate students whose primary language was Black English.

The Oakland Unified School District created linguistic pandemonium in 1996 when it recommended teaching English as a second language to black children. The contention was that their real native tongue was Ebonics. School officials even talked of seeking federal bilingual education funds for black students for the purpose of modifying the dialect.

The district was mocked internationally. Late night talk show hosts lambasted the idea, depicting black people in caricature, speaking in inarticulate mumbo jumbo. Fortunately the Oakland school board reversed its decision, removing the suggestion that Ebonics was "genetically based," as well as the directive that students be taught in their "primary" language.

Elsewhere, the effort to make black children happy in their classroom hang-ups summoned a linguistic nightmare that threatened to retard the educational progress of black kids for generations to come. Black English, after all, has its stigmas. Not the least of these is that those proficient in it – with the exception of rap artists – are culturally handicapped and at a serious disadvantage in climbing the economic ladder.

A dialect characterized by careless pronunciation and poor grammar is called "bad" English. White employers tend to react negatively to its sound. Some even see it as a lack of intelligence. Most importantly, there is no requirement for the black dialect in the sphere of education, in the business community, in arts and sciences, trades or professions. Many middle-class blacks have consciously submerged all traces of it, lest they be stereotyped as uneducated.

When employers say job applicants lack "basic skills," they mean that black applicants do not understand oral instructions or are unable to determine what customers want. No matter how impressive a job candidate's resume, if he or she speaks in ways that are associated with this speech pattern, interviewers will likely dismiss the applicant as a product of the ghetto and unworthy of anything but a menial job.

Yet many poets, authors, educators and sociologists persist in romanticizing the language of the ghetto. The hip-hop culture has deemed street talk cool. Sloppy diction is captivating. Incomplete sentences are colorful. This black dialect portrays vivid urban lifestyles.

Nothing is romantic, glamorous or enriching about those who are practitioners. Black English proponents need only look at the growing numbers of blacks who belong to a distinct, under-achieving society to see its consequences. Youths who have the weakest communication skills are significantly more likely to be out of school and out of work. Children who use the black vernacular find a fundamental language barrier to entry into the larger society for all of their lives.

Today, it is not exceptional for a black person to speak English as well as anyone else. Most of us know that the ideal speech is the one that is the least shocking to the fewest people. Millions of immigrants who followed us to this country have adjusted and embraced standard English as the bedrock principle mode of communication. Unless we do likewise, we assign generations of black people to helpless floundering among the hopeless underclass, unable to talk their way out of misery.

The Case Against Reparations

There's no question that slaves endured unspeakable injustices over a span of more than two centuries. Our forefathers were abused psychologically, physically, sexually and economically. That said, I'm inclined to believe that the ongoing debate over slave reparations is too frivolous to be taken seriously.

This foray into the impossible began about 40 years ago when groups of African Americans unleashed demands that the U.S. government compensate them for the unpaid slave labor performed by their ancestors. The contention was that most of the woes confronting black Americans today – poverty, family disintegration and a burgeoning incarceration rate – are directly connected to atrocities heaped upon slaves. However, the idea that blacks born today are somehow owed money because of what happened to their dead ancestors, failed to take root until recently. Legal scholars are now trying to determine whether past injustices can be remedied, and if so, in what form.

There are no shortages of proposals. Some include the creation of a $40 billion education fund for "resource enrichment" rather than cash payments. Besides free scholarships to any college, university, trade or vocational school, some advocates want the federal government to give each of us 40 acres of land and a mule, the restitution proposed by two Republican congressmen after the Civil War, as payment for centuries of racism.

The concept is not without precedent. In 1988 the federal government agreed to pay $20,000 each to 60,000 surviving Americans of Japanese ancestry interned on the West Coast during World War II. Back then Congress unjustly uprooted more than 110,000 loyal citizens of Japanese descent and incarcerated them out of fear of sabotage and espionage. The federal government also approved payments for several Native American tribes for land confiscated after 1836.

An argument can be made that it is the responsibility of a truly just and compassionate society to remedy what was unjust, even if there is no legal obligation. On the other end of the debate is the notion that many groups have experienced oppression of one sort or another in this country. If all are deserving, where does the line end? And are we willing to stifle the progress made in race relations until every last incident of human suffering is vindicated?

Inherent in slave reparation demands are myriad, formidable obstacles. Taking into account that almost no records were kept to identify slaves, and the names of slaves were changed several times, what methods would the government use to trace slave ancestry? How would we come up with standards of proof? What traits would qualify an individual for benefits?

Is slave ancestry determined by the color of the skin or the percentage of African blood running through a person's veins, the texture of the hair, and the size of the thighs or other biological and genetic factors? How about extensive knowledge of black history and or proficiency in Black English? If we really wanted to be facetious, we might decree that an innate love of soul food, rhythm and blues and jazz music is a must, as is the ability to dance. Would DNA tests be required? A slave mentality might be an automatic qualifier. Think of the dilemma faced by descendents of Thomas Jefferson.

I suppose if reparation merely involved compensating survivors, it might be feasible. There's precedent here, too. In 1994 the Florida Legislature passed a $2.1 million claims bill to compensate the surviving victims of racist violence that wiped out a black settlement called Rosewood more than 70 years ago. The money went to those who lost property and created scholarships for Rosewood residents' descendants.

Injustice visited upon its black brethren does color America's past. But is America being asked to purge itself of past guilt with another generation's money? Reparations will not be paid by those who inflicted the harm but by all citizens, including other blacks, Asians and Hispanics along with whites.

No one is still alive today that instituted or is responsible for the inhumane treatment slaves endured. Thousands, perhaps millions of present-day white Americans are descended from immigrants who didn't come to this country until after slavery had ended. So it is fool hardy for reparationists to hold all of America accountable for the forced servitude that took place at the hands of white slave owners who are deceased. To try and force-feed payment for past wrongs can only deepen America's racial divide.

Then consider that slavery would have been all but impossible without the help of Africans. Since they profitably sold their fellow blacks into bondage, should African countries be required to pay reparations too?

Not to be taken lightly is the fact that 360,000 Union soldiers died in the Civil War, which ultimately led to the liberation of slaves. Descendents of the war dead may feel they've already made a major contribution to the advancement of freedom for ex-slaves. Are the families of Union soldiers who died for the cause also deserving?

The last desperate argument for reparations is that blacks today have lower income and status than whites due to slavery's legacy. Do they really believe reparations will repair social, economic, and political gaps that engulf black communities through drug abuse, illegitimacy, crime and high rates of HIV infection?

Anyway, successful slavery suits against the government are probably remote. In 1995, the 9th U.S. Circuit Court of Appeals dismissed a $100-million reparations case after finding that plaintiffs had no legal basis.

So let's end the charade.

Guns Are Merely Weapons Of Choice For The Violent

There's no pride in the fact that during my time gun violence became an American epidemic without parallel among other industrialized nations of the world. I've also heard a lot of talk and pointed debate about how gun control legislation would bring about a major, and needed, interruption, to the slaughter. And I'd like to be as optimistic as I can.

But I'm not.

The rising level of violence in our communities yields an alarming casualty toll comparable to a sizeable war. During every 100 hours on the streets of America, more young men are killed than in 100 hours of ground fighting in any war zone where we're involved. Homicide is the second leading cause of death among all Americans between the ages of 15 and 34.

Gun violence takes its most critical toll among black men. With those ages 15 to 34, guns figure in almost 90 percent of all homicide cases. The firearm death rates for white and black male teenagers exceed the mortality rate from all natural causes of death. Although ripped apart by a culture of violence that is often random, I've often wondered why blacks have rarely exhibited the degree of support for stricter gun control laws the crisis would seem to warrant. Perhaps it's due to a general consensus that weapons controls miss the mark even in the face of unprecedented rates of murder.

I've also come to know that the war zone is not always in the streets. To a large extent, we've allowed our attitudes to be conditioned by misconceptions and misinformation about the protective value of having guns in the home. It's no secret that most blacks are killed at the hands of someone they know, as the result of an argument, and with a handgun that was conceivably bought to protect them from home invaders. Rarely are guns kept in the home used to kill someone on the commission of breaking in. Banning all weapons might prevent us from having ready access to the means to kill our own. But since it's also unlikely that guns would be taken out of the hands of criminals, we would become even more vulnerable to those we fear the most.

Even where strict gun laws exist, I've seen little evidence that they actually improve public safety. Washington, D.C. for example, has one of the toughest gun laws found anywhere – and one of the highest murder rates in the nation. This would appear to make the case that gun laws have no effect on crime.

That's why, I suppose, many gun control advocates have called for uniform federal laws that have application across state lines. By contrast, the National Rifle Association (NRA) says any gun control legislation passed today will lead to tougher restrictions on handgun ownership tomorrow. And, says the NRA, the ultimate goal of tenacious gun control advocates is to completely disarm the public and ban the purchase of all guns.

To help fortify their case, gun critics are leaning on both the court of law and the court of public opinion. The latest claim is that the most dangerous felons buy their firearms from licensed dealers or through other legitimate means. More than 30 lawsuits have been filed against the gun industry in an attempt to hold manufacturers accountable for what critics say is a failure or refusal to make safer guns and creating a wall of "deniability" by not monitoring the downstream path of their product. The litigation seeks to recoup from manufacturers hundreds of millions of dollars that local governments have spent in dealing with gun violence.

In retaliation, the gun lobby introduced legislation in almost every state to shield the firearm industry from city, county and even individual lawsuits. If passed, these laws would essentially place the civil justice system off limits to victims of gun violence and protect the gun industry.

Meanwhile, the gun lobby is reeling from several recent setbacks. In a Louisiana case, the U.S. Supreme Court refused to be drawn into a dispute over whether cities can sue gun manufacturers over crime costs.

New Orleans was the first city to file a lawsuit. Alleged was "willful negligence" in not stopping gun sales where buyers act as front men for felons. When the Louisiana Legislature subsequently enacted a law retroactively banning such suits, a district judge in Louisiana ruled it unconstitutional, but the state Supreme Court disagreed, prompting the appeal to the high court. The U.S. Supreme Court declined without comment to review the Louisiana Supreme Court ruling that upheld the state's prohibition. It wasn't the last time a court would render a decision in favor of gun manufacturers.

Public opinion is split over whether manufacturers should be held responsible for the alleged misuse of gun products. One study revealed that more than half of Americans oppose government lawsuits brought against gun manufacturers. The participants believe that the suits were poor use of taxpayer money.

And poll after poll shows that a majority of Americans favor tougher restrictions on guns, although the issue isn't a major priority among voters. In another poll where 67 percent of Americans supported stricter gun control laws, when asked in the same poll which issues would be "very important" or "somewhat important" to their votes, gun control placed third behind protecting Social Security and providing prescription drug benefits.

At the end of the day, I conclude that some control on weapons of urban destruction is necessary. We owe it to ourselves to more closely examine the restrictions on the tools of crime. But we should not lose sight of the fact that guns are merely the instruments, not the perpetrators of the senseless murders ripping life from our young and our neighborhoods. That's why it ultimately makes more sense to focus on caging the violent criminal among us – predators that we continue to breed.

Hope For A Color Blind Society May Be Dwindling

It has been almost three decades since I finished high school and left my beloved Texas panhandle hometown to make my mark in life. Things, I thought, could not have been more perfect.

It was the 1960s, a period that saw the rise of a new spirituality supportive of a fresh commitment to social concerns. Even then I had an unusual interest in race relations, which is fascinating since I can probably count on one hand the number of white people that I had more than a passing exchange with before finishing high school.

Change had come to America. It was a time when this country was just crossing the threshold into desegregation. Racial boundaries were constantly shifting. One visible measure of progress was the number of black faces that appeared on television. My graduating class of 1967 represented the last segregated classroom in Amarillo, Texas. Most of us graduating seniors were convinced that we had seen the last vestiges of segregation and discrimination. After all, the courts had ordered as much.

Change had come. Laws were passed. Programs were started. Poverty was reduced. Opportunities opened.

Even with all that, we were not a perfect country, and the war in Vietnam was a constant reminder of that fact. However, overall we were doing a lot of things right. Families were close knit. Neighbors respected neighbors. And even with all the social strife, things were looking up.

As we enter the mid 1990s, however, I don't hear or see much optimism anymore. It appears that far too many among us are becoming bitter, frustrated and confused.

We are becoming a society of contradiction, achieving great things while at the same time, torn apart by social economic and political struggles.

Norman Vincent Peale, the great American preacher, said not too many years ago, "America has become so tense and nervous that no one will fall asleep in church." I suppose the two things that have troubled me most over the past few years fall under the rubric of race relations and the lack of discipline some parents are providing for our youth.

My first concern was borne out when I spoke briefly with an 82-year-old black man who is tremendously respected by all who have come in contact with him. During our brief conversation, he shared with me his concern for the dramatic deterioration of race relations in this country. "I don't think I can remember things being worse," he stated in a cracking and unsettling voice.

If evidence is needed to support the elderly man's observation, take note of the recent survey that clearly suggests that blacks and whites are polarized on more than a few significant issues, with the O.J. Simpson case coming immediately to mind.

Despite the often-proclaimed view that we are finally a color blind society, nothing may be further from the truth. Listen carefully and you will hear a new kind of bitterness spurred by a sharp increase in tension. There is a rising sense of insecurity as many of us struggle to make some sense of things. It's like the question asked in the *Spoon River Anthology:* "What is this I hear of sorrow and weariness, anger, discontent and drooping hopes?"

When I think of families, I think it's fair to say that for as long as I can remember I have had a special place in my heart for the growth and development of children. It seems that during the 27 years since I left high school, our country has undergone a disturbing transformation particularly related to parent and child relationships.

Many of you have read recently about the lady in Georgia who slapped her 9-year-old son in a supermarket for what the little boy himself described as "being bratty." A store employee called the authorities and the lady was jerked away in shackles like a common criminal and charged with felony cruelty to a child. Her bail bond was set at some ridiculously high amount, and she could theoretically be sentenced to up to 20 years in the slammer.

I don't advocate that hitting children is the answer to behavioral problems, but how many among us believe (if the information reported to us is correct) that this lady should go to jail?

I wonder how many from my generation would have parents with criminal records for child abuse if they had been hauled off to jail for similar disciplinary actions. Not many I submit. As one columnist observed, "If society can't encourage a reasonable peaceful approach to child discipline without throwing parents in jail for a cuff in the face, we might as well turn over the keys to our houses and cars when our kids reach adolescence and crawl off to a retirement home."

This is a classic case of the pendulum swinging so far it's about to tip over the clock. In our zeal to protect abused and neglected children, we've lost perspective and created a system weighted in favor of the anonymous accuser.

What is needed is just a little common judgment. We don't need a myopic inability to see inappropriate behavior and stupidities that abound, we need a sense of proportion – a balancing of good about the way we do things in this country against what is bad.

When I look back on Amarillo and my graduating class of '67, I sometimes wish we could recapture the hope and promise, the buoyancy and exuberance that engulfed us. Somewhere along the way we have become a little confused.

Saving The Jewel

A recent visit to the Charles H. Wright Museum of African American History sparked my interest in its future. In addition to the many places of beauty and awe, I observed some of the people there. Attendees represented all socio-economic and age groups, but it was also a day when some school children were attending as part of a class trip.

My attention was drawn especially to the young as their eyes seemed attracted to the historic pictures and artifacts. The adolescents' behavior covered a range of emotions. They giggled and mocked. They wept and gestured in anger. Others stood in silence, some with tears of emotion as they could imagine the sorrow of hardship depicted in the displays. Their eyes looked around, in wonder and disbelief, at the disparate images and displays as if what they saw was unreal as scenes in a foreign movie.

How much could they comprehend from the symbols and messages? How much of what they saw was new to them?

I was struck on many levels as I walked around and looked at the magnificent artifacts and reminders of our history. We came against our will from a life of freedom to a life of servitude. Yet from these bonds of slavery and despite lingering hardship, when set free we found spirit and hope, and have made our way.

Our story is unique, and the black story in America is told in remarkable detail and compassion in one of the finest museums in America. The Wright Museum tells our story, shows our culture in a wide and compelling variety of displays that engage all of its visitors. The museum ranks as the largest facility of its kind in the world. It is a true jewel in the City of Detroit, yet we don't act like it.

The original, makeshift museum had difficulty attracting sponsors and patrons in a majority black city. Even after the new museum was built with substantial help from city government, support from the populace remained lacking. Attendance declined sharply.

Why?

Are we that indifferent to our past, our culture, our heritage? Do we not care enough about our story to keep it alive? Have we forgotten that our historical collections are cherished assets that enrich our lives?

Far too many of us, young and old, black as well as white, believe that black history starts in America. Thus our image of ourselves starts in bondage, brought in chains to a foreign land. Someone once said that self esteem was the greatest discovery of the 20th century – how true! If learning starts with ourselves, we must be continuously on guard in our actions and thoughts as we consider the stories our children are told every day. We are the keepers of the future, which lies in the hearts and mind of the youngsters who are so vulnerable to the multi-dimensional imagery that surrounds them, both negative and positive.

The Wright Museum shows us in rich detail the rest of who we are. How important is the Wright Museum? Need I say more?

We have overcome so much. Our history in America is that of struggle and accomplishment.

A century ago in 1903, Edward Blyden wrote, "Every race has a soul and the soul of that race finds expression in its institutions and to kill those institutions is to kill the soul…No people can profit or be helped under institutions which are not the outcome of their own character."

We have memorials to the victims of the Holocaust. Our only hope of preventing another is to be forewarned by the past. We build memorials to our veterans and war heroes, to help us remember their important story. We build cowboy museums and car museums and sports museums and natural history museums and Native American museums, all to help us about, understand and remember.

The Wright Museum is an outstanding memorial to our rich and diverse history. The postings of slave trade, memoirs and diaries, and artifacts strategically displayed throughout the museum seem to be saying to African Americans: Remember that history forgets first those who forget themselves.

We must tell what happened. The annals of culture and history will define our story, but we must be the storyteller.

Saving the museum is our collective responsibility. We all profit by it, and we all should help save and revive it. If we can't show enough interest and support to make it viable and meaningful for us, why should we expect others to do so?

The museum is ours. It speaks to us, about us, and for us – unlike any other memorial or museum in the country. It helps others learn about us. But it also helps us learn about us, too.

Let's all do our part and help save the museum.

A Final Word

"True heroism is remarkably sober and very undramatic. It is not the urge to surpass all others at whatever cost, but the urge to serve others at whatever cost..."

Author Unknown

J ust as a journey of 1,000 miles is undertaken one step at a time, so is the lifelong journey of learning, achievement, setbacks, and healings taken one step at a time. At each step, the encouragement and mentoring of others further along in the journey can be a source of inspiration and support. An old Oriental axiom says that "when the learner is ready, the teacher will come." At each step, the readiness of the learner to take the next step of self-discovery makes him receptive to the teachings of a mentor suited to the needs of the moment. Different mentors will appear at different stages of a person's growth and development. Some of these mentors will appear in educational settings, but many will also appear in family, church, business and community settings.

As we consider the role of mentoring in a person's journey of self-discovery and enlightenment, we realize that a wider definition of education has emerged. A person's education is not limited to the classroom and laboratory, but rather is the product of interactions and experiences in all spheres of life. The role of a mentor who imparts wisdom, praise, nurturing and just plain common sense to the learner can be as important as the role of the classroom teacher. Most of us can recall mentors who challenged us and supported us, at the same time creating cherished memories.

A theme mentioned a number of times in these essays is communication. I cannot emphasize enough the vital role interpersonal *communication plays in our personal growth and in the nurturing of others. I have stressed the importance of not only verbal and written communication, but also nonverbal cues. It always amazes me to realize how much nonverbal cues impact my perceptive consciousness, and I know that this is true for others. Those of us who may serve as mentors must realize that all forms of communication make an indelible mark that is permanently etched in another's psyche. We must pay attention to whether that mark will be one of discouragement or encouragement, hurt or healing. I must emphasize again in this regard the importance of personal ethics. It is a universal truth that we communicate more by personal example than by our words. Our actions based on a positive code of ethics can influence others more than any words we may utter.*

The path to enlightenment is through education and it shouldn't be taken lightly. However, one must also remember that the kind of education a person offers (and receives) is important. Academic content, of course, is crucial to building awareness, but so is praise, nurturing, and the development of critical thinking skills, all of which lead to self discovery. Such praise and nurturing should be generously available both in and outside the classroom.

Our lifetime journey is made up of numerous turns and twists. Sometimes that journey is a smooth one, filled with joy, excitement and promise. At other times that journey is filled with pain, recrimination and regret. Those who experience a successful journey have learned how to take the bad with the good. They have an optimistic, hopeful outlook. They do not look at life through rose-colored glasses in a Pollyanna sort of way. They know what their objectives in life are; they look in a clear-eyed way at the obstacles that stand in the way, and then they gather their inner spiritual resources, their talents and the support and mentoring of others needed to take the next step in the journey. Lessons learned during the good times and the bad times are added to their knowledge base as they move forward.

Ernie Boyer stated that "It is in the authentic merging of heritage and vision that an organization finds its true pulse." I think that the same could be said for our lives as individuals. We are truly the product of all the family and societal history that has preceded us, and building on that foundation we prepare for a future of change and challenges. It is by honoring our heritage and having our personal vision for the future that we find our true identity. The past may sometimes appear to be hidden in the fog of illusion, shadowed memories and myth. Even so, we can learn from the past as we look to the future and begin to create our own memories and, yes, our new myths. There are times when the best way to see the future coming toward us is to look in the rear-view mirror.

Appendix

Bibliography
(By author or, for clarity, by subject.)

Arson. See "Whites help rebuild church after building was set afire by arsonists in racial incident." *Houston Chronicle*, 25 Dec.1992.

Ashe, Arthur and Arnold Rampersad. *Days of Grace: A Memoir*. New York: Random House, 1993.

St. Augustine. "Love, and do what you like." Quote in common usage.

Baldwin, James. "An Open letter to My Sister, Angela Davis." 1970. *If They Come in the Morning: Voices of Resistance*. The Third Press. 1971.

Bennis, Warren. *On Becoming a Leader*. Addison-Wesley, 1989.

Berry, Wendell. *The Unsettling of America*. 1977. Reprinted: Sierra Club Books for Children, 1996.

Blyden, Edward. Pan African essayist. Quote commonly attributed to him: "Every race has a soul and the soul of that race finds expression in its institutions and to kill those institutions is to kill the soul … No people can profit or be helped under institutions which are not the outcome of their own character."

Bold, Stephen. "Molière and Authority: from the Querelle De L'École Des Femmes to the Affaire Tartuffe." *Romance Quarterly*: Volume: 44. Issue: 2. 1997.

Bolman, Lee G. and Terence E. Deal. *Leading with Soul: An Uncommon Journey of Spirit*. New York: John Wiley & Sons, 2001.

Boyer, Ernest L. See Altbach, Philip. "Ernest Boyer: An Appreciation." *International Higher Education*. Spring, 1996.

Bumpass, Larry L. Data relevant to socialization in the U.S. national fertility surveys. Honolulu: East-West Center, 1975.

Census Bureau. Married-Couple and Unmarried-Partner Households: 2000. Census 2000 Special Reports, 2003.

Charitable Giving. See "Poll Shows Charitable Giving, Volunteering Still on Decline." *The Washington Post*, 19 October 1994.

Cleavers. See *Leave It To Beaver*, CBS Worldwide, Inc., 1957-1963.

Clinton, William. 1997 State of the Union Address.

Colston, Freddie C. *Dr. Benjamin E. Mays Speaks: Representative Speeches of a Great American Orator*. Rowman & Littlefield, 2002.

Cooper. H. M. *The battle over homework: Common ground for administrators, teachers, and parents*. Thousand Oaks, CA: Corwin Press, 2001.

Covey, Steven R. *Seven Habits Of Highly Effective People*. New York: Simon & Schuster Adult Publishing Group, 1990.

Creature with the Atom Brain. Dir. Edward L. Kahn. Perf. Richard Denning, Angela Stevens, S. John Launer, Michael Granger. Columbia/Clover, 1955.

Detocqueville, Alexis, et al. *Democracy in America*. Washington Square Press, 1971.

Douglass, Frederick. *Autobiographies: Frederick Douglass*. Notes by Henry Louis Gates Jr. New York: The Library of America, 1994.

Douglass, Frederick. *Life and Times of Frederick Douglass, Written by Himself*. Hartford, Conn.: Park Pub. Co., 1881. Reprint, Secaucus, N.J.: Citadel Press, 1983.

Douglass, Frederick. *My Bondage and My Freedom*. With a new introduction by Philip S. Foner. New York: Dover Publications, 1969.

Douglass, Frederick. See Blassingame, John W., et al., eds. *The Frederick Douglass Papers. Series One: Speeches, Debates, and Interviews*. 5 vols. Hew Haven, Yale University Press, 1979-92.

Douglass, Frederick. See Blassingame, John W., et al., eds. *The Frederick Douglass Papers. Series Two: Autobiographical Writings*. 1 vol. New Haven: Yale University Press, 1999.

Education Reform. See A Nation at Risk: The Imperative for Educational Reform: A Report to the Nation and the Secretary of Education. National Commission on Excellence in Education, 1983.

Elders, Jocelyn on the issue of drug legalization. See Trevino, Roberto A. and Alan J.

Richard. "Attitudes toward drug legalization among drug users." *American Journal of Drug and Alcohol Abuse*, February 2002.

Elmer-Dewitt, Philip. "Some people make headlines, while others make history." *Time Magazine*.

Ezekiel, Raphael S. *The Racist Mind: Portraits of American Neo-Nazis and Klansmen.* Viking, 1995.

Frost, Robert. *Collected Poems of Robert Frost.* H. Holt and Company, 1930.

Fulghum, Robert. *All I Really Need to Know I Learned in Kindergarten: Fifteenth Anniversary Edition.* Ballantine Books, 2003.

Gardner, John W. *On Leadership*, New York: The Free Press, 1990.

Goleman, Daniel. *Emotional Intelligence: Why it can matter more than IQ.* Bantam, 1995.

Havel, Vaclav. "The Need for Transcendence in the Postmodern World." Speech in Independence Hall, July 4, 1994. Philadelphia.

Hillman, James and Brooks Haxton. *Fragments: The Collected Wisdon of Heraclitus.* Penguin, 2001.

Hofmann, Adele Dellenbaugh and Donald Everett Graydanus. *Adolescent Medicine.* Appleton & Lange, 1997.

Howard, Jane. *Families.* New York: Simon and Schuster, c1978.

I Love Lucy; CBS Worldwide, Inc., 1951-57.

Jackson, Michael. See Corless, Richard. "The Price is right: Michael Jackson's Out-of-Court Settlement of a Child Molestation Lawsuit." *Time Magazine*.

Jensen, Arthur. "How Much Can We Boost I.Q. and Scholastic Achievement?" *Harvard Educational Review*. February, 1969.

Kane, Fr. Joseph. Commentary in ABC Original Report. "Just Say No: Government's War on Drugs Fails. "The only reason that coke is worth that much money is that it's illegal," argues Father Joseph Kane, a priest in a drug-ravaged Bronx neighborhood in New York City. "Pure cocaine is three times the cost of gold. Now if that's the case, how are you gonna stop people from selling cocaine?" Kane has come to believe that while drug abuse is bad, drug prohibition is worse — because the black market does horrible things to his community. "There's so much money in it, it's staggering," he says.

Kevorkian, Jack, MD. Speech at National Press Club, 19 July 1996.

Kubler-Ross, Elisabeth. *On Death and Dying*. Scribner, 1997.

Kubler-Ross, Elisabeth. See Schoenberg, Gerber, Wiener, Kutscher, Perety, and Carr, Eds. Bereavement: Its Psychological Aspects

Lincoln, C. Eric. *Coming through the Fire: Surviving Race and Place in America*. Duke University Press, 1996.

Lippman, Walter. *The Public Philosophy*: Transaction Publishers, 1989.

Lynch, Gerald W. "Legalizing Drugs Is Not the Solution." America 13 Feb. 1993. Rpt. in "Legalizing Drugs Would Not Reduce Crime." At Issue: Legalizing Drugs. Karin L. Swisher, ed., San Diego, CA.: Greenhaven Press, Inc., 1996

Mandela, Nelson. *Long Walk to Freedom -- with Connections: The Autogiography of Nelson Mandela*. Abridgement and connecting notes by Richard W. Kelso. Austin, Texas: Holt, Rinehart and Winston, 2000.

Mansfield, Harvey C., Jr. "The Underhandedness of Affirmative Action." *National Review*. May 4, 1984.

Mantle, Mickey. See Castro, Tony. *Mickey Mantle: America's Prodigal Son*. Brassey's Inc., 2002.

Marden, Orison S. See Fishwick, Marshall W. *American Heroes, Myth and Reality*: Public Affairs Press, 1954.

Maslow, Abraham H. *Motivation and Personality*: New York: Harper & Row, 1970.

Moliere: "Everyone has a right to his own course of action." Quote in common usage.

Murray, Charles and Hernstein, Richard. *The Bell Curve: Intelligence and Class Structure in American Life*. October 1994. Free Press.

Murray, Charles. Magazine article: *Public Interest*. Spring 1994.

Nash, Gary B. *Red, white, and black: the peoples of early America*. Englewood Cliffs, N.J.: Prentice-Hall, 1974.

Pyatt, Sherman E. *Martin Luther King, Jr.: An Annotated Bibliography*: Greenwood Press, 1986.

Raspberry, Willliam. "Is American better off since Brown ruling?" *Deseret Morning News*, 18 May 2004.

Rigsbee, Ed. *PartnerShift-How to Profit from the Partnering Trend.* New York: John Wiley & Sons, 2000.

Roberts, Paul. "Risk." *Psychology Today*; Nov/Dec 1994.

Rollin, Betty, "Last Wish." *Public Affairs*, 1998.

Rollins, Ed. See Hanson, Christopher. "Insider Cynicism." *Columbia Journalism Review.* January/Feburary 1994.

Roosevelt, Franklin D. Inaugural Address, 4 March 1933.

Saul, Stephanie and Rocco Parascandola. "Man Dies in B'klyn Elevator Shaft / Marcy Houses resident may have been 'surfing.' " *Newsday*; 14 Dec. 2002.

Sexuality. See "University of California Complete Sexuality Survey." *Chicago Sun-Times*, 19 August 1992.

Shawshank Redemption, Castle Rock Productions, 1994.

Strauss, William and Neil Howe. *The Fourth Turning.* Broadway, 1997.

Swindoll, Charles. "Insights for Living." The Bible radio teaching ministry of Chuck Swindoll www.insight.org.

Thomas, Rosie. *When We Were Small.* SubPop Records, 2002.

Tuchman, Barbara. "Nothing is more satisfying than to write a good sentence. It is no fun to write lumpishly, dully, in prose the reader must plod through like wet sand. But it is a pleasure to achieve, if one can, a clear running prose that is simple yet full of surprises. This does not just happen. It requires skill, hard work, a good ear, and continued practice." -- Source unknown.

Welfare. See David T. Elwood and Elisabeth D. Welty. "Public Service Employment and Mandatory Work: A Policy Whose Time Has Come and Gone and Come Again?" Cambridge, MA: Harvard University, Kennedy School of Government, 6 March 1999.

Welfare. See National Urban League Annual Report, 1988.

Welfare. See Overview of Entitlement Programs, Committee on Ways and Means, U.S. House of Representatives. U.S. Government Printing Office, 1994.

Welfare. See Whitman, David. "War on Welfare Dependency." *US News & World Report*, April 1992.

Who's Who Among American High School Students. "Cheating, risky sexual behavior and drug and alcohol use are activities found among high-achievers in the nation's high schools, according to the 26th annual survey of students listed in "Who's Who Among American High School Students."

William James, *The Principles of Psychology*, 1892.

Wolf, David and William Piland. *Help Wanted: Preparing Community College Leaders in a New Century.* San Francisco, 2003. Jossey Bass.

Wolkomir, Richard. A biography in *Smithsonian Journeys*, October 2001.

Woodstock I & Woodstock II, Woodstock Ventures, Inc. NYC, 1969.

Zimmering, Frank. University of California Law Professor who questioned wisdom of "Two Strikes and You're Out Child Protection Act of 2001." Hearing before the subcommittee on crime of the Committee on the Judiciary, House of Representatives. One Hundred Seventh Congress, First Session, 31 July 2001.

Zinsser, William K. *On Writing Well, 25th Anniversary: The Classic Guide to Writing Nonfiction.* Harper Resource, 2001.

Author's Note

The collection of essays in this volume was (sometimes hurriedly) written as newspaper columns. Often, I made reference to recently read newspaper or magazine articles. In the "fog of years" some of those exact references have been lost. My editors and I have recovered as many of these references as possible and have placed them in a bibliography sorted by author. In instances where a person referenced in one of the essays may have been written about by another person, the reference is alphabetized by the last name of the subject of the article rather by the name of the author, which didn't appear in my essay, to make it easier for the reader to access additional subject matter.

The main purpose of this bibliography is to share the privilege of my own rich experience with the writings of others with my readers. If something in a particular essay catches your eye, you may find some references for carrying your interest further in the bibliography.